# Among the Flowers

*Translations from the Oriental Classics*

"Lady at a Dressing Table," by Su Han-ch'en, early twelfth century.
(*Courtesy Museum of Fine Arts, Boston*)

# AMONG THE FLOWERS

The *Hua-chien chi*

*Translated by*
Lois Fusek

*New York*
COLUMBIA UNIVERSITY PRESS
*1982*

Library of Congress Cataloging in Publication Data
Main entry under title:

Among the flowers.

(Translations from the oriental classics)
Translation of: Hua-chien chi / compiled by
Ch'ung-tso Chao.
Bibliography: p.
Includes index.
1. Tz'u—Translations into English.
2. English poetry—Translations from Chinese.
I. Fusek, Lois, 1934–    . II. Chao,
Ch'ung-tso, fl. 934–965. III. Title.
IV. Series.
PL2658.E3A5    895.1′13′09    81-12306
ISBN 0-231-04986-2    AACR2

Columbia University Press
New York   Guildford, Surrey

*Frontispiece:* Lady at a Dressing Table. Su Han-ch'en.
Sung Period, early 12th century. Album Leaf, H: .252m., W: .267m.
Ross Collection, 29.960. Courtesy, Museum of Fine Arts, Boston.

# Acknowledgments

I wish to express my deep gratitude to Professor David T. Roy of the Department of Far Eastern Languages and Civilizations at the University of Chicago for all his help and encouragement throughout my work on this translation. I would also like to express my appreciation to Marcia K. Moen for her kindness and patience in the final preparation of this manuscript.

# Contents

# Among the Flowers

# Introduction

## THE TRANSLATION

*Among the Flowers*, the *Hua-chien chi*, is a collection of five hundred *tz'u* lyrics compiled by Chao Ch'ung-tso (*fl.* mid-tenth century), a minor official of the Later Shu dynasty (934–965). The preface written by Ou-yang Chiung (896–971) is dated A.D. 940. It is the very first anthology of *tz'u*, a relatively new verse form that was just beginning to find acceptance among the literati. The lyrics are dedicated mainly to the celebration of love in all its many stages, the rapture of the first meeting, the secret rendezvous, the passionate embrace, and finally, love forever lost. The world depicted in *Among the Flowers* is the world of the courtesan and the singing-girl, the beautiful "flowers." In this world love's pleasures may be pursued for their own sake, without personal and social obligation. Of the eighteen poets represented, most were residents of what is now the province of Szechuan. The time covered is from the mid-ninth to the mid-tenth centuries, a time which saw the breakdown and dissolution of the once mighty T'ang dynasty (618–907) and the consequent fragmentation of the empire into a series of small local dynasties, a period known as the Five Dynasties (907–960). The Five Dynasties was a brief interregnum of 53 years before the Sung dynasty (960–1127) would once again unite China into a centralized empire.

*Among the Flowers* is divided into 10 chapters. Each chapter contains 50 *tz'u* verses with the exception of chapter 6 which contains 51 and chapter 9 which contains 49. The word *tz'u* literally means "words," and that is basically what a *tz'u* lyric is, "words" written to fit the melodies of various popular songs. However, the titles of these *tz'u* lyrics are also the titles of the melodies to which they were originally written. For example, numerous lyrics were written by many different poets to the popular song "The Taoist Nun," (*Nü-kuan tzu*), but each and every lyric is entitled "The Taoist Nun," so that the word *tz'u* also refers to the particular melody to which these lyrics were written.

Let us suppose that over a period of time many different poets had written their own lyrics to the melody of the song "Greensleeves." Each set of lyrics would continue to be entitled "Greensleeves," even if the subject matter of the lyrics hadn't the vaguest connection with the original "Greensleeves." The title "Greensleeves," however, would signal that a lyric or lyrics had been

written in accordance with the musical demands of a particular melody and
a certain verbal patterning congruent with the song "Greensleeves" is to be
expected. Now let us further suppose that in the course of time, the melody
of "Greensleeves" had been lost and there was no longer any way of knowing
how it might have sounded. Poets would remain undaunted because they
could continue to write lyrics to the tune "Greensleeves" based on the verbal
patterning of the earlier lyrics that had been written in accordance with the
original melody. Some poets would begin to add subtitles to indicate the
special topic of their poem or to give an account of the circumstances of its
composition, but the all-important title "Greensleeves," and the consequent
patterning, would remain the same.

   If we follow the Chinese precedent, all the lyrics written to "Greensleeves"
would be termed *tz'u* because they are lyric poems written to conform to the
demands of a *tz'u* tune pattern. A sonnet is termed a sonnet because lyrics
written to it follow the prescriptive pattern of the sonnet form. The difficulty
with the *tz'u* arises because there are not just several possible patterns available
as is the case with the sonnet, but quite literally many hundreds since each
individual melody in the musical repertoire adopted by *tz'u* poets established
its own unique poetic pattern.[1] Thus a lyric written to the tune "Greensleeves"
would follow one pattern, but a lyric written to the melody "Drink to me only
with thine eyes" would follow quite another. The poem "Forget not yet the
tried intent" by Sir Thomas Wyatt (1503–1542) also was written to be sung
to a particular melody. The reader will notice that each stanza is identically
constructed with three rhyming lines and a shorter refrain, and each opens
and closes with the same phrase, "Forget not yet":

```
Forget not yet the tried intent
Of such a truth as I have meant,
My great travail, so gladly spent,
        Forget not yet.

Forget not when first began
The weary life ye know, since whan
The suit, the service none tell can,
        Forget not yet.

Forget not yet the great assays,
The cruel wrong, the scornful ways,
The painful penance in denays,
        Forget not yet.
```

---

[1] The *Tz'u-p'u*, comp. Wang I-ch'ing, preface dated 1715, lists 826 tune titles and illustrates
them with 2,306 variant forms ranging from 20 to 40 characters in length. The *Tz'u-lü*, comp.
Wan Shu, author's preface dated 1687, lists 875 titles. The *Tz'u-p'u* and the *Tz'u-lü* are compendia
of such tune patterns, but since the music has long been lost, there is little information about the
original melodies to which these lyrics had been sung.

Forget not yet, forget not this,
How long ago hath been, and is,
The mind that never meant amiss,
        Forget not yet.

Forget not, then, thine own approved,
The which so long hath thee so loved,
Whose steadfast faith yet never moved,
        Forget not this.[2]

If the Chinese practice were followed, poets could continue to write lyrics in English based on the verbal patterning of Wyatt's lyric whether the music existed or not, or whether the poet was concerned with musical considerations or not. The pattern would always remain the same. In this way, poets of today can still write lyrics in Chinese to songs that were current over a thousand years ago and for which the music no longer exists, by simply writing in accord with the prescribed verbal pattern of the tune they select.

The songs to which the *tz'u* lyrics were written were popular tunes, often of foreign origin, but what made them melodies to which *tz'u* lyrics were written was simply that a poet composed one or several lyric poems in the *tz'u* manner, and as a consequence, the *tz'u* patterning for a particular song was established, and it would continue to be imitated with only occasional and minor variations. It is important to remember that the *tz'u* lyric is not written in the free and easy manner of the folksong. The *tz'u* is a rather disciplined type of verse that is based to a large extent on earlier and somewhat complex poetic forms. It adheres to a comparatively strict structure with regard to rhyme, number and length of lines, and tonal placement. The resultant pattern then is a kind of verbal notation in contrast to musical notation, although the verbal notation derives from the original music.

In summary, the *tz'u* can be defined as a song-form usually in lines of unequal length (although some tune patterns call for lines of equal length), and prescribed rhyme and tonal sequence, occurring in a large number of different patterns, each bearing the name of a tune. The lyrics were originally set to music, but as the patterns created became fixed, the direct association with music became increasingly attenuated, and eventually ceased to exist. Over the course of years, there developed many hundreds of these tune patterns, each identifiable by the tune title, so that the *tz'u* is not one verse form, but hundreds. *Among the Flowers* contains 75 of these tune patterns in all, some in variant forms. Since the lyrics in *Among the Flowers* are representative of an early phase in the development of the *tz'u*, it is probable that most lyrics were patterned directly to the music itself, or at least were written when the

[2] David Daiches and William Charvat, eds. *Poems in English, 1530–1940* (New York: Ronald Press, 1950), p. 9.

music was still extant. An index of the tune titles in *Among the Flowers* is on pp. 221–27. Each title is followed by a list of the poets who wrote lyrics for it, and the number of lyrics they wrote is indicated to the right.

Poets who wrote in the *tz'u* form may have done so because of the many and varied forms from which they could choose. The more revered and prestigious *shih* form was far less flexible, and was written entirely in lines of five characters each or entirely in lines of seven characters each. Chinese poetry is measured by the number of characters or syllables in a line, in contrast to English poetry which is measured by the number of stresses in a line. The Chinese literary language is essentially monosyllabic so that each written character represents one spoken syllable, and this one syllable is almost always the equivalent of a word. There are cases in which two or even three syllables are required to convey meaning, but these are the exceptions which prove the general rule.

A line of verse which in Chinese contains five written characters will also contain five spoken syllables, and these five syllables will usually represent five words. These words either communicate meaning or, if meaningless in themselves, indicate some aspect of grammar. The five-character line poem and the seven-character line poem were much the favored forms in traditional Chinese poetry. Even in the refrains in *Among the Flowers*, which are based on a diversity of patterns, there is a decided preference for lines of five characters and lines of seven characters. Nevertheless, it is easy to understand why the poets in *Among the Flowers* would be attracted to the much wider variety of poetic measures offered by the *tz'u*. Of course, the *tz'u* was new, and this in itself would have stimulated the creative imagination of the poets. But in addition, the *tz'u* provided a challenge that was irresistible and exciting. By utilizing the changing tune patterns, they could write endless variations on the same theme and demonstrate the full range of their poetic virtuosity.

In my translation of the poems in *Among the Flowers*, I have attempted to give some sense of the line patterning of the different lyrics. The main emphasis in *Among the Flowers* is not so much on what is expressed, but rather that it is expressed within the confines of particular poetic schemes. Most English translations of Chinese poetry, of necessity, have tended to stress substance over form. This is understandable since Chinese and English are quite different languages, and it is virtually impossible to transfer the structure of one to the other. But the different patterns are crucial in a work such as *Among the Flowers*, especially when the work is to be translated in its entirety. It is sometimes possible to adopt an English poetic form for the purposes of translation, and not infrequently this results in a moderately successful English poem. But this approach can be misleading when one is attempting to represent the Chinese experience. In addition, there are 75 different patterns in *Among the Flowers*, and the need to distinguish one from the other would prove bewildering and complex. A word-for-word literal translation of the poems would be possible, but not very effective. If Christopher Marlowe's (1564?–1593) impassioned plea, "Come live with me and be my love,/ And we will all the pleasures prove"[3] were translated literally from Chinese, it might read something like, "Come dwell love,/ All pleasures prove."

Free verse can also be employed, and this is the usual, and in most instances the desirable, compromise in English translations of Chinese poetry. However, a free translation of the lyrics in *Among the Flowers* would fail to demonstrate the importance of the role of form in the *tz'u*. Clearly there is no one satisfactory solution to the special problems inherent in the translation of a poetic anthology such as *Among the Flowers*. I have attempted, however, to suggest visually the patterning of the different tunes. Lines containing the same number of Chinese characters are equal in length in the English translation of a single *tz'u* or a series of *tz'u* lyrics written to the same tune by the same author. The number of characters in the original Chinese is indicated to the right of the English line. For example, the following is a lyric written to the tune, "The Taoist Nun," by Wei Chuang (836–910):

| 四 | 月 | 十 | 七 | | | |
|---|---|---|---|---|---|---|
| ssu | yüeh | shih | ch'i | | | (4) |
| four | month | ten | seven | | | |

| 正 | 是 | 去 | 年 | 今 | 日 | |
|---|---|---|---|---|---|---|
| cheng | – shih | ch'ü | – nien | chin | – jih | (6) |
| just | – was | past | – year | present | – day | |

| 別 | 君 | 時 | | | | |
|---|---|---|---|---|---|---|
| pieh | chün | shih | | | | (3) |
| farewell | you | when | | | | |

| 忍 | 淚 | 佯 | 低 | 面 | | |
|---|---|---|---|---|---|---|
| jen | lei | yang | ti | mien | | (5) |
| bear | tears | pretend | lower | face | | |

| 含 | 羞 | 半 | 斂 | 眉 | | |
|---|---|---|---|---|---|---|
| han | hsiu | pan | lien | mei | | (5) |
| restrain | blush | half | gather | eyebrows | | |

| 不 | 知 | 魂 | 已 | 斷 | | |
|---|---|---|---|---|---|---|
| pu | chih | hun | i | tuan | | (5) |
| not | know | souls | already | broken | | |

| 空 | 有 | 夢 | 相 | 隨 | | |
|---|---|---|---|---|---|---|
| k'ung | yu | meng | hsiang | sui | | (5) |
| only | have | dreams | together | follow | | |

[3] *Ibid.*, p. 24.

| 除 | 却 | 天 | 邊 | 月 | |
|---|---|---|---|---|---|
| ch'u | – ch'üeh | t'ien | – pien | yüeh | (5) |
| except | | sky | – edge | moon | |

| 没 | 人 | 知 | |
|---|---|---|---|
| mei | jen | chih | (3) |
| no | person | know[4] | |

In my translation of this *tz'u*, I have attempted to suggest this patterning:

| The seventeenth day of the fourth month! | (4) |
|---|---|
| It was exactly one year ago on this very same day, | (6) |
| When you had to go away. | (3) |
| I covered my tears, pretending to look away. | (5) |
| My brows came together with timid confusion. | (5) |
| | |
| We couldn't know that our hearts had broken, | (5) |
| That only in dreams would we see each other. | (5) |
| But for the moon on the far distant horizon, | (5) |
| No one could have known![5] | (3) |

In the above English translation of "The Taoist Nun," the lines which in the original Chinese contain five characters, I have made equal in length in English. The two lines which in the original Chinese contain three characters each are also equal in length to one another. The one six-character line, and the one four-character line are spaced to suggest the balanced line patterning of the original. I have followed identical patterning in the following lyric, also written by Wei Chuang to the tune "The Taoist Nun":

Last night at the very hour of midnight!
As I slept, you came to me so clearly in my dream,
And we talked on and on.
Your face was the same lovely peach blossom.
Your finely curved brows were willow leaves.

Your sweet blushes mixed with smiles of joy.
You started to leave, but still you held me.
I woke and knew it to have been but a dream.
My grief overwhelmed me![6]

It is my intent merely to suggest the line patterning of the original and not to provide a rigid structure for each and every song. Therefore, there is no

---

[4] *Sung-pen Hua-chien chi*, based on the edition of Ch'ao Ch'ien-chih with colophon dated A.D. 1148 (Taipei: I-wen yin-shu kuan, 1960), 3.5b.
[5] See chapter 3, p. 72.
[6] *Ibid.*

one inflexible pattern for each tune. The following two lyrics written by Wen
T'ing-yün (812–870) to the tune "The Taoist Nun" perfectly match each other,
but only closely approximate the spatial patterning of the lyrics by Wei Chuang
given above:

[1]

| | |
|---|---|
| Reserved beauty, restrained smile, | (4) |
| Her faded make-up, a veil of soft reds and blues, | (6) |
| Her hair, a cicada's wings, | (3) |
| Her jade hairpin, a ripple of autumn water, | (5) |
| The rolled curtain, a silken mist of azure. | (5) |
| | |
| Her breast shines snow-white in the mirror. | (5) |
| Among the magical trees fronting the tower, | (5) |
| She gives a message to a lovely fairy girl, | (5) |
| Let the immortal come soon! | (3) |

[2]

Clouds of hair fall to her collar.
Her fairylike face is as snow in the gilt mirror.
Her delicate brows painted,
She raises her dainty fan to hide her face,
And blushingly lowers the brocade curtains.

Long she looks for him from the jade tower,
Let him not come late to the flower grotto.
Eventually he will leave, riding a phoenix,
May he not forget her then![7]

Perhaps the type of patterning I have employed in my translation of *Among
the Flowers* is most readily apparent in lyrics composed in lines of equal length
such as the following three lyrics written in lines of seven characters each by
Ou-yang Chiung (896–971) to the tune "Sand of Silk-Washing Stream,"
(*Huan-ch'i sha*):

[1]

| | |
|---|---|
| The catkins fall and the orioles' cries fade at sundown. | (7) |
| Her jade face is like a sleepy flower flushed with wine. | (7) |
| Bamboos etch the window, and smoke rises from a brazier. | (7) |

[7] See chapter 1, pp. 49–50.

```
She draws the screens, and in solitary silence, grieves.     (7)
She pulls the pillow close, her hair spills to the side.     (7)
At this time, beside whom does her heart so closely lie?     (7)
```

## [2]

```
Her gown of bright azure silk gently brushes the ground.
On this occasion, her new robe is especially enchanting.
Soft winds dance in the folds, revealing her sweet skin.

She sits alone, and in solitary plaint, plays the pipes.
She walks in the garden, and plucks a blossoming branch.
What can she do when she is hopelessly smitten with him!
```

## [3]

```
They see one another, and tears take the place of words.
Done with drinking, he shares with her the joys of love.
A phoenix screen and mandarin duck quilt shield the bed.

In a mist of musk and orchid, he listens to her breathe.
Through the sheerest film of silk, he looks at her body.
Does she hate him now for being such a no-account lover?[8]
```

The following two lyrics, the first written to the tune "River Messages," (*Ho Ch'uan*) by Ku Hsiung (*c.* A.D. 933), and the second written to the tune "Immortal at the River," (*Lin-chiang hsien*) by Mao Wen-hsi (*c.* A.D. 930) provide examples of yet different patternings. Please note that all lines of equal length in Chinese are also of equal length in the English translation:

## "River Messages"

### [3]

```
The oars lift in the water.                                   (2)
The boat journeys on ahead.                                   (2)
The flashing waves reach in the distance.                     (4)
I don't at all know where we are passing.                     (4)
Flowery banks and grassy beaches extend ever farther on.     (7)
There is a fine misty rain.                                   (2)
Soaring partridges chase after one another.                   (5)
```

[8] See chapter 5, pp. 114–15.

```
At world's end, parting's ache sobs in the river's flow,    (7)
Rails from the monkey's shriek.                             (3)
But with whom can I express these thoughts.                 (5)
I lean against the orchid oars.                            (3)
I am overcome by my sorrow.                                (2)
My soul seems to melt away.                                (2)
The fragrant incense will soon burn to ash!⁹              (5)
```

## "Immortal at the River"

### [1]

```
The cry of the cicada dies away with the setting sun.     (7)
The Hsiao and Hsiang glow with silvered moonlight.         (6)
The waters rush endlessly near the Huang-ling Shrine.      (7)
Crimson trees cover the Ch'u mountains.                    (4)
Mist and rain screen the Kao-t'ang Pavilion.              (5)

The lights on the moored boats flicker with the wind.      (7)
The white duckweed spreads far its fragrant scent.         (6)
The goddesses play the se in clear and sweet harmony,      (7)
Scarlet strings, sorrowful and restive!                    (4)
Clouds scatter, unveiling the limitless sky.¹⁰            (5)
```

I believe this is the first time this particular type of translation has been done, and I hope that this approach will help to suggest the disciplined structure within which the *tz'u* poets worked. The spatial patterning is not intended to be, nor could it ever be, a duplication or a copy of the original Chinese. It is to be considered a means and not an end in itself. It is simply a reminder to the reader of the importance of form in *tz'u* poetry. The patterning will help to clarify the ways in which the poets in *Among the Flowers* sought to manipulate the different forms, as the same themes and images weave in and out of the tune patterns. This method will also indicate the concentrated structure of the original Chinese which creates a crucial tension with the subject matter so that the deep and passionate feelings expressed never seem excessive, but remain balanced and controlled. It is this distancing effect that lends a certain elegance and dignity to the lyrics in *Among the Flowers* and keeps them from being overly sentimental.

In order to keep the footnotes to a minimum, and also because so many references occur again and again, I have put such information in a Glossary, pp. 203–16. Proper names, place names, allusions, and images will be found

⁹ See chapter 6, pp. 128–29.
¹⁰ See chapter 5, p. 110.

here arranged in alphabetical order. Biographical notes for each of the eighteen poets can be found on pp. 197–201. The texts I have used are the *Sung-pen Hua-chien chi*, based on the edition of Ch'ao Ch'ien-chih with colophon dated A.D. 1148 (Taipei: I-wen yin-shu kuan, 1960); *Hua-chien chi chu*, ed. Hua Lien-p'u (Shanghai: Commercial Press, 1935); *Hua-chien chi p'ing-chu*, ed. Li Ping-jo (1935; reprint ed. Hong Kong: Lo-chih ch'u-pan she, 1960); *Hua-chien chi chiao*, ed. Li I-mang (Hong Kong: Commercial Press, 1960), and *Hua-chien chi*, ed. Hsiao Chi-tsung (Taipei: Taiwan Hsüeh-sheng shu-chü, 1977). I am especially indebted to the notes in Hua Lien-p'u's *Hua-chien chi chu*, which were extremely helpful. I am also grateful for the notes and commentary in Hsiao Chi-tsung's *Hua-chien chi*. I would suggest that both these works be consulted if one is reading the text in the original Chinese.

I hope today's reader will take pleasure in the special beauty and charm of this collection of *tz'u* lyrics. The verses in *Among the Flowers* remain fresh and appealing because they so poignantly reveal the hopes and dreams, the joy and despair, of men and women not so very different from ourselves, earnestly seeking love and fulfillment.

# AMONG THE FLOWERS

The *tz'u* lyrics collected in *Among the Flowers* represent something of a contradiction. They depict a luxurious world devoted to the pursuit of pleasure, but the reality of the times in which they were written was turbulent and harsh. By the mid-ninth century, the once powerful T'ang dynasty (618–907) was in its final years of decline. As the central government gradually deteriorated, insurrection and starvation swept across the country. In A.D. 880, the T'ang capital of Ch'ang-an was occupied by a large rebel force led by Huang Ch'ao, and the emperor and his court were forced to flee to Ch'eng-tu in Szechuan Province. In A.D. 883, the rebellion was put down, but the generals who had assisted in accomplishing this feat now had grown so powerful, and the imperial dependence on them was so complete, that the emperor became theirs to command. These warlords established themselves as independent rulers over various parts of the country, and in A.D. 907, the last puppet emperor of the T'ang was forced to abdicate. Thus a glorious age in China's history came to an end, and the period known as the Five Dynasties (907–960) began, during which time five successive dynasties ruled in and around the capital areas of Lo-yang and K'ai-feng, and ten independent states held sway in the south. There was constant warfare among the separate "kings" as they sought to consolidate and expand their positions. In addition, large bands of brigands were everywhere in the country, killing and pillaging as they went. These were years of extraordinary misery and suffering, a bleak period indeed in Chinese history. The poets in *Among the Flowers* could not help but be witness to these events, and many, in their official capacities, were actual participants. However, only occasionally do the darker notes of war and affliction penetrate the world of *Among the Flowers*, and then only by allusion to an earlier time in China's past, the ill-fated reign of Emperor Yang of the Sui dynasty (*r.* 604–618).

The lyric *tz'u* in *Among the Flowers* have been considered the products of escapism, the expression of a desire to find, in beauty and pleasure, an end to pain. Later critics would censure these poets for being shallow and trivial when death and destruction lay all about them. The traditional moralistic view would condemn this seeming flight from reality by the very class upon which the social and political structure was most reliant. However, the appreciation of poetry cannot be based either on the presumed motives or the personal characters of the poets, and the lyrics in *Among the Flowers* must be judged ultimately on their merits as poetry. From a cultural and historical point of view, *Among the Flowers* is a crucial work. It is the first anthology of *tz'u*, a verse form that would soon rise to eminence in the Sung dynasty (960–1127). The *tz'u* in *Among the Flowers* are among the earliest lyrics of this type, and since they were still closely associated with a musical setting, it is possible to study this form in its initial stages of development. These lyrics were composed to popular tunes and were not intended to be either elaborate or erudite. The melodies were taken from the vast repertoire of native folk-music as well as from new airs imported from Central Asia. And despite the fact that the lyrics in *Among the Flowers* represent an important historical link between the poetry of the T'ang and the Sung dynasties, these lyrics were assembled not for literary edification but for simple enjoyment.

But evidently even during the Five Dynasties, writers felt a certain embarrassment at devoting themselves to the *tz'u*, and Ou-yang Chiung (896–971) in his preface to *Among the Flowers* attempts to justify the *tz'u* and the competence of the *tz'u* poets found there. The preface is excessively allusive and somewhat digressive, and Ou-yang's attitude appears to be defensive. His main concern is to establish the *tz'u* in *Among the Flowers* as part of a noble and long-lived musical tradition, and he makes a special point of declaring that the poets in this anthology are every bit as good as their T'ang predecessors. It is obvious that Ou-yang senses the close resemblance to palace-style poetry, so popular in the sixth century, and to forestall comparison, he is quick to find fault with these superesthetic compositions and to classify them as inelegant and devoid of substance. But he is equally anxious to distinguish the lyrics in *Among the Flowers* from common folksongs, which in his opinion lack literary merit. Despite the ornateness of his rhetoric, Ou-yang does not claim that *Among the Flowers* offers anything new or startling in Chinese poetry. The *tz'u* in this collection are refined lyrics written by men of taste and learning. They are not only beautiful, but contribute to the pleasures of daily life.

The majority of poets represented in *Among the Flowers* either were natives of Szechuan or had fled there after the fall of the T'ang capital of Ch'ang-an. In Ch'eng-tu, the provincial capital of Szechuan, there were established two successive and brief dynasties, the Early Shu (907–925) under Wang Chien, and the Later Shu (934–965) under Meng Ch'ang. The latter dynasty is especially noted for its cultural and literary achievements, and it was during this short-lived regime that Chao Ch'ung-tso, the compiler of *Among the Flowers*, served as a minor official. The splendid and luxurious court in Ch'eng-tu sought to revive in some measure the brilliance of the T'ang. Consequently Szechuan (Shu) became known for its poets and scholars who in an age of confusion attempted to continue the cultural heritage of the T'ang, and in spite of the later criticism, the poets in *Among the Flowers* were not sounding the last frivolous notes of a dying and decadent civilization. Rather, in their songs, they were giving China a new verse form—one of the greatest gifts one generation can give to another, for by its very shape it alters human perception and experience.

What the critics lament as trivial and Ou-yang lauds as refined is a collection of verses of immense merit and appeal. But the opposition of moral and esthetic values gives rise to two contradictory ways of approaching the verses in *Among the Flowers*. The first would assume that they represent an anticlimax to the literary glories of the T'ang dynasty, and that they reflect the apathy and *déjà-vu* of a fading culture. The second view would acknowledge an artistic debt to the T'ang, but would see in the lyrics in *Among the Flowers* new devices of style and imagery blended into rich and innovative melodies. Ironically, both views are helpful in considering the verses in *Among the Flowers*, for while songs represent the commonest, simplest, and most natural kind of poetry, the lyrics in *Among the Flowers*, in spite of a close musical association, are not fully spontaneous expressions of the human spirit. They are self-conscious exercises devised and executed with respect for traditional literary values. Yet at the same time the ebb and flow of the music imposed new linguistic demands and helped to create new esthetic standards.

Love is the major theme and women the center of the poetic domain. Already in the poems of Li Ho (790–816) "there is a foretaste of the feminine, silken, flower-decked, phoenix-infested imagery of the ninth century."[11] The poetry of Tu Mu (803–852) and Li Shang-yin (813–858), contemporaries of Wen T'ing-yün (812–870), shares this luxurious world of the pleasure quarters. And as A. C. Graham notes in *Poems of the Late Tang*, "From about 800 poetry

[11] A.C. Graham, *Poems of the Late T'ang* (Baltimore: Penguin Books, 1965), p. 142.

began to move indoors, and in particular behind the doors of courtesans, from which the *tz'u* was emerging. Nature is seen increasingly in terms of the artificial."[12] Ou-yang Chiung begins his preface to *Among the Flowers* with the assertion that the contrived is, at least, the equal of the natural. "Songs are like skillfully carved jade and alabaster which duplicate the artistry of nature. They are like artificial flowers which retain the beauty and freshness of spring."[13] One of the major characteristics of the imagery in *Among the Flowers* is this tendency to blend the artificial and the natural in such a way that the real and the unreal become as one. The physical world blends into the world of the dream so that it is difficult to tell where one stops and the other begins.

This is particularly apparent in the *tz'u* of the earliest poet included in *Among the Flowers*, Wen T'ing-yün. Wen may be considered the first master of the *tz'u* form, and he is the only poet in *Among the Flowers* mentioned by name in Ou-yang Chiung's preface. Wen T'ing-yün, despite his accomplishments and brilliance, repeatedly failed the *chin-shih* examination, the all-important entry into official life, and he spent so much time carousing and philandering that he gained an unsavory reputation in the T'ang capital of Ch'ang-an. His rejection of the accepted values and his pursuit of the pleasurable are everywhere in evidence in his *tz'u*. His lyrics are written to please and entertain the *fille de joie*, and in this Wen T'ing-yün was certainly at one with the predilections of his age. A brief discussion of a few of his lyrics will show some of the features of this stylized world in *Among the Flowers*.

Wen T'ing-yün's lyrics are deceptively simple. A lone figure, usually a woman, is portrayed in the scene of a single moment, and in that moment, Wen seeks to capture the sorrow of the human condition. Consider the following *tz'u* written by Wen T'ing-yün to the tune "Deva-like Barbarian":

```
In the jade tower bright with moonlight, she remembers.    (7)
The willow branches were long and graceful that spring.    (7)
Outside the gate the grass grew luxuriantly.               (5)
As they parted, she heard his horse cry out.               (5)

Gilt kingfishers cover a sheer silk curtain.               (5)
A fragrant candle sheds tears of melted wax.               (5)
The flowers wither and the cuckoo cries out.               (5)
By the silken window, her dream goes astray.[14]           (5)
```

In this poem past and present are brought together. The former happiness is contrasted with the unhappiness of the present. the images, "spring" and "long and graceful willows," together with "the luxuriant grass" create a natural world

---

[12] *Ibid.*, pp. 141–42.
[13] See preface, p. 33.
[14] See chapter 1, p. 38.

that was in harmony with the previous joy. But "the tears of the candle," "the withered flowers," and "the cry of the cuckoo" all reinforce the desolation of the girl's longing. The "painted kingfishers" serve as a permanent reminder of a relationship that no longer exists. In this short vignette the human emotion is expressed indirectly through images drawn from the environment. The emotion is objectively detailed and subjectively felt.

Wen T'ing-yün's use of imagery is highly selective, and one might almost say stereotyped in its consistency. The following, also written to the tune "Deva-like Barbarian," reveals Wen's characteristic choices:

```
The mountains on the screen shimmer in the golden dawn.
A cloud of hair brushes the fragrant snow of her cheek.
Lazily, she rises and paints mothlike brows.
Slowly, tardily, she gets ready for the day.

Mirrors, front and behind, reflect a flower,
Face and flower shining each upon the other.
Stitched in the silk of her bright new coat,
Golden-threaded partridges fly pair by pair.[15]
```

The hills painted on the screen and the partridges embroidered on the girl's jacket show Wen's fondness for allusions to the natural world in an artificial state. The frequent mention of fragrance and cosmetics not only betrays the idle surroundings of the pleasure haunts, but also serves a function similar to the above in that the use of such aids supposedly enhances the natural state. The mirror image is important in Wen's work as it brings out the dual elements of the real and the artificial. To Wen, beauty and women are synonymous and are both described by reference to the flower image. "The partridges flying pair by pair" illustrates another important theme, that is, while the creatures of nature are pictured together, the human figure is always alone. This suggests a conflict between the natural world and the manmade world. The following lyric, also to the tune "Deva-like Barbarian," shows a use of imagery identical to that just described:

```
Two golden-stitched phoenixes lie coiled on her jacket.
Like the delicate showering of evening rain on a peony,
Her new make-up shines in the bright mirror.
But her hair is thin, and her cheeks hollow.

In the painted hall, long she waits for him.
Beyond the balcony, willow branches dip low.
Since he left there has been no news of him.
Two swallows circle above the village altar.[16]
```

[15] See chapter 1, p. 37.
[16] See chapter 1, pp. 38–39.

"A pair of embroidered phoenixes," "rain on the peonies," "the bright mirror," and "powder and rouge," together with "willow branches," and "the return of the swallows" are the familiar elements with which Wen again and again fashions his poems.

The emotion evoked by Wen T'ing-yün's lyrics, however, does not arise because of the striking originality or unusual character of the images involved, as they are all common devices of Chinese poets. Rather the author's deeper purpose is accomplished by the manner in which these images are juxtaposed with one another. Consider the following, written to the tune "Deva-like Barbarian":

```
Mandarin ducks atop a gold hairpin dip over the pillow.
Above the aloe-wood hall, Wu Mountain seems to be jade.
Once again the willow branches turn to silk.
The spring rains have shut the post-bridges.

In the painted hall, all news is broken off.
South of the river, grasses cover the banks.
A flowering spray in the glow of the mirror,
Who can know what her feelings are just now?¹⁷
```

The poem opens with the image of "the gold hairpin" decorated with "mandarin ducks." The birds caught on the pin suggest the plight of the girl, a figurative captive in the midst of luxury. Next the poet contrasts this inner image with the outside scene as he describes the view of the Wu Mountain stretching above the gate, a comparison which further emphasizes the confinement of the girl. After establishing this motif, the poet moves on and pictures the newly budding willow branches as "silk." The willow as a standard symbol of parting evokes a feeling of sadness, and the fact that they are once again in bloom shows that this particular parting has lasted for some time. But the "silk branches" give rise to the next image of the "spring rains," which fall on the bridge and make communication difficult. Here Wen has placed two images of parting together, one suggesting the past and the other very much in the present. But in the south all is loveliness as "fragrant grass lines the bank." And the girl, too, is a figure of beauty, the poet likening her to "a spray of flowers." But ironically even in the midst of all this beauty there is desolation, as she is alone and unappreciated. And the poem ends with the standard rhetorical question, "Who can know her feelings?"

On the surface this poem depicts an elegant scene of sadness and melancholy which, like the eye scanning a scroll painting, selects what it will attend to and what it will ignore. It was obviously written by a poet for whom the visual imagination is paramount. But it is in the juxtaposition of the images, which

¹⁷ See chapter 1, p. 39.

are so carefully, even artificially selected, that the poem takes on meaning and an interior life. No special significance is attached to the "golden hairpin," but when this picture is placed next to the image of "the rising mountain" a unique spatial relationship is created. Although the visual effect of this poem is one of frozen beauty, it is not completely static, and the movement is sensed in the shift of the images one to the other. The images of space, "the hairpin over the pillow" and Wu Mountain, blend with the images of time, "the willow branches" and "the spring rains." But whereas action and change take place in the space and time controlled by nature, the human world does not share in this natural course of events. Action is suspended as "all news is broken off," and life hangs in a balance. The poem closes on a curious note of tension as all the elements come together. Life will not forever hold still, and sooner or later all the beauty of the present will be caught in the space and time of the first lines. Meaning, movement, and emotion arise then not from any logically narrated idea, or from an underlying personal symbolism, they come into being through the special positioning of the images.

Another example of Wen T'ing-yün's technique is the following, written to the tune "Deva-like Barbarian":

```
The moon rises on high, shining in the sky at midnight.
It is quiet in the screens, there is no one to talk to.
In the deep recesses, incense still lingers.
As she sleeps, she wears a trace of make-up.

Long ago she held her flowering beauty dear,
But how can she endure memories of the past?
The flowers wither, and the moonlight fades.
Under the quilts she feels the cold of dawn.[18]
```

The rising moon fills the midnight sky, and the girl is alone. Something of the former pleasure remains in the lingering incense and the light make-up. But the happiness is fast fading away with the "withering flowers" and the "fading moon." The dawn of the present is cold and cheerless. The "rising moon" reaching its midnight or zenith position in the sky signals the decline to come. Once again the scene is one of loneliness as "within the screen there is no one to talk to." These two images placed together express a feeling that unlike the previous poem, events are already progressing toward an unhappy end. The sleeping girl and the reference to "what has been" create a transition between the past and the present. The girl will wake to face the harshness of reality as she already feels the cold of the dawn.

Wen T'ing-yün leaves much to his reader, and the very nature of his art is to conceal itself. His technique is a surface one, and it cannot be denied that

---

[18] See chapter 1, p. 40.

at times the surface is so skillfully presented that it distracts from the basic content. Yet Wen's subtle suggestiveness, when successful, permits him to express what cannot be directly said, or if it can, certainly not with the same power. However this approach would not be effective if there were not a sense of order in his work. It is his artistic perception, at once contained and limitless, that is able to relate all the different elements into a telling whole as the following, written to the tune "Deva-like Barbarian," reveals:

```
The wind rustles the bamboo, and the steps are chilled.
Moonlight playing on the beaded curtains casts shadows.
She hides her face against the block pillow,
A pillow of sandalwood and golden phoenixes.

Her dark brows are pale and worn from grief.
Her old home in the palace of Wu is distant.
At the moment she thinks of spring's sorrow.
In the painted hall, the water clock sounds.[19]
```

Wen T'ing-yün creates an atmosphere of total isolation. The scene is one in which everything is pale, cold, and distant. His focus is on a girl who is crying. It is a simple enough picture, but Wen does not begin with the central point. He takes the reader first by the bamboo trees, up the cold steps, and through the moonlight and the pearl curtains. Only then does Wen introduce the girl whose sadness and loneliness are exactly in key with the rest of the scene. There is a brief pause of regret for the girl, and finally Wen closes with a mention of the sound of the water clock. This brief reference contains the basic theme of the poem, which is a lament for the inexorable passage of time and, with its passage, the loss of youth, beauty, and happiness. This poem, then, becomes something more than an exercise in the rhetoric of a frustrated desire. Wen conjoins his images to suggest the frustration, but his perspective is not blinded by the tightness of his poetic structure, and he sees that the wind in the trees and the crying girl share equally the possibility of loss and change, and that the truth of this condition exists not only in the present, but for all of life and time.

One of the striking elements of the *tz'u* of Wen T'ing-yün is that while they are poems of love, they are, in fact, filled with frustration and hate, as seen in the following, written to the tune "Dreaming of the South":

```
Ever rising resentment,                                       (3)
It reaches out to him at world's end.                         (5)
The moon over the mountain cannot know what she feels.        (7)
In water and wind, flowers fall lifelessly before her.        (7)
Dark clouds tremble and drift aslant.[20]                     (5)
```

[19] See chapter 1, pp. 40–41.
[20] See chapter 2, p. 53.

Wen is described as a "poet of elegant eroticism and fastidious decor,"[21] and this is not to be denied. But even more significantly he is a poet of the desolate spirit. The following is written to the tune "Lotus Leaf Cup":

```
The chill dewdrops are like frozen pearls.              (6)
Wavy reflections,                                       (2)
Sweep the banks of the pond.                            (3)
Green stems and red flowers are piled in confusion.     (7)
Her heart breaks.                                       (2)
The water and wind are cold.22                          (3)
```

There is a quality of exhaustion in Wen's *tz'u*, as though the characters in his poems are incapable of any emotion other than self-pity. They are caught in a physical and mental torpor from which there is no escape. This lassitude is increased as the grieving women are always the same. They are beautiful and they are suffering. There is no individuality nor personality beyond these two essential qualities. This reduces the human figure to a kind of abstraction that represents not a person but rather a general feeling of aloneness. The reader is touched not by the specific situation, but by an identification with the mood. But behind the words there is neither naiveté nor illusion. This is sophisticated and knowing poetry. It depicts love not in the bright shades of morning and innocence, but in the increasingly darker shades of twilight and experience.

Wen T'ing-yün's *tz'u* are, in the main, like reflections in a mirror in which figure and replica interact. "Mirrors, front and behind, reflect a flower, face and flower shining each upon the other." Wen's world is a dream world in which sensations and images pass through the sleeping mind, and there is no longer much difference between the reflection and the reflected. But the dream resorted to by Wen's characters is not the dream of utopia, it is rather a defense against pain. His figures seek sleep and the dream as a means of oblivion or a return in memory to a happy past. It is a suspension of reality which contrasts with the movement of the present. The association of the real and the artificial colors all of Wen T'ing-yün's work. And this contrast of the live and the fabricated creates a scene that is at once immediate and changeless. But Wen's characters seek refuge in the contrived, not in the natural. The processes of nature contrast with or evoke emotion, but they do not assuage it nor enable the figure to rise above the languor of the moment. The silence and drifting of the characters indicate a rejection of reality, but such emptiness can be hollow as well as profound, and while it can sometimes mean rising above the ordinary levels of perception, it can also be symptomatic of non-

---

[21] Glen Baxter, *Hua-chien chi: Songs of Tenth Century China* (Ph.D. diss., Harvard University, 1952; Cambridge: Harvard University Microfilms, 1962), p. 222.

[22] See chapter 2, p. 55.

thinking and vegetation. Wen T'ing-yün's *tz'u* can be both empty illusion and glimpses into the bottomless pool of life and experience.

The special mood and the duality of meaning created by the skill of Wen T'ing-yün suggest the poetic ideals of the nineteenth-century Symbolists who in turn were attracted by the delicate qualities of Chinese and Japanese verse. Baudelaire attempted to project his inner vision on the outside world and sought to develop the interplay between the subjective and the objective. He strove not to make direct statements of experience but to actualize it in image and symbol. Using the stuff of common life he raised its value by making it represent something much more than itself. The emotional synthesis that takes place in Baudelaire's work arises from a mingling of earthy sense perceptions and experiences; perfumes and tears, sounds and colors. Together these stimuli produce a chain of associations that creates a strong but inexpressible mood in the mind of the reader:

```
Amongst gilt fabrics, flasks of scent and wine,
Rich furniture, white marble, precious moulds,
Fine paintings, and rich, perfumed robes that shine
Swirled into sumptuous folds,

In a warm room, that like a hothouse stifles
With dangerous and fatal breath, where lie
Pale flowers in crystal tombs, exquisite trifles,
Exhaling their last sigh--. . .²³
```

Baudelaire believed that the poetic process was as follows, "the stimulus affects the senses, the senses affect the mind, the result is language, brought together by a suprarational vigilance of the Mind. The poem emerges as a whole without the poet's having consciously put it together."[24]

But Baudelaire was preoccupied with good and evil, the angelic and the diabolic. For him the natural was evil, and the artificial represented the good. "Virtue, on the contrary, is artificial and supernatural, since at all times and in all nations it has taken gods and prophets to teach it to bestialized humanity, and since man by himself would have been powerless to discover it."[25] Baudelaire wanted to transcend the limitations of the ordinary and create a whole new world of the mind, "Imagination dissolves all creation. Remassing and reordering her materials by principles which come out of the depths of the human soul, imagination makes a new world, even a new realm of sensory

[23] Charles Baudelaire, "Une Martyre," tr. Roy Campbell in *Flowers of Evil*, ed. Marthiel and Jackson Mathews (New York: New Directions, 1955), p. 108.

[24] Anna Balakian, *The Symbolist Movement* (New York: Random House, 1967), p. 43.

[25] Charles Baudelaire, "Eloge du Maquillage" ("In Praise of Make-up") first published in *Le Figaro*, December 3, 1863. The text is in *L'Art Romantiques, Oeuvres Complète*, ed. Jacques Crépet, IV (Paris: L. Conard, 1925), pp. 95–100.

experience."[26] With his imagery of the senses Baudelaire created an intoxi-
cation that drew forth the extraordinary and the unusual, and within this
scheme he delineated the conflict between good and evil, the artificial and the
natural.

Wen T'ing-yün, too, presents a series of sensual associations and creates a
mood similar to that of Baudelaire. But Wen is not concerned with good and
evil. His imagery is designed to portray a world that for all its loveliness and
luxury is essentially empty. In this respect Wen's lyrics resemble those of
Mallarmé, who also sought escape in memory and the dream:

```
                            O mirror!
cold water frozen by ennui in your frame,
how many times and through what hours, distressed
by dreams and searching my memories, like leaves
under your ice in the deep hole, have I
appeared in you like a shadow far away,
but, horror! in the dusk, in your austere pool
I have known the nakedness of my scattered dreams![27]
```

In Mallarmé's poetry as in Wen's a powerful ennui of existence is translated
into objects and projected onto the character. In Mallarmé as in Wen there
is the acute sensitivity and the tendency to reduce life to inaction and the
dream, the mere reflection of reality.

Of course Wen T'ing-yün is not a Symbolist poet. His effects rise from a
combination of visual and emotional factors and are easily apprehended. But
Wen's interplay of the artificial and the natural, the objective and the subjective
create an overall poetic effect that is both touching and intriguing. They
construct a scene in which the human figure is virtually removed from the
stream of life. Added to this are the repeated references to the inevitable
passage of time. Thus Wen's basic theme is both tragic and ironic, and the
"painted screens" and the "golden partridges" become symbols of the poet's
attempt to stop the inevitable and to protect the beautiful from decay and
death. The poet's conflict is never excessively nor passionately expressed. All
is contained and contrived within the restrictions of the tz'u form itself, a fact
which further strengthens the air of tension that surrounds Wen's poems.

But quite apart from the impression produced in his lyrics by the skillful
interplay of the real and the artificial, Wen's technique represents a departure
from the traditional Chinese concept that poetry ought to serve a moral pur-
pose. In him can be seen an alternative view which stressed a kind of esthetic

[26] Charles Baudelaire, "Salon de 1859," in *Curiosités Esthétiques*, as cited in *A Short History of
Literary Criticism*, ed. Cleanth Brooks and William K. Wimsatt, Jr. (New York: Vintage Books,
1967), p. 481.
[27] Stéphane Mallarmé, "Herodiade," tr. C.F. MacIntyre in *Stéphane Mallarmé, Selected Poems*
(Berkeley: University of California Press, 1957), pp. 30–33.

autonomy, and the expression of this idea in an emphasis on sensory and emotive pleasure. It is not unlike Poe's praise of Beauty in *The Poetic Principle*:

we struggle by multiform combinations among the things and thoughts of time, to attain a portion of that Loveliness whose very elements, perhaps, appertain to eternity alone.[28]

And in China by the ninth century, the idea of the "beautiful" had developed into a system based on "taste" in which the appreciation of the beautiful became somewhat fixed and complex.

The second poet who had a deep influence on the early *tz'u* was Wei Chuang (836–910). He was born in the capital district of Ch'ang-an. When the rebellion of Huang Ch'ao interrupted his official examinations, he fled to Lo-yang where in A.D. 883 he wrote his most famous ballad, "The Lament of the Lady of Ch'in." He wandered about eastern and southern China for about ten years, and then returned to Ch'ang-an in A.D. 893. A year later he received his *chin-shih* degree. Wei Chuang's own life is a testament to the uncertainty of the times. Serving the T'ang government in a minor capacity, Wei made the acquaintance of Wang Chien who, while nominally serving the emperor, made himself the virtual ruler of Szechuan. In A.D. 901 Wei went to serve in Wang Chien's administration. When the last T'ang emperor was forced to abdicate in A.D. 907, Wei urged Wang Chien to proclaim himself emperor. The state thus founded was the Early Shu, and Wei Chuang was a power in the Shu government, instrumental in the formulation of political policy.

Compared to the lyrics of Wen T'ing-yün, Wei Chuang's verses are less allusive and less subtle. His style is openhearted, and although his lyrics lack the dreamy dimension of Wen T'ing-yün's, still they convey a mood that is in some ways more appealing in its forthrightness. The following is written to the tune of "Sand of Silk-Washing Stream":

```
Each night, I think of you until the water clock is still.      (7)
Sorrowing, I stand on the balcony in the bright moonlight.      (7)
I think you too feel the cold all alone within your quilt.      (7)

The painted hall is so near, yet it seems a depthless sea.      (7)
I think of you, but all I can do is read your old letters.      (7)
When can we be together again, hand in hand, in Ch'ang-an?[29]  (7)
```

It is difficult to analyze a poet who writes so simply, and so directly. Any kind of extensive discussion will inevitably appear to labor the obvious.

[28] Edgar Allan Poe, *The Poetic Principle*, as cited in Brooks and Wimsatt, *A Short History of Literary Criticism*, p. 478.
[29] See chapter 2, p. 59.

The mood established by Wen T'ing-yün has delicacy and perception, but it tended to be enervating in the hands of his imitators. Wei Chuang, in contrast, contributed a personal and direct manner to the *tz'u* which enabled it to convey a more intense lyric feeling, but the brevity of the tune patterns limited progression and climax. The short lyric can be extremely effective, but it is generally restricted to the depiction of one quality.

*Among the Flowers* is significant because the *tz'u* became one of the finest representations of Chinese verse. But though Chao Ch'ung-tso's collection shows the growing popularity of the *tz'u* as a poetic form in the ninth and tenth centuries, it also reveals certain weaknesses that had to be overcome before the *tz'u* could flower as a fully mature literary vehicle. Ironically these obstacles are the very features that identify the lyrics in *Among the Flowers*. These poems explore but one main theme—love and pleasure. They do so with great urgency, but without much variety. The *tz'u*, for all its lyric excellence, might never have made the transition from popular song to full-fledged literary genre if later poets had not developed and expanded the melodic lines, and admitted a greater range of topics and themes. But it was the poets in *Among the Flowers* who were among the first to explore the possibilities of the *tz'u*, and in their verses of love gave it a special dignity and beauty.

A second major contradiction in *Among the Flowers* is that although its poetic world is largely dominated by women, it is very much a man's world. Some poems make this explicit as they depict the poet's joy at succeeding in the civil-service examination, or as they describe places visited by the poet in the course of his travels. Others tell of his homesickness, and the sadness felt when he and his friends must part, while other verses speak of the poet's sorrow and longing for his beloved. Still others praise the pleasures of feasting and drinking, and on occasion the poet finds a kind of literary escape as he casts himself in the role of the carefree fisherman and rustic. But by and large, the world of *Among the Flowers* is a feminine world seen through the eyes of men who assume the female persona. It is not the real world of family and social obligation, but a world of pleasure and entertainment, whose lovely inhabitants literary convention and conceit have stylized to an exquisite perfection.

The women are the palace-ladies, the courtesans, the singing and dancing girls, and the prostitutes who were so much an accepted part of the court and social life of the times. Since the public and private aspects of a man's life were to be kept separate, professional and political matters were handled outside the home in the congenial atmosphere of food and drink, music and song, and pretty women. These women were an accepted and important part of the social structure, and were not considered déclassé as in the West. It is Van Gulik's belief that their sexual role was secondary to their social role as hostesses and entertainers.[30] The lyrics in *Among the Flowers* would not entirely support this thesis. Nevertheless given the restrictions imposed in the family and the home, it was in the company of these women, not unlike the Greek hetaerae, that the scholars and poets, officials and generals spent much of their time in informal and relaxed companionship. And it was for just such gatherings that the lyrics in *Among the Flowers* were composed, to the delight of all concerned.

It is not the purpose of this discussion to relate the inequities and injustices that were a woman's lot in traditional China. Suffice it to say, it was a male-dominated society and, as in the West, women had few choices to make about their lives. The lyrics in *Among the Flowers*, dedicated to these women, might have depicted their sorry plight in somewhat more realistic terms, but instead the women are not really true to life, but are highly stylized representations based much more on the conventions of Chinese love poetry than on the actual experience or revelation of the moment.

The theme of love is as old as Chinese poetry itself. Many of the lyrics in the *Book of Songs*, the *Shih-ching*, composed between the twelfth and the seventh centuries B.C., are forthright declarations of love and desire. The subject matter of the verses ranges from the niceties of courtship and marriage to the intrigues of illicit love and moments of stolen passion. Not much is known about the period represented by the *Book of Songs*, the early Chou (1122–770), and much of what is known is based on materials found in the *Book of Songs* itself. It is therefore difficult to determine with any accuracy the actual background of the love verses in this collection. Some critics have chosen to emphasize their possible folk origin, while others see them as products of the court, and still others opt for a middle view by saying that they are folk songs which have been revised and polished by men-of-letters. Chinese tradition holds that the *Book of Songs* was compiled and edited by Confucius (551?–479?). Whether or not this was actually the case, the connection with Confucius elevated the *Book of Songs* to the status of a classic, and as such it was to exert a powerful influence on the subsequent development of Chinese poetry, most partcularly Chinese love poetry.

When Confucianism was accepted as imperial dogma during the first part of the Han dynasty (second and first centuries B.C.), the Confucian scholars found themselves in something of a dilemma. How could they possibly reconcile the frank, even erotic, expressions of love in the *Book of Songs* with the precepts of Confucianism, which placed a heavy emphasis on the moral and the didactic. Allegorical and symbolic interpretations of the poems were formulated, and by the second century after Christ the denotive became the accepted way to read the *Book of Songs*. The plaint of the frustrated lover

---

[30] R. H. Van Gulik, *Sexual Life in Ancient China* (Leiden: E. J. Brill, 1961), p. 178.

became the plea of the government official yearning for a return to stability and good government. The story of a reckless love affair was taken to indicate just how far from the straight and narrow the government of the time had strayed. The loving and even lingering descriptions of one's lover became an image for the "good prince." In short, the prescriptions for one world view were imposed on the literary works of another, and not always to the advantage of either. However in the absence of much real information about the early Chou period, it is possible to assume that at least some of the poems in the *Book of Songs*, even some of the love poems, were written to convey hidden meanings now lost with the passage of time. Nevertheless, the Han Confucians made the lyrics in the *Book of Songs* conform so wholeheartedly to the Confucian tradition that some of the explanations seem quite ridiculous. Chinese scholars such as Chu Hsi (1130–1200) saw the fragile substance of such formulations, and were at pains to place the verses in the *Book of Songs* in a more coherent framework. Yet the idea that the verses in the *Book of Songs* were meant to convey a lesson and illustrate philosophical truth never quite disappeared from the Chinese tradition.

This belief was reinforced by another tradition surrounding the *Book of Songs* and that is that the songs were collected originally from the various parts of the Chou kingdom by emissaries specially dispatched by the king. It was felt that the songs sung by the people would reveal whether or not a particular area was being governed for good or for ill. There is no evidence to support this story, but it strengthened all the more the already close connection between songs, song lyrics, and the quality of government. This close connection established, rather early in the Chinese tradition, the literary convention of the "neglected wife," in which a woman abandoned and rejected by her husband or lover becomes a metaphor for the misunderstood and unappreciated courtier or official. Lyrics expressing the grief of the lost woman could be read, at this level, as the veiled complaint of the government official. The whole notion that the relationship between the sexes was to be read symbolically, and from a Confucian viewpoint, derives from the attempt of the scholar-officials to find hidden allegorical meaning in the revered lines of the *Book of Songs*.

The love lyrics in the *Book of Songs*, whatever the symbolism, deal with relationships between very real men and women. Myth and legend are largely confined to the poems dealing with the divine and semidivine origins of the Chou people, the dynastic hymns. The love poems, on the contrary, are remarkably centered in this world. Man and nature are seen in constant interaction. The harmony or disharmony of the natural scene is used as an image to exemplify the human condition, but always the action takes place within the confines of the human world.

The selections in the *Ch'u-tz'u*, translated by David Hawkes as *The Songs of the South*, represent a second ancient tradition, a southern tradition as opposed to the northern tradition of the *Book of Songs*. *The Songs of the South* was compiled in the second century by Wang I (*fl.* 114–119), long after the composition of its earliest works in the fourth century B.C. In the "*Li-sao*," "Encountering Sorrow," by Ch'ü Yüan, the fourth-century-B.C. poet from the state of Ch'u, we find the same metaphor of ruler and minister as lover and rejected mistress. King Huai (*r.* 329–299), influenced by slanderers at court, has refused to heed the counsel of Ch'ü Yüan and has sent him into exile. Ch'ü Yüan bemoans his fate and laments the indifference of the king, until he can no longer bear it, and he drowns himself in the Mi-lo River. Although the verse form, the *sao*, and the language and imagery differ from that of the *Book of Songs*, the literary convention, although carried to an extreme, remains the same, the "neglected wife." However the background has changed greatly. The poem is no longer earth-centered, but rather opens in boundless directions as Ch'ü Yüan in his frustration embarks on a magical and wonderful tour of the cosmos in a marvelous flying chariot. The spirits of the four quarters are his to command as he ceases to be a devoted minister, and becomes a master magician. David Hawkes believes the poem, "Encountering Sorrow" is written in imitation of material that was originally shamanistic in nature and was based on the ancient religious practices of the state of Ch'u, and as such represents the secularization of such material.[31]

The cycle of poems in *The Songs of the South* entitled the *Nine Songs*, also attributed to Ch'ü Yüan, contains two poems addressed to the Goddess of the Hsiang River, the "Hsiang *fu-jen*," and the "Hsiang-*chün*," as well as a poem to a mountain goddess, simply entitled "*Shan-kuei*," "The Mountain Goddess." In these poems, the poet-shaman attempts to coax the reluctant goddesses to come to join him. The intent is frankly sexual, but the goddesses do not heed the pleas of the poet-shaman, and his hopes are frustrated. Other poems in *The Songs of the South* imitate these motifs, which David Hawkes has termed the *tristia*, the unendurable sorrow attendant on the poet's plaint, and the "quest of the goddess," the attempt to flee from an impure and hostile world to an ideal world of beauty and harmony.[32] In the later poems in *The Songs of the South*, probably composed at successive intervals between the second century B.C. and the second century after Christ, the poet seeks to magically escape from this world of suffering to a better world inhabited by the gods and goddesses, but he also attains to immortality as well. With the rising popularity of religious Taoism, in which the adept sought by various

---

[31] David Hawkes, "The Quest of the Goddess," *Asia Major* 13 (1967), pp. 72–73.
[32] *Ibid.*, p. 82.

means such as diet, yoga, special elixirs, and sexual practices to attain im-
mortality and to live forever among the lovely and charming inhabitants of
Paradise, the image of the goddess becomes even more frankly seductive and
erotic.

In the "Kao-t'ang *fu*," and the "Shen-nü *fu*," attributed to Sung Yü, the
third-century-B.C. poet from the state of Ch'u who was believed to be a disciple
of Ch'ü Yüan, this view of the goddess, most specifically the Goddess of the
Wu Mountain, becomes apparent. King Hsiang (*r.* 298–265), the son and
successor of King Huai, is strolling with Sung Yü by the Kao-t'ang Pavilion,
a site associated with the rituals devoted to the Goddess of the Wu Mountain.
The king asks Sung Yü to describe for him the lovely goddess that once
favored a king of Ch'u in a dream. Sung Yü replies with a rhapsodic description
of the goddess, and promises King Hsiang that such pleasure, and even long
life, can be his if only he will practice good government, a powerful incentive
for the promotion of a well-ordered administration. But the beauty of the
immortal goddess, on the contrary, also represented a temptation to the would-
be supplicant who sought to "still the passions," to turn away from worldly
desire and pleasure in order to attain a spiritual purity in which all desire,
including sexual desire, is absent. The topic "Stilling the Passions" became a
popular subject for poetic treatment in which the lovely goddess is described
in sensuous detail, but although the goddess is eminently desirable, the poet
seeks to remain celibate, "My heart rejoices in her chaste beauty / And I am
bound to her in unrequited love."[33]

The "neglected wife" and the "goddess," the human and divine represen-
tations of woman, are two of the most enduring images in Chinese love poetry,
and because of their ancient associations and political symbolism, two of the
most powerful. But it will be noted that in both conventions the emphasis is
on unrequited, and unconsummated love. The overwhelming majority of
Chinese love poems are characterized by a mood of sadness and melancholy
because for one reason or another the desired union does not take place. This
is a curious aspect of Chinese love poetry. Since most of the poems were
written by men, even though they frequently assumed the female persona,
the viewpoint is nonetheless masculine, and one would expect a much more
vigorous celebration of physical pleasure and desire. Of course, many such
poems do exist, but the tendency in Chinese poetry is in the opposite direction,
it tends to depict the pain and suffering that come from frustration.

The two major male types that occur in such poetry, the *chün-tzu*, the lord
(later the emperor) and husband, and the *tang-tzu* or *yu-tzu*, "the wanderer,"
"the exile," and in some contexts, "the profligate" are long absent and distant

---

[33] Ts'ai Yung (132–192), "Curbing Excess," tr. James R. Hightower in "The *Fu* of T'ao Ch'ien,"
in *Studies in Chinese Literature*, ed. John L. Bishop, Harvard Yenching Institute Studies XXI
(Cambridge: Harvard University Press, 1966), p. 190.

from the poetic scene. This derives, at least in part, from the early political associations just discussed, so that the plight of the woman becomes a device for the expression of regret and unfulfillment, and in a society that little honored the celibate, the theme of love can be strangely negative. An odd tension is therefore created between what we know of Chinese culture and the manner in which love finds expression in Chinese poetry. In the West, a somewhat similar situation occurs in the "courtly-love tradition" which praises and exalts women, and the reality which finds them in a rather unhappy situation. We can be sure that the importance given to "frustrated feelings" in Chinese love poetry is also such a literary device or convention and may or may not in any given poem reflect a true situation.

The symbolism inherent in the "neglected wife" and the "goddess" is present also in the figure of the palace lady, and by extension, the courtesan and the prostitute as well. Though their beauty is that of the fair goddess, they must live lonely and desolate lives, surrounded by every luxury but without human love and companionship. Nowhere is this image of the palace lady made more explicit than in the palace-style poetry that became the vogue in the sixth century. From the real world of the *Book of Songs*, and the supernatural realms of *The Songs of the South*, we move into the aristocratic setting of palace and court. Examples of this style of poetry are to be found in the *Yü-t'ai hsin yung, New Songs from the Jade Terrace*, compiled by Hsü Ling (507–583), and containing over 600 love poems from the Han dynasty to the Liang, from about the second century B.C. to the sixth century after Christ.

The poetic world created in "palace-style poetry" is devoted entirely to women. The development of this style of poetry owes much to the folk song tradition in the region of Wu, the lower Yangtze area around Nanking and Shanghai, and many such lyrics are preserved in the *Yüeh-fu shih-chi*, a collection of song lyrics compiled in the twelfth century. They are generally short, playful, given to puns, and concentrated on the longing for an absent lover. But whereas the Wu-Songs deal with the lives of merchants and traders, palace-style poetry is concerned with the rarefied lives of the aristocracy and the upper classes. The literary image that emerges is once again that of the dazzling beauty of rare accomplishment who languishes all alone and unappreciated. The metaphor is unmistakable, and all-pervasive. In the lyrics in *Among the Flowers*, the poets sing of the tragedy of unrequited love and the grief of the woman who waits for her loved one in vain, but they sing, too, of their own hopes and dreams lost in the imperfect world around them.

The poetic world of *Among the Flowers* is a world closed to outside demands or responsibility and duty. Elegantly clad men and women move gracefully in silken garments amid luxurious furnishings. The women of the T'ang period wore a long robe, lined in winter and of lighter weight in summer, over a pair of trousers. (The robes of the women resemble the Japanese kimono, which was derived from the T'ang models, and the large sashlike obi was also derived from the T'ang custom of wearing an elaborately wound sash which was tied in a bow in the front.) Over the long robe, the women of the T'ang wore a long apron, tied below the bosom with a ribbon. For outside wear, a loose outer robe with wide flaring sleeves was added. Women of the T'ang and Sung dynasties are often pictured wearing long scarves, the ends of which reached to the floor. Paintings also show that during the T'ang dynasty the neck and a portion of the bosom were exposed. This seems to have been particularly true of dancing girls. During the Sung dynasty, however, the style changed and a high-collared gown similar to the one worn today became the fashion.

Hair was worn piled high in a chignon with softly coiled tresses at the temples. Elaborate gold and jeweled hairpins, flowers, and feathers were worn on the head. The lips were reddened with a cream, and large round patches of rouge were placed under the eyes. Black, red, and gold beauty marks were painted on the forehead, chin, and cheeks, and often a large beauty spot was painted on the forehead with a yellow salve or powder. Eyebrows were an important part of the face, and artificial brows were painted at various angles above the natural brow line.

The practice of footbinding did not begin until a time shortly before A.D. 950 or just about the time Ou-yang Chiung wrote the preface to *Among the Flowers*. It is mentioned just once in a lyric to "Sand of Silk-Washing Stream" written by Mao Hsi-chen (*c.* A.D. 940).[34] The women of the T'ang lived active lives and were fond of athletics. Dancing was an especially admired part of any entertainment. It was not until the Sung dynasty that the practice of footbinding became so widespread. During the T'ang, women and men both wore boots or shoes with upturned points.

The men wore wide loose trousers indoors under a long robe. A silk sash was used to hold the robe in place. Outdoors men added a second robe, a little smaller so the collar and sleeves of the first robe could still be seen. Their hair was long and wound up in a topknot, and held with a hairpin. Pieces of black gauze stood out from the head like wings. In addition, they also wore caps of different shapes and sizes. The shape of the cap, the design on the robe, the style of the belt, and various insignia suspended from the belt all were indications of official rank. The ideal male figure seems to have been the bearded and mustachioed bravo. The ideal female figure was somewhat rounded, the waist was slender and the hips full. Again during the Sung dynasty, the fashion changed and a slim delicate figure became the ideal for both men and women.

Rooms were furnished with low benches of carved and lacquered wood. There were different kinds of low tables, and small cupboards. The floors

---

[34] See chapter 9, p. 175.

were covered with rush mats or rugs, and the people seem to have removed
their shoes upon entering a room and, just as in Japan today, thick-soled socks
were worn while inside. There were movable screens decorated with paintings
and elaborate carvings. Samples of calligraphy were hung on the walls. Incense
burners of various shapes and degrees of elegance were placed in the room,
and they not only served to scent the room, but to dry and fumigate clothes
as well. The bed was placed on a raised dais over which was a frame. Curtains
were hung from this frame, and the bed became a private and separate room
of its own. Life for the upper classes in the T'ang capital of Ch'ang-an, and
later during the Five Dynasties in Ch'eng-tu, was cosmopolitan, sophisticated,
and comfortable. The scenes created in the lyrics in *Among the Flowers* are of
luxury and beauty dimmed only by the mists and clouds of dreams.

A third major contradiction in *Among the Flowers* is that although the music
came from the popular tradition, the lyrics were written in accordance with
a carefully prescribed tonal and rhyme sequence that belied too direct a de-
rivation from folk tunes. The origin of the *tz'u* as a distinct poetic genre is
still very much a matter of speculation. Some scholars see it as an outgrowth
of the *yüeh-fu*, or the folk song tradition, most particularly the popular songs
of the region of Wu, much imitated in the Six Dynasties (222–589) and the
early years of the T'ang dynasty. Others hold that it developed from the
regulated verse, the *lü-shih*, a rigid and somewhat difficult poetic form in
which, however, much of the greatest T'ang poetry is written. Those who
adhere to the former view do so because any new type of poetry in the history
of Chinese literature is closely connected with the introduction of new fashions
in music and singing, and the rise and development of a new poetic form has
always depended in large part on the influence of folk songs.

This interaction can be seen in the emergence around the second century
of the five-character and the later seven-character *shih* form of poetry from
the Han *yüeh-fu*, the folk songs of the Han dynasty associated with the Music
Bureau established by Emperor Wu around 120 B.C. In the process of this
development, the irregular line lengths of the earlier folk songs more and
more often tended toward the regular five-character line length of the *shih*,
until textually there was no difference between them. The distinction at the
time seems to have been that one set of lyrics was written to be sung, and
another set of lyrics was not. But it was the interaction of the folk tradition
with the genius and skill of the literati that gave rise to the *shih*, the most
durable and popular verse form in Chinese history.

Those who adhere to the latter view trace the development of *tz'u* from the
"song-words," the *ko-tz'u* of the seventh and eighth centuries. These "song-
words" are nearly always written in lines of equal length with symmetrical
stanzas, and it would seem that the term *ko-tz'u* did not apply to a particular
genre of musical lyrics, but rather to the function of the poem as "song-

words."[35] Many of these "song-words" turn out to be *chüeh-chü*, four-line verses, written in accord with the rhyme and tonal sequences of the regulated-verse form, or in accord with the ancient-style verse, the earlier and tonally freer *ku-shih*. In the attempt to make a regular pattern of words fit an irregular line of music for purposes of performance, a word might be held for several notes (melisma), short pauses could be taken while the music played on, exclamations and even nonsense words could be thrown in, filler words could be used and so on. The poetic patterns that resulted from the inclusion of these interpolations would consist largely of lines of unequal length.

The *tz'u* began to emerge in the ninth century as a recognizable poetic genre, different and distinct from other forms of poetry, yet still very similar to *shih* in that there was a strong preference for five- and seven-character lines, and most similar to regulated-verse because the *tz'u* form, too, had to follow specific rules for tonal sequence and rhyme. The Chinese language is characterized by a large number of homophones, and to help ease the confusion of so many similar sounds, a system of musical accents or "tones" is employed. The standard pronunciation in Peking today has four tones: the level or even tone, the rising tone, the low tone, and the falling tone. In modern Cantonese there are nine tones. (Modern Cantonese, it may be noted, more closely approximates the pronunciation of the T'ang dynasty than do the other dialects in China today.) In the sixth century there were eight tones. Shen Yüeh (441–512), a poet of the Six Dynasties, devised a system of versification based on the deliberate manipulation of these tones for greater euphony, and these strictures were influential in T'ang verse and in the development of regulated-verse. The tones were divided into two groups, the *p'ing* referred to the level or even tones, and the *tse* referred to the deflected or oblique tones. The patterning of regulated-verse stipulated the tonal sequence for each line, although there was some flexibility. Rhymes had to be either words from the *p'ing* group or words from the *tse* group. In other words, a word pronounced with a *p'ing* tone would not be considered to rhyme with a word of the *tse* group even if they were otherwise identical in sound.

These basic rules were retained for the *tz'u*, but because of the greater variety of line length due to the influence of music, there is a far greater range of tonal and melodic possibilities than is offered by the *shih*. The following pattern is one of three for "The Deva-like Barbarian" as listed in the *Tz'u-p'u*.[36] O indicates where a tone from the *p'ing* group is called for, X indicates where a tone from the *tse* group ought to occur, and R indicates the rhyme

---

[35] Glen W. Baxter, "Metrical Origins of the *Tz'u*" in John L. Bishop, *Studies in Chinese Literature*, p. 190.

[36] Based on a *tz'u* written by Chu Tun-ju (1080?–1175?), *Tz'u-p'u*, 5.2a.

sequence:

```
0 0 X X 0 0 X      (RX)      (7)
0 0 X X 0 0 X      (RX)      (7)
0 X X 0 0          (RO)      (5)
X 0 0 X 0          (RO)      (5)

X 0 0 X X          (RX)      (5)
0 X 0 0 X          (RX)      (5)
X X X 0 0          (RO)      (5)
X 0 0 X 0          (RO)      (5)
```

In contrast, the following is a tonal pattern for "The Water Clock at Night"[37] as listed in the *Tz'u-p'u*:

```
X 0 0                        (3)
0 X X              (RX)      (3)
X X X 0 0 X        (RX)      (6)
0 X X                        (3)
X 0 0              (RO)      (3)
X 0 0 X 0          (RO)      (5)

0 X X                        (3)
X 0 0              (RO)      (3)
X 0 X X 0 0        (RO)      (6)
0 X X                        (3)
X 0 0              (RO)      (3)
0 0 X X 0          (RO)      (5)
```

A final illustration of the way the tone and rhyme are used in *tz'u* poetry is the following, a pattern for "The Song of the Heavenly Immortal," by Huang-fu Sung (*c.* A.D. 859), as listed in the *Tz'u-p'u*.[38] In this pattern there is some flexibility, and the brackets indicate that the tone may be either *p'ing* or *tse* as the poet chooses:

| ch'ing | yeh | lu — ssu | fei | i — chih | | (7) |
|---|---|---|---|---|---|---|
| [0] | X | [X]  0 | 0 | X    X | (RX) | |
| clear—sky | fields | egret | flies | alone | | |

| shui — hung | hua | fa | ch'iu | chiang | pi | (7) |
|---|---|---|---|---|---|---|
| [X]   [0] | 0 | [0] | 0 | [0] | X | (RX) |
| water—pepper | flowers | bloom | autumn | river | jade—green | |

---

[37] Based on a *tz'u* written by Sun Kuang-hsien (898?–968), *Tz'u-p'u*, 6.2b–3a.
[38] *Tz'u-p'u*, 19b–20a.

```
Liu  -  lang      tz'u   jih   pieh   t'ien   hsien              (7)
[0]     0         [X]    X     X      0       0
Liu  -  master    this   day   part   heavenly  immortal
  (young man)


teng       ch'i   hsi                                            (3)
[0]        [X]    X      (RX)
move-to    silk   mat


lei        chu    ti                                             (3)
[X]        [0]    X      (RX)
tears      pearls drop


shih  -  erh   wan      feng    kao    li - li                   (7)
[X]      X     [X]      0       0      X    X        (RX)
twelve        evening  peaks   high   in-succession
```

Such complexities of rhyme and tonal sequence cannot possibly be conveyed
in English. But I have made an attempt in this translation of *Among the Flowers*
to suggest the *importance* of the line-pattern even though it is also impossible
to reproduce the original in English. I have translated this *tz'u* as follows:

```
A lone egret flies in a clear sky across the open fields.        (7)
Water pepper blooms along the jade green river in autumn.        (7)
This day, the young man must part from his fair immortal.        (7)
He moves up close to her side,                                   (3)
Her teardrops are like pearls.                                   (3)
The twelve peaks of Mount Wu loom across the evening sky.[39]    (7)
```

It is easy to see why the *tz'u* became such a popular poetic form. The chang-
ing tune patterns were a stimulus and a challenge to the poets and they would
work the same theme over and over in a variety of different forms, much as
musical instruments play in their own way variations on the same melody. In
the Sung dynasty, the *tz'u* would rival even the hallowed *shih* for supremacy.
The *tz'u* remained a favored form, and even so redoubtable a figure as Mao
Tse-tung wrote *tz'u* in the time-honored tradition. The poets in *Among the
Flowers*, some known, others virtually unknown, have left an enduring and
beautiful legacy to the literature of China.

[39] See chapter 2, pp. 55–56.

# Preface to *Among the Flowers* by Ou-yang Chiung (896–971)

Songs are like skillfully carved jade and alabaster which duplicate the artistry of nature. They are like artificial flowers which retain the beauty and freshness of spring. When the Queen Mother of the West[1] feasted with King Mu[2] at the Yao Pond, she sang the "White Cloud Song."[3] The rosy wine was poured, and King Mu's heart was carried away.[4] The one who was famous for singing the "White Snow Song"[5] sang every note in harmony with the cry of the marvelous *luan*.[6] The one whose song stilled the drifting clouds[7] sang every

---

[1] The Queen Mother of the West (Hsi wang mu) is a deity who dwells to the west in the fabulous K'un-lun mountains. In the *Shan-hai ching,* she is described as having a human shape, a leopard's tail, tiger's teeth, a terrible snarl, and a kind of headdress over her tangled hair. *Shan-hai ching, Ssu-pu pei-yao,* 2.19ab. In later Taoist literature, she became a beautiful and gracious personage who acted as the guardian of the herb of immortality.

[2] King Mu of Chou is a semi-legendary figure who is supposed to have flourished around 900 B.C. There are various accounts of his purported travels to fantastic realms such as the K'un-lun mountains.

[3] According to one version of their famous meeting, King Mu feasted with the Queen Mother of the West at the Yao Pond in K'un-lun. The Queen Mother sang the "White Cloud Song," "*Pai-yün yao*":

White clouds are in the sky,
Coming forth from the hills.
The road is distant and far,
Hills and rivers lie between.
I want you not to die,
So you will come again!

*Mu t'ien-tzu chuan, Ssu-pu pei-yao,* 3.1a.

[4] The "rosy wine" is a kind of nectar of the gods believed to confer the *Tao* and immortal life.

[5] The "White Snow Song," "*Pai-hsüeh ko*," is the name of an ancient tune supposed to have been composed by Shih K'uang, the court musician of Duke P'ing of Chin (r. 557–532) and the most famous musician in Chinese history. Lyrics to a "White Snow Song" are found in the *Yüeh-fu shih-chi,* comp. Kuo Mao-ch'ien (twelfth century) (Taipei: Shih-chieh shu-chü, 1961), 57.2b–3a. In the "*Tui Ch'u-wang wen,*" Sung Yü (a third century B.C. Ch'u poet) tells the king that the "White Snow Song" and the "Spring Song," "*Yang-ch'un ch'ü*" are the most beautiful melodies in the kingdom, and that it is the rare musician who is capable of mastering them. *Wen-hsüan,* comp. Hsiao T'ung (501–531) (Taipei: Kuang-wen shu-chü, 1965), 45.1a–2a.

[6] The *luan* is a mythical bird resembling a phoenix.

[7] This is an allusion to Ch'in Ch'ing, a musician of ancient times who "beating time, chanted a mournful strain. The sound shook the trees, and stilled the drifting clouds." *Lieh-tzu,* ed. Yang Po-chün (Taipei: T'ai-p'ing shu-chü, 1965), pp. 110–11.

word in accord with the harmony of the phoenix.[8] The songs, "Picking the Willows," and "The Great Embankment" were handed down by the Music Bureau.[9] And gentlemen of the most prominent families wrote lyrics about "hibiscus" and "winding river banks."[10]

Poets competed for precedence before their patrons as in the story of "the three thousand guests and the tortoise shell pins."[11] They strove to outdo each other at their feasts, as did the rivals with their "coral trees."[12] There were gentlemen on the silken mats, and ladies behind ornamented curtains.

---

[8] This refers to the twelve semitones in the Chinese octave arranged by Ling Lun, a musician believed to have lived during the reign of the legendary Yellow Emperor. Ling Lun is said to have derived the tones by listening to the singing of the phoenix, the male giving him six tones, and the female giving him six tones. *Han-shu*, vol. 3, ed. Yen Shih-ku (Peking: Chung-hua shu-chü, 1962), 21.959.

[9] "Picking the Willows," "*Che Yang-liu*," is a *yüeh-fu* song. There are several different tunes in the *Yüeh-fu shih-chi* with this title, but the lyrics referred to here are undoubtedly those in 25.7ab. "The Great Embankment," "*Ta-t'i ch'ü*," is also a *yüeh-fu* song. It is found in the *Yüeh-fu shih-chi*, 48.7b–8b. The phrase "*ta-t'i*" can also refer to the "Hsiang-yang *yüeh*," "Melody of Hsiang-yang," *Yüeh-fu shih-chi*, 48.6a–7a.

[10] The lyrics referred to here are somewhat unclear. Hua Lien-p'u in the *Hua-chien chi chu* (Shanghai: Commercial Press, 1935), p. iii, suggests that the "hibiscus," "*fu-jung*," is a reference to the first line in the sixth of the "Nineteen Old Poems of the Han," "I cross the river to pick hibiscus." Ting Fu-pao, ed. *Ch'üan Han san-kuo Chin nan-pei ch'ao shih*, vol. 1 (Taipei: Shih-chieh shu-chü, 1969), p. 160. And Hua further suggests that the "winding banks," "*ch'ü-chu*," is an allusion to a poem by Ho Hsün (d. *circa* A.D. 527), "*Sung* Wei *Ssu-ma pieh*," "I say farewell near the winding river banks." Ting Fu-pao, vol. 3, p. 1146. However, these two poems do not apply to Ou-yang's discussion very well. There is a *yüeh-fu* to a tune entitled "*Fu-jung hua*," "The Hibiscus Flowers," by Hsin Te-yüan (*fl. c.* A.D. 570) in the *Yüeh-fu shih-chi*, 77.3a. And if the character for *chu*, "banks," is emended to a similar character, *ch'ih*, "pond," there is a *yüeh-fu* entitled "*Ch'ü-ch'ih shui*," "The Waters of the Winding Pond," by Hsieh T'iao (464–499) in the *Yüeh-fu shih-chi*, 75.3a. These two songs and their authors are more in keeping with Ou-yang's statement about "gentlemen of the most prominent families writing lyrics about 'hibiscus' and 'winding river banks.'" But it is also possible that the "hibiscus" and the "winding river banks" are references to general topics rather than to specific poems, and on this point there can be no argument, for "gentlemen" did indeed write many poems about "hibiscus" and "winding river banks."

[11] Lord P'ing-yüan of Chao (third century B.C.) sent an envoy to Lord Ch'un-shen of Ch'u (third century B.C.). The emissary wished to show off in front of the courtiers of Ch'u, and so he had pins made of tortoise shell, and a sword decorated with pearls and jade. When he joined the retainers of Lord Ch'un-shen, numbering more than three thousand, they were all wearing shoes made of pearls. The man from Chao was greatly ashamed. *Shih-chi, Ssu-pu pei yao*, 78.5b–6a.

[12] The "coral trees" refer to a rivalry of riches between Shih Ch'ung (249–300) and Wang K'ai (*fl.* late third century). Since Emperor Wu of the Chin dynasty (*r.* 265–290) was Wang K'ai's nephew, he frequently assisted Wang in his attempts to outdo the ostentatious display of Shih Ch'ung. On one occasion, he presented Wang with a coral tree about two feet high. When Shih Ch'ung saw it, he struck it with an iron baton, and the tree shattered. Wang was, of course, furious since the tree was so valuable. Shih Ch'ung replied that the tree wasn't so precious as to be worth great distress, and he ordered his attendants to bring out all his own coral trees. Every one of them was some three or four feet in height and surpassed in beauty anything seen in the world. There were six or seven trees in all, more than had ever been possessed by Wang K'ai. Wang stood speechless and dismayed. *Chin-shu*, vol. 4, comp. Fang Hsüan-ling (578–648) (Peking: Chung-hua shu-chü, 1974), 33.1007.

Page after page, they passed around the flowered paper,[13] and their literary offerings were like beautiful embroideries. The women raised their delicate fingers and beat time with the fragrant wood.[14] There was no lack of splendid lines to enhance the graceful postures of the singers. However, during the southern dynasties, the palace-style of poetry[15] revived the music of Pei-li.[16] Not only were the words inelegant, the ideas though flowery were without substance!

From the time of the T'ang dynasty [618–907], in all parts of the country, on the fragrant paths amid spring breezes, every household had its own beauty of Yüeh.[17] And wherever the evening moon shone on the red towers,[18] there the Lady of the Moon herself was to be found.[19] At the time of the Emperor Hsüan-tsung of the T'ang dynasty [r. 713–756], Li Po [701–762] under imperial order wrote the four "*Ch'ing-p'ing*" songs.[20] More recently, there is the *Golden Weir Collection* of Wen T'ing-yün [812–870].[21] Present-day writers are not inferior to their predecessors.

Now the Lesser Lord of the Imperial Insignia, Chao Ch'ung-tso [*fl.* mid-tenth century], has collected extraordinary songs from near and far, and their literary merit far excels common folk music. Chao has many friends, and often they gave him good suggestions. Consequently, he was able to collect five hundred *tz'u* which he divided into ten chapters. Because I have some slight knowledge of music, Chao was kind enough to ask me to title this collection,

[13] The "flowered paper" is a kind of elegantly decorated stationery.

[14] The "fragrant wood" refers to a type of musical clapper which consists of two pieces of sandalwood.

[15] The palace-style of poetry is a slow-moving erotic type of poetry that was extremely popular during the sixth and seventh centuries. It was based on critical precepts developed by Hsiao Kang (503–551), who was to become Emperor Chien-wen of the Liang dynasty (r. 550–551). He felt that poetry ought to be the unrestrained expression of feelings. The palace-style is important in Chinese literary development, and its influence is very much apparent in the *Hua-chien chi.* However, Ou-yang Chiung probably considered the basic premise of the palace-style to be in excess.

[16] The music of Pei-li was supposed to have been composed for the last and infamous ruler of the Shang dynasty, Chou Hsin, whose crimes caused the downfall of the dynasty in 1122 B.C. The term came to be used more commonly for music associated with the pleasure quarters.

[17] This is a reference to Hsi Shih, the famous beauty from the ancient state of Yüeh who was sent by the King of Yüeh, Kou Chien (r. 496–465) to the King of Wu, Fu Ch'ai (r. 495–473), to distract him from his official duties. Wu fell to Yüeh in 473 B.C.

[18] The red towers are the apartments of women, most specifically, the quarters of courtesans and singing girls.

[19] The Lady of the Moon is Ch'ang O, who stole the elixir of immortality from her husband, I the Archer, and fled with it to the moon. Despite the fact that she was turned into a toad as punishment, the reference here is to great beauty.

[20] Sources now agree that Li Po wrote only three sets of lyrics and not four as Ou-yang states. These songs were set to music and were believed to have been written to praise the beauty of the emperor's favorite, Yang Kuei-fei.

[21] The *Golden Weir Collection, Chin-ch'üan chi,* was an anthology of Wen T'ing-yün's poetry in ten chapters, but it is no longer extant.

and to write a preface. In ancient times in the city of Ying,[22] they sang the "Spring Song,"[23] and it was praised as being the most exceptional of lyrics. It was with this in mind that I named this book, *Among the Flowers.* It will add to the pleasure of those gentlemen who ramble in the West Garden in the early spring.[24] And the ladies from the south can stop singing songs about the lotus boat.[25]

Written by Ou-yang Chiung A.D. 940, summer!

[22] Ying was the name of the capital of the ancient state of Ch'u.

[23] The "Spring Song" is the name of an ancient tune. See above, note 5. Ou-yang's point here is to emphasize the elegance and artistry of the lyrics in the *Hua-chien chi* as compared with ordinary folk songs.

[24] The image intended by the West Garden is simply one of men at leisure, drinking wine and composing poetry. Ou-yang Chiung echoes the line from the *"Kung-yen shih,"* or "The Banquet Poem" by Ts'ao Chih (192–232), "On a clear night I wander in the West Garden, / The flying carriages pursue one another." Ting Fu-pao, vol. 1, p. 160.

[25] Songs about the lotus boat refer to the continuing popularity of songs about picking the lotus, some of which are found in the *Yüeh-fu shih-chi,* 50.4b–8a.

# CHAPTER ONE

## Wen T'ing-yün (812–870)

### "Deva-like Barbarian" (*P'u-sa man*), Fourteen Lyrics

### [1]

```
The mountains on the screen shimmer in the golden dawn.      (7)
A cloud of hair brushes the fragrant snow of her cheek.      (7)
Lazily, she rises and paints mothlike brows.                 (5)
Slowly, tardily, she gets ready for the day.                 (5)

Mirrors, front and behind, reflect a flower,                 (5)
Face and flower shining each upon the other.                 (5)
Stitched in the silk of her bright new coat,                 (5)
Golden-threaded partridges fly pair by pair.                 (5)
```

### [2]

```
Within crystal curtains, she rests on a crystal pillow.
In a mandarin duck quilt, warm fragrances rouse dreams.
The willows on the river are hazy like mist.
Wild geese fly in the sky as the moon fades.

She wears an ivory gown, pale as lotus root,
In her hair, a cluster of fine silk ribbons.
At her temples, sweet buds frame her beauty.
On high, a jade hairpin shivers in the wind.
```

### [3]

```
Her forehead seems powdered with crushed yellow pollen.
In her evening make-up, she smiles shyly by the window.
They were together when the peonies bloomed,
But time is short and soon they had to part.

From the blue-green tip of her gold hairpin,
A pair of butterflies dances back and forth.
Who knows the sorrow that lies in her heart?
In the moonlight flowers cover the branches.
```

## [4]

The blue tufts of the mandarin ducks are threaded gold.
In spring the azure pond is awash with shallow ripples.
A cherry-apple tree is standing by the pond.
Red blooms fill its branches after the rain.

With her sleeve she hides her dimpled smile.
Butterflies seem pasted to a mist of greens.
Her doorway faces the lush expanse of grass,
But there is little news from the Jade Pass.

## [5]

The dew-drenched apricot flowers are sweet snowy balls.
On the willow-lined path there have been many partings.
In the waning moonlight, the lamp is bright.
She wakens to the sound of the dawn orioles.

A jade hook catches the blue-green curtains.
Her make-up is pale and worn from the night.
Her dreams are filled with thoughts of love.
In the mirror, her hair looks much too thin.

## [6]

In the jade tower bright with moonlight, she remembers.
The willow branches were long and graceful that spring.
Outside the gate the grass grew luxuriantly.
As they parted, she heard his horse cry out.

Gilt kingfishers cover a sheer silk curtain.
A fragrant candle sheds tears of melted wax.
The flowers wither and the cuckoo cries out.
By the silken window, her dream goes astray.

## [7]

Two golden-stitched phoenixes lie coiled on her jacket.
Like the delicate showering of evening rain on a peony,
Her new make-up shines in the bright mirror.
But her hair is thin, and her cheeks hollow.

In the painted hall, long she waits for him.
Beyond the balcony, willow branches dip low.
Since he left there has been no news of him.
Two swallows circle above the village altar.


## [8]


The peonies fade, and the orioles' songs are at an end.
Willows fill the garden, and moonlight fills the court.
Because she thinks of him, she cannot sleep.
A flickering lamp burns dimly at the window.

A feathered hairpin falls close to her face.
She is lonely in the fragrance of her rooms.
Tears flow down her cheeks for one far away.
The swallows fly off leaving spring to fade.


## [9]


Bright moonlight in the house whitens the pear blossom.
Unending miles of mountains and passes keep them apart.
A pair of golden geese soar through the sky.
Traces of tears dampen her embroidered robe.

In the small garden the lush grass is green.
Once she dwelt near the winding Yüeh stream.
The rich beauty of the willow has not faded.
The swallows return, but he does not return.


## [10]


Mandarin ducks atop a gold hairpin dip over the pillow.
Above the aloe-wood hall, Wu Mountain seems to be jade.
Once again the willow branches turn to silk.
The spring rains have shut the post-bridges.

In the painted hall, all news is broken off.
South of the river, grasses cover the banks.
A flowering spray in the glow of the mirror,
Who can know what her feelings are just now?

## [11]

Piles of catkins cover the grounds in the south garden.
Sadly she had listened as it rained on ch'ing-ming day.
It was sundown when the rain came to an end.
Fallen apricot petals spread sweet perfumes.

Without a word, she strokes her sleepy face.
The screen above the pillow is still closed.
Twilight is coming, the hour of yellow dusk.
Cheerless and alone, she stands by the door.

## [12]

The moon rises on high, shining in the sky at midnight.
It is quiet in the screens, there is no one to talk to.
In the deep recesses, incense still lingers.
As she sleeps, she wears a trace of make-up.

Long ago she held her flowering beauty dear,
But how can she endure memories of the past?
The flowers wither, and the moonlight fades.
Under the quilts she feels the cold of dawn.

## [13]

After the rain the mimosa are graceful in the sunlight.
Their red flowering branches are delicate and fragrant.
She daydreams, recollecting the golden hall.
Tall day-lilies spread across the courtyard.

Tassels hang down from the brocade curtains.
Her brows are the green of the far mountain.
The waters of spring cross under the bridge.
By the railing, her heart is about to break.

## [14]

The wind rustles the bamboo, and the steps are chilled.
Moonlight playing on the beaded curtains casts shadows.
She hides her face against the block pillow,
A pillow of sandalwood and golden phoenixes.

Her dark brows are pale and worn from grief.
Her old home in the palace of Wu is distant.
At the moment she thinks of spring's sorrow.
In the painted hall, the water clock sounds.

# "Song of the Water Clock at Night" (*Keng-lou tzu*), Six Lyrics

## [1]

| | |
|---|---|
| The willow branches are long. | (3) |
| The spring rain is a drizzle. | (3) |
| A distant water clock echoes beyond the flowers. | (6) |
| The wild geese start in fear, | (3) |
| And crows rise from the wall. | (3) |
| Golden partridges decorate the screen. | (5) |
| | |
| A delicate mist of fragrance, | (3) |
| Spreads through the curtains. | (3) |
| Sadness permeates the grand ponds and pavilions. | (6) |
| The red candle is behind her. | (3) |
| Brocaded curtains trail down. | (3) |
| Long she dreams, but he does not know. | (5) |

## [2]

The stars are thin-scattered.
The watch bells have stopped.
Orioles and a faded moon are beyond the curtain.
The orchids lie heavy in dew.
The willows bend in the wind.
Piles of fallen petals fill the court.

Up above her empty apartment,
She watches from the balcony.
Her grief is the same as it was the year before.
Spring is drawing to a close,
Her thoughts go on endlessly.
Past joys return as though in a dream.

## [3]

Gold birds adorn her hairpin.
Her face is dusted with pink.
Among the flowers, they are together so briefly,
"You understand my affection!"

"I am moved by your feelings!"
Only Heaven can appreciate their love.

The incense burns into ashes.
The candle weeps waxen tears.
Just so is the sorrow they felt in their hearts.
Her tears burnish the pillow.
Cold fills her silken covers.
She wakens to the echoing water clock.

[4]

Their meetings were so brief,
Their partings are very long.
Her brows are colored a pale mist like a willow.
She lowers the azure curtain,
And ties it with a love knot.
Waiting, she perfumes the silk covers.

The moon above the city-wall,
Shines like the whitest snow.
The beautiful woman feels the deepest of sorrow.
The trees are in dark shadow.
The magpies fashion a bridge.
The clock's jade tally points to dawn.

[5]

The river tower is behind me.
The moon shines on the water.
The dawn watch horn seems to sob above the city.
Willows tremble on the shore.
Mist swirls along the island.
Two rows of wild geese part in flight.

Along the way to the capital,
Homeward-bound sails pass by.
The fragrant grasses are soon to wither and die.
A silvery candle burns dimly.
The Jade Cord hangs down low.
In the village, a cock starts to crow.

[6]

The aroma from a jade censer,
The wax tears of red candles,

Reflect the sorrow felt within the painted hall.
Her darkened brows are faded.
Her hair, once full, is thin.
The night is long and the bed is cold.

On a clump of wu-t'ung trees,
The midnight rain pours down.
She didn't know being apart could be such agony.
One leaf followed by another,
Sound followed upon by sound,
Echoes from the empty steps till dawn.

## "Returning to my Distant Home" (*Kuei-kuo yao*), Two Lyrics

### [1]

Face fair as jade!                                              (2)
A gold mesh tassel falls from an azure phoenix hairclasp.       (7)
Two golden rectangles are coupled high on her chignon.          (6)
Her silken gown ripples like the spring waters.                 (5)

In the painted hall, a candle flickers on the curtain.          (6)
Her dream ends with the quickening water clock.                 (5)
There is no limit to the emotions she must be feeling.          (6)
The mountain screen shimmers in the dawn light.                 (5)

### [2]

Two lovely cheeks!
A small golden phoenix swings back and forth from a comb.
Her dancing robe moves softly in the gathering breeze.
Her gown is of ivory as pale as the lotus root.

The brocaded hangings and silken curtains fall aslant.
Dewdrops glisten on the mats in the clear dawn.
Her face is dusted yellow and graced with flower dots.
Her blackened brows are like distant mountains.

## "Song of the Wine Spring" (*Chiu-ch'üan tzu*), Four Lyrics

### [1]

The flowers shone on the willows,                               (4)
Now idly they fall into the green duckweed pond.                (6)
She leans against the railing,                                  (3)

And watches the fragile waves.                                    (3)
The rain murmurs in sad sighs.                                    (3)

In past days there has been little news between them.            (7)
It is lonely and still within her chamber.                       (5)
The silver screen stands shut.                                   (3)
The azure curtains hang loose.                                   (3)
So she bears the spring night.                                   (3)

[2]

The sun shines in a gauze window,
Lighting a golden censer and a landscape screen.
It will be spring in her home,
But fog and mists divide them.
The orchid lamp is behind her.

Her make-up faded, sadly she stands by the high hall.
Shadowy clouds reach across endless miles.
The grass is at its very peak.
Flowers are beginning to fall.
Two by two the swallows leave.

[3]

The southern lady cannot go home.
Spring waters flow in the stream near the tower.
The lone moon shines brightly.
Gusts of wind rise once again.
Few apricot blossoms are left.

A jade hairpin slants across a cloud of upswept hair,
A golden-threaded phoenix trims her skirt.
If she could send on a letter,
Saying that she dreams of him,
Wild geese could fly it south.

[4]

Fragrance rises from a silk sash,
Still bound are the love seeds given at parting.
The traces of tears are fresh.
The gold silk threads are old.
Her heart aches in separation.

Two graceful swallows chatter among the carved beams.
A full year has passed since he went away.
The trees grow dark and thick.
The lush grasses are fragrant.
Willow flowers wildly scatter.


## "Pacifying the Western Barbarians" (*Ting hsi-fan*), Three Lyrics

In ancient times when an officer had to say goodbye,        (6)
He took down a lithe willow branch,                         (3)
Or broke off a wintry plum blossom,                         (3)
As a farewell offering to his lady.                         (3)

The spring snows cover the borders so very far away.        (6)
The wild geese return, but he does not return.             (5)
The piping of a foreign flute gives rise to sadness.       (6)
An uncertain moon flits to and fro.                        (3)


### [2]

A seagull shakes its wings as it starts to fly away,
The day-lilies turn green as grass,
The apricot flowers are bright red,
Out beyond a latticework partition.

Ornaments of green, rose, and gold set off her hair.
She is like a branch of lovely spring flowers.
Above the high tower, the full moon shines brightly,
Lighting the grille at the windows.


### [3]

A late spring shower greets the orioles at the dawn.
Her beauty is like the finest jade.
Her brows are like willow branches.
Just now she is thinking about him.

She rolls up the silken hangings and azure curtains.
In the mirror she is like a branch of flowers.
Her heart aches at so little news from the frontier,
Few are the wild geese flying past.

# "The Willow Branches" (*Yang-liu chih*), Eight Lyrics

## [1]

| | |
|---|---|
| The very longest willow branches grow in I-ch'un Park. | (7) |
| They bow in the spring wind with the ease of a dancer. | (7) |
| Just now the woman fair as jade feels her heart break. | (7) |
| The waters of spring flow by the red-railinged bridge. | (7) |

## [2]

East of the South Palace wall, he drives his carriage.
Well he knows the willow is a pallid yellow in spring,
While an apricot flower would never be so halfhearted.
Why then is the traveler so profoundly broken-hearted!

## [3]

Willows stand in profusion at the gate of the Lady Su.
Their fine gold branches brush the flat-topped bridge.
The yellow orioles are silent in the rising east wind.
Behind the red gate, the willows bend with easy grace.

## [4]

Golden branches trail along the canals tiled in green,
Like the dark brows of palace ladies bent with sorrow.
But at night, the rains favor them at the Dragon Pond.
The branches graze the balcony and reach to the tower.

## [5]

Beyond the Kuan-wa Palace and west of the city of Yeh,
Willows frame the far sails and caress the near shore.
Willows can bind the prince making him want to return,
Unlike the fragrant grasses which grow lush and green.[1]

---

[1] An allusion to the "*Chao yin-shih*" in the *Ch'u-tz'u* anthology, "A prince went wandering and did not return / In spring the grass grows lush and green." See David Hawkes, *Songs of the South* (Boston: Beacon Press, 1962), p. 119.

[6]

Two by two, yellow orioles tinged with brightest gold,
Sing on the graceful willow branches covered with dew.
With spring, the willows delight in their slenderness.
How very sad they have entangled the wanderer's heart!

[7]

The willows shine like brightest silk upon the palace.
At a phoenix window, they light the hibiscus curtains.
By the Ching-yang Tower, they reach in all directions.
In burgeoning color, they await the winds of the dawn.

[8]

By the loom, there is the constant chatter of orioles.
She holds the shuttle and weeps for one gone far away.
In the third month the frontier is a barren wasteland.
Even if willows grew there, they wouldn't know spring.

## "A Southern Song" (*Nan-ko tzu*), Seven Lyrics

[1]

| | |
|---|---|
| Two golden parrots perch atop her hand. | (5) |
| Two phoenixes are sewn across her coat. | (5) |
| Secretly she observes the paired forms. | (5) |
| They seem not as good as being married, | (5) |
| And being mandarin ducks. | (3) |

[2]

Her waist seems a silken willow branch.
Her face is a smooth snow-white flower.
A jade hook fastens the rolled curtain.
She watches the dusty roads until dusk,
Speeding carriages go by.

[3]

Her hair is bound loosely in a chignon.
Her painted eyebrows are finely arched.
Day and night, her thoughts are of him.
Because of him, she is worn with grief,
When flowers are so lush.

[4]

A gold curtain shimmers above her face.
A patch of azure glows on her forehead.
She rests on a pillow, beneath a quilt.
Beyond the window screen, orioles sing,
Making her miss him more.

[5]

She dusts her face with crushed pollen.
Her breath warms a flower for her hair.
Pillow and screen shine on one another.
The full moon brightens the dark night,
Lighting her lovely face.

[6]

Her gaze is like gently swelling waves.
She moves with the grace of the willow.
Among the flowers, they met in secrecy.
She thinks of him, and her heart aches,
Hating the spring nights.

[7]

Idly she shakes a mandarin duck pillow,
And leaves off mending her azure skirt.
Fragrance no longer fills the curtains.
Lately her heart breaks more than ever,
For thinking only of him.

# "The Spirit of the Yellow River" (*Ho-tu shen*), Three Lyrics

## [1]

| | |
|---|---|
| She views the clustered shrines by the river. | (5) |
| Spring rains pour down the facades of the temples. | (6) |
| Slow-moving birds fly over the endless southern mountains. | (7) |
| Alone in the boat, she feels the grief of parting. | (6) |

| | |
|---|---|
| Somewhere a cuckoo is crying out, sobbing on without stop. | (7) |
| Flowers in full bloom are as red as spilled blood. | (6) |
| The beautiful woman experiences an intense sorrow. | (6) |
| This is the time the flowers and grasses flourish. | (6) |

## [2]

The solitary temple faces the winterly tides.
Wind and rain over the west mound sigh mournfully.
In her sadness the beautiful woman leans against the boat.
The tears pour down her face in countless streams.

At sunset, she is grieved by the song "Thoughts of Return."
The scent of early plums fills the mountain's rim.
She turns her head, desolate with longing for him.
Where is it that he enjoys such ease and pleasure?

## [3]

A beating brass drum calls forth the spirits.
In front of the hall, banners flutter in the wind.
A clash of wind and thunder whirls across the river banks.
Above the southern mountains, the clouds open out.

The sound of the oars on the departing boat is melancholy.
Her beautiful face is grieving, her make-up faded.
Forlorn swallows fly across fields of green wheat.
Lifting a curtain, she sadly faces the pearl hall.

# "The Taoist Nun" (*Nü-kuan tzu*), Two Lyrics

## [1]

| | |
|---|---|
| Reserved beauty, restrained smile, | (4) |
| Her faded make-up, a veil of soft reds and blues, | (6) |

Her hair, a cicada's wings,                                          (3)
Her jade hairpin, a ripple of autumn water,                         (5)
The rolled curtain, a silken mist of azure.                         (5)

Her breast shines snow-white in the mirror.                         (5)
Among the magical trees fronting the tower,                         (5)
She gives a message to a lovely fairy girl,                         (5)
Let the immortal come soon!                                          (3)


## [2]

Clouds of hair fall to her collar.
Her fairylike face is as snow in the gilt mirror.
Her delicate brows painted,
She raises her dainty fan to hide her face,
And blushingly lowers the brocade curtains.

Long she looks for him from the jade tower,
Let him not come late to the flower grotto.
Eventually he will leave, riding a phoenix,
May he not forget her then!


# "Jade Butterflies" (*Yü hu-tieh*), One Lyric

## [1]

The cold autumn winds cut sharply at her grief.                     (6)
The traveler has not yet made his return.                           (5)
Beyond the frontier, grass will soon die.                           (5)
South of the river, wild geese come late.                           (5)

Her fragile face is like the faded lotus.                           (5)
Her brows are like tumbled willow leaves,                           (5)
The heart breaks to see them so atremble.                           (5)
Who can know what she feels in her heart?                           (5)

# CHAPTER TWO

## Wen T'ing-yün (812–870)

### "Pure Serene Music" (*Ch'ing-p'ing yüeh*), Two Lyrics

#### [1]

| | |
|---|---|
| Late spring in the Shang–yang Palace! | (4) |
| Her delicate eyebrows are pale with sorrow. | (5) |
| In the new year's calm, she thinks of the imperial outings. | (7) |
| Why is the road to Ch'ang–an so distant and remote? | (6) |

| | |
|---|---|
| In vain, the curtains and quilts have been scented. | (6) |
| She sits all alone, locked within a thousand gates. | (6) |
| If only she had gold enough to buy a splendid poem,[1] | (6) |
| A poem could plead for her to his glorious majesty. | (6) |

#### [2]

Sorrowful and dismal in Lo–yang city!
Willow catkins whirl like snow in the wind.
Throughout the day, travelers pull at the hanging branches.
Waters cry and sob as they flow beneath the bridge.

The parting company is urged to have another drink.
South of the river, the oriole cries out its grief.
These bravos of P'ing–yüan feel the deepest sorrow.
They turn aside to wipe away their streaming tears.

### "Hatred of Distant Places" (*Hsia-fang yüan*), Two Lyrics

#### [1]

| | |
|---|---|
| She leans on a carved railing. | (3) |
| She unties the silken curtain. | (3) |
| She has yet to receive his letter. | (4) |

---

[1] "Buy a poem" is an allusion to the payment of a hundred catties of gold by the Empress Ch'en, wife of the Emperor Wu of the Han dynasty (r. 140–86), to the poet Ssu-ma Hsiang-ju (179–117). It is believed that Ssu-ma Hsiang-ju then wrote the *Ch'ang-men fu* in honor of the empress who resided in the Ch'ang-men Palace. Because of this poem, the empress was restored to the good graces of the emperor who had been neglecting her in favor of someone else.

Her heart breaks as the wild geese return in spring.        (7)
She knows not when the traveler's horse will return.        (7)
The cherry—apples will fade and die away.                   (5)
The freezing rain will follow.                              (3)


                                    [2]


The flowers begin their bloom.
The rain is starting to clear.
The beaded curtains remain undone.
Her dream fades as she sadly hears the dawn orioles.
Her pale brows rise and bend like distant mountains.
She ties her hair in front of the mirror.
The silk of her gown is light.


## "Speaking of Love" (*Su chung-ch'ing*), One Lyric

                                    [1]

Orioles chirp.                                              (2)
Flowers dance.                                              (2)
Spring is at its peak.                                      (3)
Droplets of rain fall.                                      (3)
A gold banded cushion,                                      (3)
Of royal silk.                                              (2)
Phoenixes on curtains.                                      (3)
Butterflies dart by the yielding willow.                    (5)
Far, far away,                                              (2)
Few letters have arrived from Liao—yang.                    (5)
He returns in a dream.                                      (3)


## "Thoughts of Paradise" (*Ssu ti-hsiang*), One Lyric

                                    [1]

Flowers, flowers,                                           (2)
They cover the branches like rosy clouds.                   (5)
Silk sleeves and painted curtains hide her grief.           (6)
She stops the carriage,                                     (3)
And turns round to join him in idle conversation.           (6)
A gold phoenix sways on her shaking comb.                   (5)
He will remain only until spring comes to an end,           (6)
And he will not return.                                     (3)

# "Dreaming of the South" (*Meng chiang-nan*), Two Lyrics

## [1]

| | |
|---|---|
| Ever rising resentment, | (3) |
| It reaches out to him at world's end. | (5) |
| The moon over the mountain cannot know what she feels. | (7) |
| In water and wind, flowers fall lifelessly before her. | (7) |
| Dark clouds tremble and drift aslant. | (5) |

## [2]

Her toilette completed,
She gazes alone from the river tower.
A thousand sails have drifted by, but not one was his.
The setting sun is aflame, but the water reaches away.
She grieves to see the duckweed isle.

# "River Messages" (*Ho ch'uan*), Three Lyrics

## [1]

| | |
|---|---|
| On the river bank, | (2) |
| She calls for him. | (2) |
| At dawn, she is so beguiling. | (3) |
| In a scene of enchantment, she is gathering lotus. | (6) |
| "Please do not go to that other bank across the river! | (7) |
| Oh handsome youth, | (2) |
| These pretty flowers will fill up your boat." | (5) |

| | |
|---|---|
| Her red sleeves flutter in the warm and gentle breeze. | (7) |
| Her wrists appear to be jade. | (3) |
| Her heart grieves to see the broken willows. | (5) |
| Has he gone toward the south? | (3) |
| Has he gone toward the north? | (3) |
| She does not know. | (2) |
| Since evening, not many people have come by! | (5) |

## [2]

On the lake shore,
She looks for him.
The rain is sad and mournful.

By misty banks, by flowery bridge, the way is far.
Sorrow yet clings to the brows of the beautiful woman.
From break of day,
She hazily dreams she is adrift on the tide.

The distant traveler's boat still lies at world's end.
It is already late in spring.
Orioles chatter as her heart breaks in vain.
"Waters of the Jo—yeh Stream!
Waters moving on to the west!
Willow embankment!
You will not hear the neighing of his horse!"

### [3]

For her companion,
She is crying out.
The apricot blossoms are few.
So often in her dreams, she is grieved by parting.
Like a crane so soon gone, or a swallow taking flight,
No more to return.
Stains of tears shed in vain cover her robe.

Birds on the cloudy horizon draw her feelings far off.
It is already late in spring.
A smoky mist passes across the south garden.
The snow plums were fragrant.
The willow branches are long.
Oh beautiful girl,
Their passing can only make a person suffer!

## "The Foreign Woman's Complaint" (*Fan-nü yüan*), Two Lyrics

### [1]

Masses of sweet snowy apricot blooms cover the branches.        (7)
A pair of swallows in the misty rain,                            (4)
Inlaid cicadas on the cheng,                                     (3)
And gilded birds on the fan,                                     (3)
Seem to gaze in wonder at each other.                            (4)
There has been no word from the distant frontier passes.        (7)
The swallows circle and fly.                                     (3)

### [2]

Wild geese fly up in alarm from the endless rocky sands.
They fly across the far distant snow.

His bridle carved from jade,
His arrows barbed with gold,
Year after year, he rides for battle.
In the painted tower, she grieves by the vacant screens.
The apricot blooms grow red.

## "Lotus Leaf Cup" (*Ho-yeh pei*), Three Lyrics

### [1]

The chill dewdrops are like frozen pearls. (6)
Wavy reflections, (2)
Sweep the banks of the pond. (3)
Green stems and red flowers are piled in confusion. (7)
Her heart breaks. (2)
The water and wind are cold. (3)

### [2]

The autumn moon shines in a watery mirror.
Petals like snow,
Drift from the picked lotus.
The pretty woman faces into the chill rising waves.
She feels sorrow.
She is thinking only of him.

### [3]

The woman from the south longs to go home.
A morning shower,
Bathes her sorrowing beauty.
In rising tides, his skiff sails among the flowers.
The waves billow.
A west wind is between them.

# Huang-fu Sung (*c.* A.D. 859)

## "Heaven's Immortal" (*T'ien-hsien tzu*), Two Lyrics

### [1]

A lone egret flies in a clear sky across the open fields. (7)
Water pepper blooms along the jade green river in autumn. (7)

This day, the young man must part from his fair immortal.    (7)
He moves up close to her side,                               (3)
Her teardrops are like pearls.                               (3)
The twelve peaks of Mount Wu loom across the evening sky.    (7)


[2]


The flowering rhododendron shine crimson upon the waters.
Partridges fly above the lush green of a mountain valley.
He stayed for the year, but now he must start his return.
In their world so far removed,
They were constantly together.
Her deep sadness at their parting is only to be expected.


## "Ripples Sifting Sand" (*Lang-t'ao sha*), Two Lyrics

[1]


Delicate river grasses spread into the tangled undergrowth.   (7)
In the rising waves, a fishing boat is very nearly swamped.   (7)
Sleepy egrets and drowsy seagulls fly toward the old banks.   (7)
The sandy beach of a year ago has now drifted to mid-river.   (7)


[2]


Southern songs and southern nutmeg sadden the northern man.
Rain on the banks, wind in the pines, his skiff tumbles on.
In the churning waves, there is no sleep for the wild duck.
Chill grains of sand softly slip away into the watery flow.


## "Willow Branches" (*Yang-liu chih*), Two Lyrics

[1]


Spring fills the palace, and the sun sets beyond the hills.    (7)
Like graceful dancers entertaining the Emperor Hsüan-tsung,    (7)
The willows are burgeoning green within the abandoned city.    (7)
But who is there to take up a jade flute and play for them?    (7)

## [2]

When bright spring returns to the watery land of the south,
Willows arch elegantly among the palaces of the king of Wu.
The cries of the orioles echo long in the empty apartments,
But the beautiful Hsi Shih can have no way of knowing this.


# "Picking Fresh Flowers" (*Che-te hsin*), Two Lyrics

## [1]

| | |
|---|---|
| Fill up the cups to the full! | (3) |
| Let the piping music of the jade flutes begin! | (5) |
| The mats are embroidered, the candles are red, | (5) |
| You must not arrive too late! | (3) |
| Blossoming buds, in the wind and rain of the night, | (7) |
| Leave but the empty branches! | (3) |


## [2]

Let's pick the fresh flowers!
Branch after branch, leaf upon leaf in spring!
Some very good music, and some very good wine,
Have real influence on a man!
How many tens of years will a man get in this life?
So open up the perfumed mats!


# "Dreaming of the South" (*Meng chiang-nan*), Two Lyrics

## [1]

| | |
|---|---|
| The orchid lamp burns low. | (3) |
| The banana trees on the screen darken red. | (5) |
| She idly dreams of the plums full ripening in the south. | (7) |
| On a boat, a flute cries in the night as the rain sighs. | (7) |
| Voices carry from the post-station bridge. | (5) |


## [2]

In a bedroom in the tower,
A fading moon shines beneath the curtains.
In her dreams, she is in Mo-ling sorrowing for the past.

Peach flowers and willow catkins covered the river city,
Where a girl in pigtails played the sheng.


## "Gathering Lotus" (*Ts'ai-lien tzu*), Two Lyrics

### [1]

| | |
|---|---|
| Fragrant lotus spread across the banks of the river. | (7) |
| Raise oars! | (2) |
| A girl merrily picked lotus until the hour was late. | (7) |
| Youngsters! | (2) |
| Come evening, she got splashed by the passing boats. | (7) |
| Raise oars! | (2) |
| She slipped off her petticoat and bundled the ducks. | (7) |
| Youngsters! | (2) |

### [2]

The boat glided across the lake shining with autumn.
Raise oars!
She eagerly eyed a handsome young boy sailing along.
Youngsters!
Suddenly, she threw him a lotus seed over the water.[2]
Raise oars!
As word got around, she blushed for the shame of it.
Youngsters!


# Wei Chuang (836–910)

## "Sand of Silk-Washing Stream" (*Huan-ch'i sha*), Five Lyrics[3]

### [1]

| | |
|---|---|
| A clear dawn graces the morning of the Cold Food Festival. | (7) |
| A cluster of willow blossoms sets off her golden hairpins. | (7) |
| She rolls up the curtain and goes out of the painted hall. | (7) |

---

[2] The lotus seed is a token of love.

[3] Slightly different versions of my translations of Wei Chuang's lyrics to this tune and to the following tune, "Deva-like Barbarian," are included in *Sunflower Splendor,* ed. Wu-chi Liu and Irving Yucheng Lo (Bloomington, Indiana: Indiana University Press, 1975), pp. 281–84.

The tiny peony buds are just starting to burst into bloom.          (7)
The sun is on high, and yet she stands by the red railing.          (7)
She quietly frowns, hating the spring that will fade away.          (7)

### [2]

She yearns to climb on the swing, but she is too hesitant.
She would ask him to push the swing, but she is too timid.
The curtains in the painted hall glisten in moon and wind.

On a night such as this, who does not feel a deep emotion?
The snowy pear blossoms by the wall come to full splendor.
A faint red blush touches the sorrow in her jadelike face.

### [3]

My lonely dream fades as the moon dips over the mountains.
A solitary lamp shines on the wall from the silken window.
The beautiful woman dwells in a room high up in the tower.

I see her lovely jadelike face, yet how can I describe it?
It is like a branch of snowy plum flowers in early spring,
Sweetly scented, and flushed like the rosy clouds of dawn.

### [4]

The orioles chatter hidden away in the green of the trees.
The willow branches brush the slopes of the Pai-t'ung Dam.
Along the Pearl-Sporting River, the grass grows luxuriant.

I return after a night of drinking, where else could I go?
My horse, finely saddled and ready to ride, softly neighs,
But I, covered with a heavy perfume, am stone blind drunk!

### [5]

Each night, I think of you until the water clock is still.
Sorrowing, I stand on the balcony in the bright moonlight.
I think you too feel the cold all alone within your quilt.

The painted hall is so near, yet it seems a depthless sea.
I think of you, but all I can do is read your old letters.
When can we be together again, hand in hand, in Ch'ang-an?

# "Deva-like Barbarian" (*P'u-sa man*), Five Lyrics

## [1]

| | |
|---|---|
| The night we parted in the red tower was hard to endure. | (7) |
| The fragrant lamp was half-hidden by a tasseled curtain. | (7) |
| I went out into the light of the fading moon. | (5) |
| The beautiful lady said her tearful farewell. | (5) |

| | |
|---|---|
| Gold and azure streamers hung from a p'i-p'a. | (5) |
| Its stringed melody was like a crying oriole, | (5) |
| Urgently beseeching me to return before long. | (5) |
| She was like a flower in a green silk window! | (5) |

## [2]

Everyone says how good it is to live south of the river.
A traveler ought to remain there until he has grown old.
The spring waters are more blue than the sky.
Adrift in the boat, drowsily I hear the rain.

The girl pouring wine is as fair as the moon.
Her wrists shine white like the frosted snow.
Do not return home before you have grown old,
To return home is surely to break your heart!

## [3]

I can still remember how happy I was south of the river.
Then I was young, and my spring robes were a light silk.
I would ride my horse by the slanting bridge,
From the tower came a flutter of red sleeves.

Gold ties held the folds of the azure screen.
Drunk, I stopped the night among the flowers.
So now when I see a lovely blossoming branch,
This white-haired head swears not to go home!

## [4]

Host:
I urge you this night to drink until you are very drunk!
You must not speak of tomorrow in front of the wine jar!

Guest:
I appreciate the kindness of your sentiments.
The wine is deep, but my feelings are deeper.
Host:
Grieve for the shortness of the spring night,
And do not complain when your cup is so full!
When we yet have wine, we can laugh together,
For after all, how long does man's life last?

[5]

The spring scene is splendid within the city of Lo—yang.
But the gifted man of Lo—yang grows old in another land.
Willows shade the Prince of Wei's Embankment.
At this time, I feel restless and bewildered.

Clear waters run beside the blossoming peach.
Mandarin ducks dip themselves in a cool flow.
In an agony of grief, I face the setting sun.
I think always of you, but you don't know it!

## "Returning to My Distant Home" (*Kuei-kuo yao*), Three Lyrics

[1]

Spring is almost over.                                          (3)
Red petals spattered with raindrops cover over the ground.     (7)
The cockatoo is forlorn within its cage of fine jade.          (6)
Alone it perches without friends or companions.                (5)

I look south at the road and wonder where can you be?          (6)
I question the flowers, but they do not answer.                (5)
Surely a time must come when we can go back together.          (6)
It is a matter of sad regret that I lack wings.                (5)

[2]

Oh, golden kingfisher,
Would you take up my thoughts and carry them south for me?
The waters of spring flow on past the painted bridge.
How long have I been drunk among these flowers?

After a parting, there remains only a painful memory.
Teardrops cannot easily be sent such distances.
Screened by curtains of silk, wrapped within a quilt,
Past happiness returns to me as though a dream.


## [3]

Spring is almost over.
Saucy butterflies and gadabout bees frolic in the flowers.
The sun's last light falls on the pond and pavilions.
Willow branches like golden threads lie broken.

She wakens with hair tousled as if blown by the wind.
Clouds and rain vanish from within the screens.
Listless, she draws near the censer and deeply sighs.
A rush of tears moistens her moon—white wrists.


# "Echoing Heaven's Everlastingness" (*Ying t'ien-ch'ang*), Two Lyrics

## [1]

The branches of the locusts shade the chattering orioles.       (7)
The inner courtyard is deserted on this spring afternoon.        (7)
On the hanging curtain,                                          (3)
Golden phoenixes dance.                                          (3)
A thin wisp of incense awaits her solitude by the screen.        (7)

Clouds in the blue sky,                                          (3)
Drift aimlessly beyond.                                          (3)
Only in her dreams does his spirit come back to her.             (6)
Night after night, wind and rain beat on the window.             (6)
"Do you believe the truth of my broken heart?"                   (5)


## [2]

I have not heard from you since we parted six months ago.
An inch of separation's sorrow ties into a million knots.
Hard to meet once more,
So easy to say goodbye.
Again the flowers by the jade tower bloom like the snows.

My thoughts are of you,
But where to tell them?

In the sadness of the night, a mist covers the moon.
As I dwell on this, feelings arise from deep within.
Teardrops have stained the red of my sleeves.

## "Lotus Leaf Cup" (*Ho-yeh pei*), Two Lyrics

### [1]

| | |
|---|---:|
| It is difficult to meet with so exquisite a beauty, | (6) |
| A ruin of states.[4] | (2) |
| We may not rendezvous among the flowers. | (5) |
| Her darkened brows are like the far distant mountains. | (7) |
| No longer can I bear the thought of her. | (5) |
| | |
| Idly I close an azure screen golden with phoenixes, | (6) |
| My dreams ending. | (2) |
| I am very alone within the painted hall. | (5) |
| The sky has no road by which I could send on a letter. | (7) |
| My heart grows heavy in these old rooms. | (5) |

### [2]

I well remember that year we met among the flowers,
So late at night.
When first the beautiful one came to me,
The curtains hung round us in the hall near the water.
Hand in hand, we secretly drew together.

The dawn orioles and a fading moon were our sorrow.
We said farewell.
"Today, we must go on our separate ways!
Today, we become as strangers living in foreign lands!
Never again will we be with one another!"

## "Pure Serene Music" (*Ch'ing-p'ing yüeh*), Four Lyrics

### [1]

| | |
|---|---:|
| Spring's sadness lines the south road. | (4) |
| No letters have come with news of my home. | (5) |
| The rain falls in a fine sleet on the white pear blossoms. | (7) |
| Swallows whir by the golden tablets atop the gates. | (6) |

---

[4] "Ruin of states" is a cliché for a *femme fatale*. The expression comes from a song by Li Yen-nien, whose sister was a favorite of Emperor Wu of the Han (r. 140–86). "A look from her will overthrow a city./ A second look will overthrow the state."

All the day through, I have looked in hope for you.          (6)
Tear stains have mixed with the dust on my clothes.         (6)
Who is it who plays the flute alongside the bridge?         (6)
I stop the horse and look west with a broken heart.         (6)


## [2]

The flowers and grasses are luxuriant.
It must be desolate on that mountain road.
Willows sputter a fine gold, and orioles start to chatter.
In the sadness of her fragrant room, she grows old.

She regrets the lover's knot tied in her silk sash.
Alone, she stands by a red railing lost in thought.
Awake, she sees a band of moonlight across her bed.
The wind in the window strikes a note on the ch'in.


## [3]

Where can that wanton little wench be?
Shu's domains abound with clouds and rain.
She is a cloud that can feel, and a flower that can speak,
And there is a rustling of silks as she goes along.

Her make-up is done, but her hairpin is not placed.
Coyly she sits on a swing waiting for the moonrise.
Her home is in the shade of the green locust trees.
Her gate is by the bridge where spring waters flow.


## [4]

Orioles trill in the fading moonlight.
At the side door, the lamp is burning low.
At the gate, his horse neighs as the man gets ready to go.
It is that time of year when flowers fade and fall.

Her make-up is done, but her brows are not painted.
Stifling her sorrow, she leans on the gold shutter.
"Don't sweep the dust on the path of his departure!
If you sweep it, then he will be slow to come back!"

# "Gazing after the Distant Traveler" (*Wang yüan-hsing*), One Lyric

## [1]

| | |
|---|---|
| Silently she waits by the screen as he prepares to leave. | (7) |
| She holds back the anguish in her heavy heart. | (5) |
| From a tree in the courtyard comes the sound of cockcrow. | (7) |
| The moon is setting over the border barricade. | (5) |
| | |
| They make their final farewell. | (3) |
| His horse cries and he must go. | (3) |
| Locust trees stretch endlessly along the embankment. | (6) |
| Beyond the gate, lush grass covers the far-reaching road. | (7) |
| The clouds and rain sweep away in an irrevocable parting. | (7) |
| After his departure, it is unbearable for her, | (5) |
| To go back once again to those fragrant rooms. | (5) |

# CHAPTER THREE

## Wei Chuang (836–910)

### "Paying Homage at the Golden Gate" (*Yeh chin-men*), Two Lyrics

#### [1]

```
Springtime hurries to its end.                              (3)
In the gloom, she stirs the wick of the dying candle.      (6)
At night, the winds rattle the bamboos beyond the curtain. (7)
Unquiet dreams come in restless starts.                    (5)

Here is a woman as beautiful as the very finest jade.      (6)
Night after night, she stays all alone by the screen.      (6)
She cradles a p'i-p'a and lightly strums the old melodies. (7)
Her dark brows seem a distant mountain.                    (5)
```

#### [2]

```
It is useless to think of him.
She doesn't have a way by which to send him a letter.
She would ask the Lady Ch'ang O, but she doesn't know her.
And if it could be sent, send it where?

She awakes from her fitful sleep exhausted and spent.
She cannot bear to take up his few remaining letters.
Fallen petals cover the court in the desolation of spring.
Her heart breaks at the fragrant grass.
```

### "Song of the River City" (*Chiang-ch'eng tzu*), Two Lyrics

#### [1]

```
She is very loving, very beautiful, and very easily hurt. (7)
The water clock drags along.                               (3)
He pulls aside the curtains.                               (3)
Before her crimson lips can move,                          (4)
He knows the sweet fragrance of her mouth.                 (5)
Slowly, she opens the quilt and reaches her hand for him.  (7)
Yielding the phoenix pillow,                               (3)
She goes to her young lover.                               (3)
```

## [2]

Her hair is disheveled, and her blackened brows are long.
She leaves her scented room,
Saying goodbye to her lover.
The cry of a watch horn is a sob.
The stars grow pale and fade from the sky.
The dew is chill, the moon is faint, and no one is astir.
He cannot remain any longer.
Tears run across her cheeks.

# "River Messages" (*Ho ch'uan*), Three Lyrics

## [1]

| | |
|---|---:|
| What place can it be, | (2) |
| So shrouded in mists?[1] | (2) |
| In late spring on the Sui Embankment, | (4) |
| The willows grew full and lush green. | (4) |
| The painted oars dripped silken gold. | (4) |
| The azure banners flew high in the fragrant wind. | (6) |
| The water was bright and smooth. | (3) |
| | |
| The girls pulling the dragon boats had fine painted brows. | (7) |
| In a drifting gossamer of cloud, | (3) |
| The Keeper of the Flower was enchanting. | (5) |
| Through the palace gate of Chiang-tu, | (4) |
| Moonlight mirrored in the Huai shone on Mi Tower. | (6) |
| Such sadness lasts for all time! | (3) |

## [2]

At the end of spring,
So gentle the breeze.

[1] In this *tz'u*, Wei Chuang evokes the last extravagant progress made by the Emperor Yang (*r.* 604–618) of the Sui dynasty in A.D. 616 down the Grand Canal (constructed by him at great cost and suffering to the people) from Ch'ang-an to Loyang and thence to Chiang-tu (Yang-chou) near present-day Nanking. Wei Chuang makes reference to the hundreds of young girls employed by the Emperor Yang to pull the boats of the flotilla. These girls were selected for their beauty and fairness of skin, and in order to maintain their attractiveness, they were provided with a rare and costly eyebrow coloring imported from Persia.

Wei Chuang also alludes to the emperor's arrival in Loyang where he was presented with a strange and wonderful double-blossomed flower. Since no one knew what to call it, it was named "Welcoming the Emperor's Carriage Flower." The emperor was very pleased with it and turned it over to one of his favorites, a female carriage driver named Yüan Pao-erh, and she was promptly commissioned the "*Ssu-hua nü*" or "The Keeper of the Flower." The Mi Tower or "The Maze Tower" mentioned in line twelve was in Chiang-tu, and it was so named because of its labyrinthine passages and apartments in which the emperor could pursue his sexual pleasures in privacy.

Flowers bloom in the City of Brocade,
Arousing excitement in the travelers.
With our jade whips and gold bridles,
We gallop in a flurry of dust seeking for beauty,
Holding dear the moments of day.

Beautiful women press us to drink the wine of Lin-ch'iung.
Their slender, delicate fingers,
Are willow branches caressing our faces.
When we return, the mists are rising,
And the drums are just sounding the hour of dusk.
Secretly, my soul seems to melt.


## [3]

By the Brocade River,
So fair is the woman.
Her silken gown is trimmed with gold,
Like a mist of silk, a chiffon cloud.
She is a flower in darkening willows.
It is now the season of the ch'ing-ming festival,
And the rain has begun to clear.

My heart breaks as I ride in the dawn haze along the road.
Orioles cry out for one another.
I gaze at the rains falling on Mount Wu.
Fragrant dust screens the bright sun.
I look for the green door and red tower far away,
Her dark brows bend with sorrow.


## "Heaven's Immortal" (*T'ien-hsien tzu*), Five Lyrics

### [1]

She yearns for those times they came together in dreams.     (7)
Silently she looks at the flowers with sad deliberation.      (7)
She is a dewy peach blossom on a lithe and slender body.     (7)
Her brows are finely delicate.                                (3)
Her hair is a billowing cloud.                                (3)
But only the romantic Sung Yü would understand all this!      (7)


### [2]

It is late at night when he returns magnificently tipsy.
He clutches the bed-curtain since he is giddy with wine.

Silly and besotted, he reeks of drink and heavy perfume.
Roused from her sweet slumber,
She laughs and giggles at him.
But as it is said, how much of life do we get after all!


## [3]

A shimmering frost of silvery moonlight fills the night.
From my pillow I hear the wild geese cry in the far sky.
I am too lazy to freshen the fading scent on the quilts.
Everything is quiet and still,
But for the whispering leaves.
Just now I slept, and as always, I saw him in my dreams.


## [4]

She wakes from dreaming to find the screens still empty.
The sobbing cry of a cuckoo is heard outside the window.
Coldly callous, her lover abandoned her without a trace.
One day follows after another.
Her anger deepens and deepens.
Strands of crimson teardrops flow down her lotus cheeks.


## [5]

Raiment like dazzling gold, skin like pure glowing jade!
Eyes like the autumn waters, hair like a floating cloud!
Dressed in the pink light of dawn, cloaked in moonbeams,
The fairies stand by the cave,
Watching the mists whirl away.
Liu and Juan do not return, and spring comes to a close.


# "Delight in the High-Flying Orioles" (*Hsi ch'ien ying*), Two Lyrics

## [1]

| | |
|---|---|
| A tumultuous clamor of voices, | (3) |
| A thunderous booming of drums, | (3) |
| A morning breeze whipping at my jacket, | (5) |
| A pale fading moon in the upper reaches of the heavens, | (7) |
| I ride on as though galloping in space. | (5) |

Sweet fragrance fills my robe.                                      (3)
Myriad chariots fill the road.                                      (3)
Flying phoenix banners sweep against my body.                       (6)
The imperial insignias and emblems stand in vast array,            (7)
As I come before her imperial presence.                             (5)


[2]


Drums sound along the streets.
The imperial gates swing open,
The examiners withdraw from the palace.
The list of the fortunate candidates is placed on high.
Shouts like thunder resound from below.

These are high-flying orioles.
These are transformed dragons.
Their carriages crowd the city all the night.
In every house and pavilion, bevies of beautiful women,
Press to see the heaven-soaring cranes.


## "Thoughts of Paradise" (*Ssu ti-hsiang*), Two Lyrics

[1]

Her cloudlike hair tumbles free.                                    (3)
A phoenix hairpin dangles loose.                                    (3)
Flowing hair, falling pin, how languorous and tender,              (6)
As she lazes against the pillow.                                    (3)
Fading moonlight falls deep within the azure screens.             (6)
The water clock is a low murmur.                                    (3)
Together they pledged their love, each for the other.             (6)
Their two hearts are now as one!                                    (3)


[2]


[Variation]
On a spring day, I wander about.                                    (3)
A shower of apricot petals drifts round my head.                   (5)
Wherever did that handsome boy on the path come from?             (6)
How truly too romantic he looks.                                    (3)
Why I think I really will have to get married to him,             (6)
And be happy my whole life long.                                    (3)
And if it be that he cold-heartedly abandons me,                  (5)
Still, I'd not be ashamed of it!                                    (3)

# "Speaking of Love" (*Su chung-ch'ing*), Two Lyrics

## [1]

| | |
|---|---|
| A candle dies, and incense fades by the closed curtains. | (7) |
| She awakes with a sudden start. | (3) |
| The flowers are soon to wither. | (3) |
| In deep night, the moon rises bright and splendid. | (5) |
| From somewhere comes the faintest murmur of music. | (5) |
| So low, so soft the song. | (2) |
| Her dancing robes lie dark and dusty with neglect. | (5) |
| He turned his back on her love. | (3) |

## [2]

A green pond and red flowers lie in the soft misty rain.
She rests on the magnolia boat.
Drops of jade hang at her side.
Her sash winds around her slim and delicate waist.
Love's dream is kept apart by the Bridge of Stars,
So far, so very far away.
The sweet scent from her silken gown slowly fades.
A coronet of feathers dips low.

# "A Toast to the Traveler" (*Shang hsing pei*), Two Lyrics

## [1]

| | |
|---|---|
| Spring grasses grow luxuriantly on Pa-ling's shores. | (6) |
| Willows stand deep in the mists. | (3) |
| Strings and pipes play within the tower. | (4) |
| The song of farewell breaks my heart, inch by slow inch. | (7) |

| | |
|---|---|
| Now I say goodbye as you leave on a distant journey. | (6) |
| Rare fish fills plates of jade, wine fills cups of gold. | (7) |
| I want the best for you! | (2) |
| Take very good care of yourself! | (3) |
| Savor every drop to the fullest! | (3) |

## [2]

His white horse, jade whip, and golden bridle ready,
The young man looks so handsome.

This parting moment seems to be so easy,
But he leaves on a journey over many thousands of miles.

I grieve that you are going to live in another land,
And tearfully beg you to drink of this full cup of wine.
I want the best for you!
Take very good care of yourself!
Drain every drop to the fullest!

## "The Taoist Nun" (*Nü-kuan tzu*), Two Lyrics

### [1]

| | |
|---|---:|
| The seventeenth day of the fourth month! | (4) |
| It was exactly one year ago on this very same day, | (6) |
| When you had to go away. | (3) |
| I covered my tears, pretending to look away. | (5) |
| My brows came together with timid confusion. | (5) |
| | |
| We couldn't know that our hearts had broken, | (5) |
| That only in dreams would we see each other. | (5) |
| But for the moon on the far distant horizon, | (5) |
| No one could have known! | (3) |

### [2]

Last night at the very hour of midnight!
As I slept, you came to me so clearly in my dream,
And we talked on and on.
Your face was the same lovely peach blossom.
Your finely curved brows were willow leaves.

Your sweet blushes mixed with smiles of joy.
You started to leave, but still you held me.
I woke and knew it to have been but a dream.
My grief overwhelmed me.

## "Song of the Water Clock at Night" (*Keng-lou tzu*), One Lyric

### [1]

| | |
|---|---:|
| The bells and drums lie cold. | (3) |
| The towers stand in darkness. | (3) |

The moon shines on the <u>wu-t'ung</u> trees by a golden well.   (6)
The inner gardens are closed.   (3)
The small courtyard is empty.   (3)
The falling flowers redden the fragrant dew.   (5)

The smoky willows grow heavy.   (3)
The spring fog rolls lightly.   (3)
A lamp still shines in a high window facing the waters.   (6)
Idly I lean against the door.   (3)
Hidden tears fall on my robe.   (3)
I wait for a gentleman never more to return.   (5)

## "Song of the Wine Spring" (*Chiu-ch'üan tzu*), One Lyric

### [1]

The moon dips low and the stars grow dim.   (4)
In the tower, a lovely girl sleeps in sweet abandon.   (6)
Her radiant hair falls tousled.   (3)
Her pillow glistens with tears.   (3)
It is quiet within the screens.   (3)

The sudden cry of the cuckoo shatters love's tender dream.   (7)
A pale shimmer lights the east as she first awakens.   (6)
A thin mist covers the willows.   (3)
The flowers are heavy with dew.   (3)
Her thoughts become unbearable.   (3)

## "The Magnolia Flower" (*Mu-lan hua*), One Lyric

### [1]

Alone she climbs the small tower as spring comes to an end.   (7)
Sadly she gazes at the thick grass along the frontier road.   (7)
All news has come to a stop.   (3)
No travelers are to be seen.   (3)
Her fine brows caught in a frown, she returns to her rooms.   (7)

She sits and watches the flowers fall, of no use her sighs.   (7)
Teardrops, stained with rouge, spill on her silken sleeves.   (7)
She has never been across the endless mountains and rivers,   (7)
So even in her dreams, she wouldn't know where to find him.   (7)

## "Manifold Little Hills" (*Hsiao ch'ung shan*), One Lyric

### [1]

```
In spring I came to the Chao-yang, now spring comes again.    (7)
The drone of a water clock fills the cold night.             (5)
I dream of your goodness and favor.                          (3)
I think of things as they used to be, and my heart breaks.   (7)
My silken gown is wet from weeping.                          (3)
A tracery of tears runs down my crimson sleeves.             (5)

Faint melodies filter through the serried doors.             (5)
A rich plush of green grass rings the courtyard.             (5)
My gaze is drawn toward Ch'ang-men.                          (3)
So many untold sorrows, but with whom can I speak of them.   (7)
With ever growing emotion, I stand.                          (3)
It is almost the hour of twilight in the palace.            (5)
```

# Hsüeh Chao-yün (*c.* 900–932)

## "Sand of Silk-Washing Stream" (*Huan-ch'i sha*), Eight Lyrics

### [1]

```
Red smartweed flowers fill the ford in the autumn rains.     (7)
The tracks of the seagulls make a path across the sands.     (7)
She smooths her hair, sleeves rising in the heady winds.     (7)

Silent and sorrowful, she stands alone on the far shore.     (7)
Again and again, she turns to look with growing sadness.     (7)
The swallows return, the sail is gone, the waters go on.     (7)
```

### [2]

```
At a mirror set with caltrops, her silken sash is loose.
In the hush of her doorway, she lets down her long hair.
Fixing a topknot, earrings abob, she reckons his return.

Flowers and grasses bloom along the banks of the Hsiang.
In her reverie, she hears a water clock in the distance.
Two years, day after day, her fragrant beauty must fade.
```

## [3]

Traces of scattered teardrops stain her powdery make-up.
From her room, she sees flowers fall in the coming dusk.
She suffers the agony of parting, but whom can she tell?

She recalls the day of the Cold Food Festival last year.
Just beyond the Yen-ch'iu Gate, his carriage had paused.
The sun has set, he has gone, and her soul melts unseen.

## [4]

Their hands touched by the gold willows near the bridge.
A bee gently nuzzled a flower, rousing its inmost heart.
In the sweet wind, her love is in the song of the ch'in.

Her thoughts rush on like the flooding waters of spring.
Her feelings run deep like the wine bubbling from a cup.
The Ch'u mists and the Hsiang moon evoke a heavy sorrow.

## [5]

Drawing the curtain to her room, she stands at the door.
Drooping willows cast long green shadows along the path.
Soft shades of red and azure blend in her vivid make-up.

The briefest of looks shows her beauty still flourishes.
But in her lonely life, she secretly thinks only of him.
The far spheres of the immortals lie between their love.

## [6]

Beside a river inn, a boat moors in the chill of autumn.
Old friends come to say goodbye feast through the night.
A smoky perfumed haze drifts around the beautiful women.

Just then their hearts break in the magic rains of Ch'u.
The pain of parting cries out from the southern strings.
The rising moon, the white frost, water and sky are one!

## [7]

That beauty, the ruin of city and state, had much grief.[2]
How many rouge-stained tears fell in the Ku-su Pavilion?
She faces the wind, her gaze fixed, her skin snow-white.

The domains of the lord of Wu stand empty in the sunset.
The palaces of the king of Yüeh lie buried in the weeds.
Lotus and caltrops, layer upon layer, overflow the lake.

## [8]

A lovely woman of Yüeh pans gold from the spring waters.
Her hair sways, her waist pendants ring with every step.
The winds rippling the river grasses are pure and sweet.

It is not the far mountains that make her brow so tense.
She holds back her anger and regret for the setting sun.
The peach blossom is fading with only her memory of him.

## "Delight in the High-Flying Orioles"
## (*Hsi ch'ien ying*), Three Lyrics

### [1]

| | |
|---|---|
| The moon is slowly sinking. | (3) |
| The dawn watch is sounding. | (3) |
| This brand-new immortal feels a litheness of body. | (5) |
| Suddenly I am awake, still reeling from the night's wine. | (7) |
| In the Apricot Garden, the snows are melting away. | (5) |
| | |
| The royal road reaches far. | (3) |
| The chill fills my sleeves. | (3) |
| The scenery is quite beyond the world of ordinary men. | (6) |
| I turn and look back as though witnessing my former life. | (7) |
| No longer will I envy those orioles in the valley. | (5) |

[2] "Ruin of city and state" is an expression for a *femme fatale*. See ch. 2, n. 4, p. 63. Here it is used in reference to Hsi Shih, who was believed responsible for the fall of the ancient state of Wu.

### [2]

Dawn is at the palace gate.
Spring attends the capital.
On my splendid horse I ride through the hazy dust.
My new robe is white in the torchlight of the inner hall.
One knows that this is a newly transformed dragon.

Shouts rise along the road.
Windows and doors fly open.
Fragrant cassia fills my sleeves in the gentle breeze.
In the Apricot Garden, we gaily feast by the Ch'ü-chiang.
From now on, it will be an endless time of spring.

### [3]

It is time for ch'ing-ming.
The sky is cleared of rain.
I have achieved my success just at this very time.
My horse proudly paces the mud, secure in silk trappings.
The whip is half-concealed by my fragrant sleeves.

Flowers blossom in harmony.
Men vie to delight in them.
Every saddle is ornamented and every bridle is beaded.
The sun is setting, the joy ending, yet I hesitate to go.
I take to the road through the mist-covered grass.

## "Manifold Little Hills" (*Hsiao ch'ung shan*), Two Lyrics

### [1]

Spring has come, and the grass by Ch'ang-men grows green.  (7)
The jade steps glitter with droplets of dew.  (5)
Mist blurs the bright moon.  (3)
The east wind cuts short the wailing melody of the flute.  (7)
The water clock hurries on.  (3)
Beyond the curtain, the orioles cry at dawn.  (5)

Such intense grief makes dreaming difficult.  (5)
Tears shed in the night stain my red cheeks,  (5)
Exhausting me with emotion.  (3)
My sash is crumpled in my hands as I go around the steps.  (7)

My every thought is of you. (3)
Dust quietly gathers on the silken hangings. (5)


## [2]

Autumn has come, and the grass by Ch'ang—men is yellowed.
A pair of swallows depart the painted beams.
They leave the palace wall.
Never again will the jade pipes play the "Rainbow Skirts."
A gold hairpin hangs loose.
The mirror conceals fine powders and rouges.

I remember the Chao—yang Palace of long ago.
My dancing gown was sashed with red ribbons,
Banded with mandarin ducks.
Still the fragrance of the palace incense clings to them.
My heart's dream is broken.
Sadly I hear the water clock's slow advance.


# "The Difficulty of Parting" (*Li-pieh nan*), One Lyric

## [1]

Your horse stands saddled and ready in the dawn. (6)
By the curtains, suddenly it is so hard to part. (6)
How can I endure the beautiful spring scene? (5)
I will watch you go thousands of miles away. (5)
My make—up undone, a pearl hairpin dips low. (5)
The drops of dew lie chilled. (3)
Red candles burn so brightly. (3)
Green strings play so softly. (3)
But the tears rush down my cheeks in a steady stream. (7)

Our happy night went so fast, (3)
Drifting petals on the grass! (3)
My soul is lost and confused. (3)
I bow my head to hide the suffering on my brows. (6)
You've not gone, but my heart begins to sob. (5)
I try to speak, but I can't say what I feel. (5)
You leave the teeming growth. (3)
The road opens east and west. (3)
I raise my trembling sleeves. (3)
The spring wind hurries past. (3)
The bleak rain soaks the cherry blossoms and willows. (7)

# "The Joy of Meeting" (*Hsiang-chien huan*), One Lyric

## [1]

```
Silk jacket, embroidered sleeves, a beautiful girl,      (6)
In the painted hall.                                     (3)
Delicate tufts of grass, level sands, a fine horse,      (6)
On the small screen.                                     (3)

Curtain lifted high,                                     (3)
In her make-up room,                                     (3)
Her thoughts run on.                                     (3)
Rain at sunset, a scattered mist, a breaking heart,      (6)
Out beyond the door.                                     (3)
```

# "The Drunken Gentleman" (*Tsui-kung tzu*), One Lyric

## [1]

```
Leisurely she binds her shining black hair.             (5)
Her Wu silk stockings are sleek and glossy.             (5)
A steaming rack nestles warm above the bed.³            (5)
A new gown in a stylish pink hangs over it.             (5)

Inexplicably, and without any clear reason,             (5)
He manages to get it all twisted and dirty.            (5)
Vexed and angry, she slowly opens her eyes,             (5)
Only to be scolded with lots of silly talk!             (5)
```

# "The Taoist Nun" (*Nü-kuan tzu*), Two Lyrics

## [1]

```
I'm off in search of the immortals!                     (4)
I've put aside all my plumed pins and golden combs.     (6)
Entering the high mountain peaks,                        (3)
The fog enfolds me in a cape of yellow silk.            (5)
The clouds clothe me in a cap of white jade.            (5)

Mist on the wilds, the watery cave is chill.            (5)
Moon over the trees, the rock bridge is icy.            (5)
In the quiet night a breeze stirs the pines.            (5)
I worship at the altar of heaven!                       (3)
```

³ A "steaming rack" is a frame that fitted over an incense burner and on top of which clothes were spread for both drying and perfuming.

[2]

In cloudlike silks and filmy gauze,
I receive the bright and awesome secret of the Way.
The True Word is handed on to me.
I bind up my hair dark as the deepest black.
I pull out the emerald jade pin atop my cap.

Back and forth I go through the Five Clouds.
Back and forth I go above the Three Islands.
Just then a messenger comes from Master Liu.
I open this most precious letter!

## "Paying Homage at the Golden Gate" (*Yeh chin-men*), One Lyric

[1]

| | |
|---|---|
| Spring overflows the garden. | (3) |
| Gold threads on her robe are worn with folding. | (6) |
| When she wakens, the crystal curtains are yet unrolled. | (7) |
| A pair of swallows chatter by the eaves. | (5) |
| | |
| A gold knocker is poised on the half-open door. | (6) |
| A thousand fallen petals scatter on the ground. | (6) |
| So long her thoughts of him, her heart will soon break. | (7) |
| So hard to bear, the meetings in dreams! | (5) |

# Niu Chiao (850?–920?)

## "Willow Branches (*Liu-chih*), Five Lyrics

[1]

| | |
|---|---|
| In the first spring winds, my branches grow new green. | (7) |
| I let fall my silken sleeves and bow to the gentlemen. | (7) |
| Delicate and graceful, I wait aimlessly near the road. | (7) |
| My whole life long, I dance for the parting travelers. | (7) |

[2]

In the palace of the king of Wu, a willow ripens dark.
Its slender branches fall like myriad strands of gold.

The willow is really vexed by the Lady Su Hsiao-hsiao.
She led her lover to tie the love-knot beneath a pine.


## [3]

Thousands of my branches spread out across the bridge.
I hate Chang Hsü for not admitting my superior beauty.
On a gold-bridled white horse, a youth faces the wind.
He recalls the slim-waisted dancer of the family Yang.[4]


## [4]

Snowy catkins racing the wind pelt the passing horses.
Powerless in the rising mist, I am beguiled by spring.
Please do not move me from here to the Ling-ho Palace.
Thousands of lovely ladies there will only be jealous.


## [5]

My mist-covered branches gently caress the warm waves.
I wear a newly dyed dancing skirt of pale yellow silk.
I grow by the Chang-hua Palace and the Sui Embankment.
Here, so many willows take delight in the spring wind.


[4] This line is a pun on the graceful waist of the willow, *yang,* and the Yang family's slim-waisted dancer, Chang Ching-wan. She is mentioned in the biography of Yang K'an who lived during the Liang dynasty (502–556). *Nan-shih,* 6 vols., compiled by Li Yen-shou and completed in A.D. 659 (Peking: Chung-hua shu-shü, 1975), ch. 63, p. 1547.

# CHAPTER FOUR

## Niu Chiao (850?–920?)

### "The Taoist Nun" (*Nü-kuan tzu*), Four Lyrics

#### [1]

| | |
|---|---|
| Her shining black hair is swept high. | (4) |
| A spot of azure on her rouged face is the fashion. | (6) |
| Her eyebrows are crescent moons. | (3) |
| She softly smiles and dimples dot her cheeks. | (5) |
| Her voice a whisper, she sings a little tune. | (5) |
| | |
| Her eyes betray fear that he will not return. | (5) |
| Her unsettled soul seeks to follow after him. | (5) |
| With dainty steps, she gracefully turns back. | (5) |
| He has set a time to meet again! | (3) |

#### [2]

Mist rises on the waters of the Chin.
A beautiful woman serves the warm and savory wine.
She is a gossamer cloud of rose.
A brocade sash winds round her hibiscus gown.
Peony blossoms grace the gold of her hairpin.

Yellow on her brow touches her gleaming hair.
A tissue of red chiffon reveals her bracelet.
Orioles sing in the shade of the willow tree.
We know a gentleman dwells here!

#### [3]

Stars form a cap, rosy clouds a cape.
She dwells in Fairyland within the Jui–chu Palace.
Her waist pendants softly sound.
A pin of bright azure trembles atop her hair.
Her slender hands repair the night's make–up.

Round the altar the spring grass grows green.
In the herb garden the apricots are fragrant.
The Bluebird will carry her heart's feelings.
He will send them to Master Liu!

[4]

Two by two, birds take wing to dance.
On a spring morning orioles chatter in the garden.
She rolls up the silken screens.
Her elegant letter is sealed and ready to go,
But the wild geese linger near the Milky Way.

A row of mandarin ducks decorate the curtain.
Branches of nutmeg are stitched in the folds.
She is without words as tears wet her cheeks.
It is the time the flowers fall!

## "Dreaming of the South" (*Meng chiang-nan*), Two Lyrics

### [1]

A swallow, mud in its beak,                                   (3)
Flies to the front of the painted hall.                       (5)
It has found a safe and secure haven in the beams.           (7)
The fragile swallow has stirred the master's pity.           (7)
One can only envy this fortunate union!                       (5)

### [2]

On a red embroidered quilt,
Mandarin ducks parade, pair after pair.
It isn't that I like them better than other birds,
But throats entwined, dozing on the southern bank,
They care more than that heartless man!

## "Deep Gratitude" (*Kan-en to*), Two Lyrics

### [1]

He:
Her tears fell in two reddening streams.                      (5)
So often I think of those scented rooms.                      (5)
I clutch the branches of peach and pear,                      (5)
My brow is so very sad.                                        (3)

She:
On the path, orioles cry and butterflies dance.                    (6)
Blossoms of willow fly!                                            (3)
Blossoms of willow fly!                                            (3)
I want his loving heart to be mine.                                (4)
May he remember my home and soon return!                           (5)


[2]


[Variation]
He:
Ever since I left those southern shores,
I sorrow at the lilacs in knotted bloom.
Recently my feelings have grown so deep.
I think of us together.


She:
Often I wanted to send a letter with the wild geese.              (7)
Tears spill on my robe!
Tears spill on my robe!
I honor the moon and beg to Heaven.
Please understand what lies in my heart!


## "Echoing Heaven's Everlastingness" (*Ying t'ien-ch'ang*), Two Lyrics


[1]


A fading mist unveils spring's scene by the jade tower.           (7)
Her dancing skirt hangs in folds from a golden circlet.           (7)
The sweet harmonies of the orioles have come to a stop.           (7)
Fallen apricot petals are like drifts of mountain snow.           (7)

Her phoenix hairpin dips low as the song ends.                    (5)
He joins in the revels but with the utmost sadness.               (6)
They are mandarin ducks holding to a silken thread.               (6)
Their love grows ever deeper in the moonlight.                    (5)


[2]


[Variation]
Her pale brows hide what lies so deep within her heart.           (7)
In the lamplight, her rare beauty is flushed with wine.           (7)

Her hairpin falls to the side.                        (3)
Her teardrops blot the pillow.                        (3)
On the screen, mandarin ducks doze contented in spring.  (7)

When they had to say farewell,                        (3)
Their affection had no bounds.                        (3)
His promises of enduring love were hollow promises.   (6)
"Don't believe a letter even if on exquisite paper!   (6)
Its words will cheat you and break your heart."       (5)


# "Song of the Water Clock at Night" (*Keng-lou tzu*), Three Lyrics

## [1]

The stars slowly fade from view.                      (3)
The water clock rolls on faster.                      (3)
From somewhere comes a plaintive song of the frontier.  (6)
The fragrant door has been shut.                      (3)
Red is the bloom on the apricot.                      (3)
The moon is bright, and wind blows the willows.       (5)

She stitches characters on silk,                      (3)
A reminder of her every feeling.                      (3)
Her only longing is for their two hearts to be as one.  (6)
She stops this tearful phrasing,                      (3)
And drowses in the lamp's light.                      (3)
Her jade hairpin falls askew beside the pillow.       (5)


## [2]

It is late on a night in spring.
The water clock races on faster.
The fading candle flares into golden ash and goes out.
She wakes startled from a dream.
It is hushed within the screens.
Parted, the same bright moon makes them as one.

The grass by her rooms is green.
She watches afar for his return.
She still has not gotten any word or message from him.
He is without gratitude for her.
She regrets her feeling for him.
She cries to Heaven, but Heaven doesn't listen.

[3]

She was saddened as they parted.
Her tears wet her rouged cheeks.
How would they bear their deep longing for each other?
She lowered her blackened brows,
And bundled up his army clothes.
His horse cried amidst the frost-tipped leaves.

She lifted her hand in farewell.
Her heart broke with the sorrow.
Now the season is the same but a full year has passed.
The wild geese take her letters.
She dreams of his return to her.
When she wakes the moon is just over the river.


## "Sorrow on Gazing at the River" (*Wang chiang yüan*), One Lyric

[1]

| | |
|---|---|
| The east wind rises in hurried gusts. | (3) |
| With a clasp of hands, they parted among the flowers. | (7) |
| She grieves to enter the silken curtains alone. | (5) |
| The horse cries out, and rain soaks the spring grass. | (7) |
| She stands, leaning against the gate. | (3) |
| She sends her love to that heartless gentleman. | (5) |
| Her fragrant powder mixes with her quiet tears. | (5) |


## "Deva-like Barbarian" (*P'u-sa man*), Seven Lyrics

[1]

| | |
|---|---|
| A golden phoenix swirls across her warmly fragrant skirt. | (7) |
| Swallows chattering in the beams wake her from her dream. | (7) |
| Beyond the gate, catkins float through the air. | (5) |
| The handsome young man still has not come home. | (5) |
| | |
| Pink powdery tears cover the grief on her face. | (5) |
| Her brows are the blue of a mountain in spring. | (5) |
| Where is that faraway place known as Liao-yang? | (5) |
| By the silken screens the spring days are long. | (5) |

## [2]

Catkins soar on high to the anxious cries of the orioles.
On a sunny street in the warm spring the carriage stands.
Its curtain banded with a golden phoenix opens.
In her eyes there is a look of deep melancholy.

Tonight, she will search for him in her dreams.
It is so hard to think of their times together.
She can only realize an extra measure of grief.
Whose head will lie by hers beneath the quilts?

## [3]

The wind blows her hairpin in a flurry of spring ribbons.
Mist covers the twined apricot branches like quiet tears.
From the tower she watches for his return home.
The window is chill as a drizzling rain clears.

An azure coverlet hangs over the steaming rack.[1]
On the embroidered curtain mandarin ducks doze.
Where is the man who was dearest to her of all?
She loved that first time he painted her brows.

## [4]

Wu Mountain is brushed in azure along the folding screen.
The goddess of Ch'u still desires to be a floating cloud.[2]
Day and night, so many feelings fill her heart,
But he has taken advantage of her love for him.

Romance today is just as it was in olden times.
He, too, is a false traveler to the Ch'ü-t'ang.[3]
The moon on the mountain shines on the flowers.
When she wakes, the lamp's shadow falls aslant.

---

[1] A "steaming rack" is a frame that fitted over an incense burner and on top of which clothes and other items were spread for both drying and perfuming.

[2] Yao Chi, the goddess of the Wu Mountain.

[3] Ch'ü-t'ang Gorge is one of the three famous Yangtze gorges. Rocky configurations make this gorge hazardous to shipping and travel, especially during the monsoon season. Travelers and merchants who went beyond this point could expect to be away a long time. Chinese poetry contains many laments of wives for their husbands gone to Ch'ü-t'ang.

[5]

Wind blows the curtain, swallows dance, and orioles sing.
At her dressing table, hands so soft, she combs her hair.
Her hairpin hangs heavy above her flowing hair.
She fastens a cluster of red—flowering peonies.

A happy traveler is making his way to the gate.
His white horse whinnies in the spring scenery.
Again and again, he lets fall his whip of gold.
He turns and looks round with a burning desire.

[6]

Gilded birds fly in the shining dark hair at her temples.
She frowns with grief at the thinness of the spring mist.
Her fragrant door is hidden by hibiscus blooms.
Mountains reach across the folds of the screen.

The window is cold, but soon the sun will rise.
Their love knot made of rush is still fastened.
Tears mixed with powder stain her silken robes.
She asks whenever will the gentleman come home?

[7]

The mats and the coverlets lie waiting in the jade tower.
Her powder blends with her moist fragrance on the pillow.
Outside she hears the sound of the well—pulley.
Suddenly a smile wipes the gloom from her face.

The willows are dark, and the mist without end.
Her hair is loose as the cicada pin falls away.
Even if it is necessary to forfeit life itself,
May this day be filled with complete happiness!

## "Song of the Wine Spring" (*Chiu-ch'üan tzu*), One Lyric

[1]

She holds in memory this time last year.                              (4)
In the warm mists of the Apricot Garden, flowers bloomed.             (7)
Petals drifted like sweet snow.                                       (3)

River grasses grew thick green.                                      (3)
Willow branches stretched long.                                      (3)

She raises the curtains of the gilt carriage to look out.            (7)
Her eyebrows are like the mountains in spring.                       (5)
Her phoenix hairpin dips low, and azure curls in a crown.           (7)
Her make-up is a fragile bloom.                                      (3)

## "Pacifying the Western Barbarians" (*Ting hsi-fan*), One Lyric

### [1]

The moon shines across miles of purple frontier.                    (6)
The metal armor is cold.                                             (3)
The guard tower is cold.                                             (3)
Ch'ang-an is in a dream.                                             (3)

He looks at the wide heavens and thinks of home.                    (6)
The water clock slows, and the stars fade.                          (5)
The sound of the watch horn is a melancholy cry.                    (6)
Snow fills the distance.                                             (3)

## "Song of the Jade Tower in Spring" (*Yü-lou ch'un*), One Lyric

### [1]

Spring comes to the pond in a ripple of shallow waves.              (7)
Flowers fall in the garden, and she is sad and lonely.             (7)
Who would believe her feelings for a good-for-nothing?             (7)
Azure and red from hatred and grief run on the pillow.             (7)

Beyond Little Jade's window swallows jabber and scold.             (7)
Reddened tears fall on the golden-threaded embroidery.            (7)
The wild geese return but cannot report on his return.            (7)
Verses stitched in silk lie ready as her gift for him.            (7)

## "Song of the West Stream" (*Hsi-ch'i tzu*), One Lyric

### [1]

A pair of golden phoenixes wind round the lute.                   (6)
Jade hairpins at her temples tremble and shake.                   (6)
In front of the painted hall,                                     (3)

People say not a single word.                              (3)
The music is able to say all.                              (3)
The melody tells of the sad exile of Chao–chün.           (6)
The lovely girl is sorrowful,                              (3)
And cannot raise up her head.                              (3)

## "Song of the River City" (*Chiang-ch'eng tzu*), Two Lyrics

### [1]

A red–capped egret rises high flying east of the city.     (7)
The green river is deserted.                               (3)
Winds cross the tiny island.                               (3)
The palaces of the king of Yüeh,                           (4)
Stand amid the duckweed and the lotus.                     (5)
Beyond the rolled curtains, waves lap the water tower.     (7)
A thousand petals like snow!                               (3)
A drizzling scatter of rain!                               (3)

### [2]

[Variation]
In the melting mist of the river bank birds rose high.
When you took your leave of the feast,                     (5)
I gave you a goblet of wine.
At the ford the willow blossoms,
Blew in the winds like a driving snow.
At twilight the waves churn across the deserted river.
Luxuriant grass on the bank!
Silken showers of fine rain!

# Chang Pi (*c.* A.D. 961)

## "Sand of Silk-Washing Stream" (*Huan-ch'i sha*), Ten Lyrics

### [1]

The golden–wheeled carriage passes the willow embankment.  (7)
Torches light his departure as his horse urgently whines.  (7)
Because of him, she is very drunk, but not entirely numb.  (7)

Flowers cover the post-station, softly perfuming the dew.         (7)
The cry of the cuckoo abruptly ends, and the moon is low.         (7)
Restrained, wordless, she turns to the west of the tower.         (7)


[2]


On horseback, he recalls with emotion a love of long ago.
Shining flowers overran the bamboo near a flowing stream,
A gold zither, silk curtains, and a hairpin made of jade!

When he left in early morning, the moon was still bright.
How did he bear to part from her and live another autumn?
In the evening wind at sunset, he is overcome with grief.


[3]


All alone on the cold steps she looks at the bright moon.
The dew is thick, and a flowery bouquet scents the court.
By the silken screen she grieves in flickering lamplight.

Since he left the clouds and rain are scattered and gone.
Humans have no roads to reach the dwellings of immortals.
Only by way of dreams can she search the distant horizon.


[4]


She freshens the color of her smudged and faded eyebrows.
She pulls away the long hairpin and her hair falls loose.
In warm breezes and a clear light she finishes making-up.

She picks a cherry-apple bloom, twisting it in her hands.
Her frail fingers are touched with a lingering fragrance.
With feelings such as these who can face the setting sun?


[5]


An azure screen is open, and the silken hangings are red.
She is listless, her make-up for the day carelessly done.
The curtain and quilt hold the fragrances from the night.

Fine rains wet the courtyard in the loneliness of spring.
Outside the curtains, swallows wheel and orioles chatter.
Bitterly the apricot blossom surrenders to the east wind.

## [6]

A pillow screen and a brazier stand outside the curtains.
For two years, every day, their hearts were close as one.
He must remember the apricot blossoming in the moonlight.

Where in the reaches of heaven or this world could he be?
When sleep comes, the old pleasures return in new dreams.
Rain mists the air at dusk, and the curtains trail loose.

## [7]

Bright moonlight and fresh coolness fill the quiet night.
At the feast, he secretly sees her, and secretly suffers.
She seems to be a beautiful portrait painted on a screen.

When no one is watching, he undertakes a few brief words.
Only after she drinks in her turn does she deign a frown.
All the Yüeh silks and Pa brocades cannot surpass spring!

## [8]

A white jade hairpin hangs rakishly from her flowery cap.
Sleep covers her face, and she sighs deeply at waking up.
A circlet of azure fringed with gold presses on her brow.

The sun's last rays and a quiet breeze enter the lattice.
Behind the curtains, an apricot flower languishes unseen.
Its faded perfume and frail green lock grief deep within.

## [9]

At evening, he follows after her carriage to the capital.
The east wind lightly tosses aside the brocaded curtains.
With a charming smile, she turns her shining eyes to him.

Since he can't speak to her, what is there for him to do?
He just pretends to be tipsy, and goes along with it all.
And she can be heard to say, "What a really crazy fellow!"

## [10]

At the east gate of the small market it is about to snow.
Among the crowd, he seems to glimpse his lovely immortal.
A gold cicada dangles above her brow brushed with yellow.

At twilight, the revel over, she grows ever more anxious.
Tipsily, silently, she stands and waits outside the gate.
His horse cries out, and the road swirls with smoky dust.

## "Immortal at the River" (*Lin-chiang hsien*), One Lyric

### [1]

In the calm of the autumn river, mist rises on the Hsiang.          (7)
Dew soaks the flowering banana in red tears of grief.               (6)
A pair of cranes vanish into the empyrean without a trace.          (7)
Her heart breaks over and over again,                              (4)
As she stares at the emptiness of the vast sky.                    (5)

The pearl tears shed in mourning lie hidden on the bamboo.[4]       (7)
Idly, she plays a precious se amid the surging waves.               (6)
Her upswept hair rises in a billow of dark shining clouds.         (7)
By ruined shrines and sunken palaces,                             (4)
The fragrant chill is mixed with wind and rain.                   (5)

## "The Taoist Nun" (*Nü-kuan tzu*), One Lyric

### [1]

Dew for flowers, mist for grass!                                  (4)
Loneliness and desolation cover this magic land.                  (6)
Now it is late springtime.                                        (3)
Her beauty fades away like dissolving jade.                       (5)
A delicate fragrance lingers at her throat.                       (5)

The bamboo are thin, the empty door hushed.                       (5)
The pines are thick, the spirit—altar dark.                       (5)
Why did that Liu gentleman have to go away?                       (5)
No word has come from him.                                        (3)

## "River Messages" (*Ho ch'uan*), Two Lyrics

### [1]

Distant clouds churn the waters.                                  (4)
A boat sails in the somber dusk.                                  (4)

---

[4] The tears shed by the wives of Shun, the Hsiang River goddesses, were believed to have fallen on the bamboo, and to have created the speckled pattern characteristic of certain bamboo that grow in Hunan and Kuangsi.

Ahead stretches the far journey.                                (4)
At sunset, the grasses are lush.                                (4)
Past thousands of endless miles,                                (4)
The cries of the wild geese never stop.                         (5)

Among the mist and waves, her dream comes to an end.           (7)
Her heart seems dizzied.                                        (3)
Where will they meet one another again?                        (5)
She lies sleepless in the chill of the screen.                 (6)
Teardrops, uncounted, lie on the quilt!                         (5)


## [2]

[Variation]
Twining apricot branches shine on one another.                 (6)
Fine rain falls in a light mist.                               (4)
In the court, pungent flowers turn to the east wind.           (7)
A steamy fragrance,                                            (2)
Penetrates the curtains.                                        (3)

The setting sun seems to chat with the spring scene.           (7)
Rival butterflies dance.                                       (3)
The flitting orioles grow more jealous.                        (5)
Her heart shatters in tiny pieces near the wine cup.           (7)
Celestial immortal,                                            (2)
At twilight he lies drunk in fairyland!                         (5)


# "Song of the Wine Spring" (*Chiu-ch'üan tzu*), Two Lyrics

## [1]

The spring rains beat at the window.                            (4)
Suddenly roused from her dream, she awakens to the dawn.        (7)
In the depths of the hall,                                      (3)
A sliver of reddish flame,                                      (3)
Burns in the scented lamp.                                      (3)

She smells the wine's fragrance, and idly opens the jar.        (7)
She is heartsick that there is no one to drink with her.        (7)
Dwelling in the old nests,                                      (3)
The newly paired swallows,                                      (3)
Converse with one another.                                      (3)

[2]

[Variation]
From the royal roads to Ch'ing Gate,                              (4)
The imperial palaces grace the spring scenery.                   (6)
Along the water of the palace drain,                             (4)
Once went secret messages.[5]                                    (3)
Wind stirs Apricot Garden.                                       (3)

The wine shops and the women of Hsien-yang are all gone.         (7)
Smiling, he points to Wei-yang for his return.                  (6)
A flower atop his head, he gallops across fallen petals,        (7)
In a shimmer of moonlight.                                       (3)


## "Mountain Hawthorns" (*Sheng-ch'a-tzu*), One Lyric

[1]

Their meetings were so few,                                      (3)
But oh, so very delightful.                                      (3)
Their every meeting was to be a parting.                         (5)
Red lichees are painted across her gown.                         (5)
A dragonfly of soft gold holds her hair.                         (5)

Her letters have gone away,                                      (3)
His messages of love ended.                                      (3)
Flowers fall, and the garden grows dark.                         (5)
Have pity for her skin like finest jade,                         (5)
As she grows thin and frail with sorrow.                         (5)


## "Thoughts of the Yüeh Beauty" (*Ssu Yüeh-jen*), One Lyric

[1]

Paired swallows soar above.                                      (3)
Orioles warble their songs.                                      (3)
The long bridge runs below the Yüeh Embankment.                 (6)
Flowers, richly encrusted with gold, overlay her hair.          (7)
Her dancing gown is sheer silk, her waist slim.                 (6)

---

[5] During the reign of the T'ang emperor Hsi-tsung (r. 874–889), Yü Yu sent a poem entitled "Red Leaves" along the imperial drains into the palace where it was received by the Lady Han.

In the stillness of the east wind, she feels listless.          (7)
The fresh green of her brows gathers in sorrow.                 (6)
Fallen flowers cover the ground, but no news has come.          (7)
In the moonlight, vain memory breaks her heart.                (6)

## "Flowers Fill the Palace" (*Man-kung hua*), One Lyric

### [1]

The flowers bloom in abundance.                                (3)
The tower is like cutwork silk.                                (3)
It is desolate within the Shang-yang Palace.                   (6)
Mandarin ducks doze in a gilt cage locked with gold.           (7)
The dew on the curtains makes a pearl crown.                   (6)

She is lovely and graceful with skin smooth as snow.           (7)
A pair of orioles rise up in the misty rain.                   (6)
It is almost ch'ing-ming, and the east wind grieves.           (7)
That man by the bridge must really be drunk!                   (6)

## "Willow Branches" (*Liu-chih*), One Lyric

### [1]

Behind a cloud of green gauze is her jadelike face,            (7)
Putting even snow to shame.                                    (3)
A golden phoenix hairpin dangles across her temple.           (7)
Her hair falls in a tangle.                                    (3)

She turns to the cloud screen when she first wakes.            (7)
Her dreams make her giggle.                                    (3)
The ornamented pillow has left marks on her cheeks,            (7)
Just a few, here and there!                                    (3)

## "A Southern Song" (*Nan-ko tzu*), Three Lyrics

Willow trees screen the tower in darkness.                     (5)
Fallen wu-t'ung flowers perfume the steps.                     (5)
The chill of a distant wind fills the painted hall.            (7)
The crystal curtains are rolled to the very top,               (6)
Burnished by the setting sun.                                  (3)

## [2]

The willows on the shore trail green mist.
The garden flowers redden in the sunlight.
The cry of the cuckoo enters the gathered curtains.
Her dreams are suddenly shattered at the window.
The painted screen is vacant.


## [3]

Mandarin ducks lie red on the silken mats.
Phoenixes are stitched on her silken gown.
At the window, snow rages wildly in the north wind.
The loosened curtains are closed and motionless.
There is a scent of turmeric.

# CHAPTER FIVE

## Chang Pi (*c.* A.D. 961)

### "Song of the River City" (*Chiang-ch'eng tzu*), Two Lyrics

#### [1]

| | |
|---|---|
| Beyond the green railings there is a small garden. | (7) |
| The rain has just passed. | (3) |
| The orioles sing at dawn. | (3) |
| Flowers fall amid the flying catkins. | (4) |
| It is almost the time of the ch'ing-ming. | (5) |
| She wakes with little to do but raise the curtain. | (7) |
| She has done her make-up. | (3) |
| She feels dull and weary. | (3) |

#### [2]

| | |
|---|---|
| [Variation] | |
| On the Brocade River he glimpses his dear darling. | (7) |
| Her eyes shine like the waters in autumn. | (5) |
| Her brows are a gossamer. | (3) |
| A cloud of dark hair is brushed high. | (4) |
| A dragonfly clings to her golden hairpin. | (5) |
| He asks her for a time when they can get together. | (7) |
| She answers with a smile, | (3) |
| "You needn't get excited!" | (3) |

### "Spirit of the Yellow River" (*Ho-tu shen*), One Lyric

#### [1]

| | |
|---|---|
| Crows are cawing from the ancient trees. | (5) |
| Maple leaves and rush tassels fill the court. | (6) |
| At noon, the sanctuary lamp burns behind a silk curtain. | (7) |
| A pearl screen casts a shadow along the room. | (6) |
| | |
| Beyond the gate, pious pilgrims come and go from prayer. | (7) |
| A billowing sail disappears over the horizon. | (6) |
| I turn and see smoke rising across the river. | (6) |
| A few families are settled close to the ford. | (6) |

## "Song of the Butterflies" (*Hu-tieh-erh*), One Lyric

### [1]

| | |
|---|---|
| There are butterflies! | (3) |
| It is late springtime! | (3) |
| A pretty lady in a brand—new pale yellow gown, | (7) |
| Paints the butterflies from the window. | (5) |
| So real, they seem to be in the garden! | (5) |
| Two by two, pair after pair, they soar. | (5) |
| Unwitting tears splash from her rouged cheeks, | (7) |
| Slowly a pair of wings starts to droop. | (5) |

# Mao Wen-hsi (*c.* A.D. *930*)

## "The Beautiful Lady Yü" (*Yü mei-jen*), Two Lyrics

### [1]

| | |
|---|---|
| Mandarin ducks swim in the warmth of the clear pond. | (7) |
| Stubby reeds break the water's surface. | (5) |
| Trailing willow branches brush the pale amber waves. | (7) |
| The dew, like pearls scattered on a gossamer cobweb; | (7) |
| Splashes the budding lotus. | (3) |

| | |
|---|---|
| Far away, I think of the T'ao—yeh Ford in Wu—chiang. | (7) |
| My home is as distant as the Milky Way. | (5) |
| Lacy scales and red fins are vanished in the depths.[1] | (7) |
| I think of you, and in vain, seek for you in dreams. | (7) |
| Thoughts so hard to endure! | (3) |

### [2]

Mandarin ducks embroidered in gold adorn the pillow.
Ribbons encircle the brocaded hangings.
The setting sun shines brightly on the small window.
In the south garden, orioles gossiping in the trees,
Make dreaming so difficult.

I add incense to the warm aromas of the jade censer.
Catkins lightly whirl along the ground.
The smoky scent of aloes passes the closed curtains.
The swing stands deserted in front of the courtyard.
Such a splendid lovely sky!

[1] "Lacy scales" and "red fins" refer to fish, a common image for news or a letter.

# "Song of the Wine Spring" (*Chiu-ch'üan tzu*), One Lyric

## [1]

| | |
|---|---|
| The trees are green in the late spring. | (4) |
| Now and then, swallows chat and orioles sing a tune. | (7) |
| An orchid-scented breeze stirs the flowering shrubs, | (7) |
| And red petals flutter down. | (3) |

| | |
|---|---|
| Willow branches are softly swaying in the misty air. | (7) |
| I never decline a wine-cup, but keep it always full. | (7) |
| Beneath the wild plum, my thoughts are in confusion. | (7) |
| And I lie drunk in the wind! | (3) |

# "Delight in the High-Flying Orioles" (*Hsi ch'ien ying*), One Lyric

## [1]

| | |
|---|---|
| The spring scenery is luxuriant. | (3) |
| It is shimmering in a hazy mist. | (3) |
| The orioles flit about among the tall trees. | (5) |
| Chirping, they gather twigs and nestle in the leaves. | (7) |
| They skip in and out of a tracery of bushes. | (5) |

| | |
|---|---|
| Their lovely wings shine bright. | (3) |
| Their golden down is silky soft. | (3) |
| In melody and harmony, they call to one another. | (6) |
| Dawn is at the window but some fear to hear the song. | (7) |
| It will surely wake the cozy mandarin ducks. | (5) |

# "In Praise of Merit" (*Tsan ch'eng-kung*), One Lyric

## [1]

| | |
|---|---|
| The budding wild plum has yet to burst. | (4) |
| It is thick with dots of deepening red. | (4) |
| In knotted clusters, the sweet buds pile on one another. | (7) |
| It seems as if they are shyly blushing, | (4) |
| As if they are snaring the spring wind. | (4) |
| The bees come while the butterflies go, | (4) |
| Freely they circle its abundant beauty. | (4) |

```
Last night, rain fell in a fine shower,              (4)
And raindrops splattered the courtyard.              (4)
Water suddenly spills from the wu-t'ung beside the well.  (7)
The beautiful lady awakes with a start.              (4)
She sits and listens to the dawn bells.              (4)
"Quickly," she says, "Pick some for me!"             (4)
She puts the dainty blooms in her hair.              (4)
```

## "Song of the West Stream" (*Hsi-ch'i tzu*), One Lyric

### [1]

```
Yesterday, I amused myself at the western stream.    (6)
Lush trees and rare flowers grow in extravagance.    (6)
I was locked in spring's beauty.                     (3)
My gold cup was full to the top.                     (3)
Strings and pipes filled my ear.                     (3)
The graceful dancer's robe was fragrant and warm.    (6)
Before I knew it, the bright sun was setting,        (5)
And my horse carried me on home!                     (3)
```

## "Joy at Renewal" (*Chung-hsing le*), One Lyric

### [1]

```
In the mist, the flowering nutmeg is beautiful.      (7)
The lilac buds are like fragile love-knots.          (6)
A touch of azure trims her hair.                     (3)
They are together,                                   (2)
And together they wash for gold.                     (3)

Chimpanzees are jabbering in the banana leaves.      (7)
Mandarin ducks sit on the shore.                     (3)
A phoenix dances on a shining mirror.                (4)
Behind the soft drizzling rains,                     (3)
The lichee bloom lies in shadow.                     (3)
```

## "Song of the Water Clock at Night" (*Keng-lou tzu*), One Lyric

### [1]

```
Late in the spring night,                            (3)
Spring's grief cuts deep.                            (3)
```

Beyond the flowers, the cuckoo mourns the moon.                    (6)
They can't meet together.                                          (3)
She can't rely on dreams.                                          (3)
A single flame burns by the curtain.                              (5)

She resented his leaving.                                          (3)
The year is in its prime.                                          (3)
Lilacs in the garden swarm with knotted blooms.                   (6)
The nighttime mist fades.                                          (3)
The dawn clouds are rosy.                                          (3)
Paired swallows fly among the beams.                              (5)

# "Welcoming the Worthy Guest" (*Chieh hsien-pin*), One Lyric

## [1]

A scented cloth and tooled flaps outfit his fine horse.          (7)
In early spring, the earth begins to stir.                       (5)
Beads of foam fleck the horse's mouth.                           (4)
Blood—red sweat splashes from its every stride.[2]               (6)

The young gentleman rides his horse with supreme skill.          (7)
The gold bit and jade bridle are finely chased.                  (6)
He is kindhearted and doesn't bear down the coral whip.          (7)
The spirited horse gallops in quickening steps.                  (6)
They saunter through the flowers.                                 (3)
They idly brush away the willows.                                 (3)
Toward the open road, they chase the wind.                       (5)

# "The Barbarian Chieftain" (*Tsan-p'u tzu*),[3] One Lyric

## [1]

The silk curtains will be fragrant as she sleeps.                (5)
Fresh incense has been added to the gold brazier.                (5)
She is too lazy even to fasten her hibiscus sash,                (5)
And her skirt of azure trails loosely behind her.                (5)

---

[2] The very finest horses came from Ferghana and were known from Han times as the "blood-sweating" horses or the "heavenly" horses.

[3] *Tsan-p'u tzu*, the title of this tune, is a transliteration of a Tibetan expression which means a "barbarian chieftain" or "general." See Ts'ui Ling-ch'in (*fl.* second half of the eighth century), *Chiao-fang chi chien-ting*, ed. Jen Pan-t'ang (Peking: Chung-hua shu-chü 1962), p. 135.

Just now the peach is tender and the willow beguiling.        (6)
How can she bear the evening rains and morning clouds.        (6)
Her thoughts are much with Sung Yü and Kao-t'ang.            (5)
She wishes pretty words would convey this to him.            (5)

## "Roaming in Kan-chou" (*Kan-chou pien*), Two Lyrics

### [1]

The spring scene is splendid.                                (3)
The gentleman likes to leisurely ramble about.              (5)
He really is so good-looking.                                (3)
His white horse is saddled with gold.                        (4)
He has a carved bow and a rare sword.                        (4)
In red hat-strings and silken chaps, he roams the lanes.    (7)

His horse has rich trappings.                                (3)
A jade bit bridles its mouth.                                (3)
The gentleman seeks beauty and the joys of a feast.         (6)
The music of pipes and strings goes on and on.              (5)
A pretty lady sings the song.                                (3)
The song is that well-known melody, "Kan-chou."            (5)
He is drunk in the red tower.                                (3)
It is the golden age of Yao and Shun.                       (4)
Rejoice in the sages and never ever be gloomy!              (5)

### [2]

The autumn wind surges ahead.
Over the sandy flats, the wild geese file low.
Clouds rise in ordered ranks.
The whistling wind is a sharp scream.
The frontier sounds sweep all around.
Sadly, we listen to the watch horn and the battle drums.

North from Chao-chün's grave,
And west of the Hei Mountain,
The swirling sands toss and turn in unending waves.
Travelers are often confused and lose the way.
The frozen armor is like ice.
Blood drips from the hooves of the war horses.
The tartars have been beaten.
The emperor proclaims his kind favor.
Step by step, we move up the vermilion stairs!

# "Feeling Regret at the Silk Window" (*Sha-ch'uang hen*), Two Lyrics

## [1]

```
The swallows return in the freshness of spring.      (7)
A pair is flying about.                               (3)
The oozy mud of their nest often splashes down,      (7)
Spattering one's robes.                               (3)

The flowers teem with bloom in the back garden.      (7)
A sweet wind brushes the gilt door to her room.      (7)
Moonlight shines on a silk window.                   (4)
Her regret is unending!                              (3)
```

## [2]

```
[Variation]
The wings of the butterflies are powdery white,
From snuggling flowers.
They come to rest on a silk window in her room.
Shadow covers the hall.

In spring, they fly the winds with the catkins.
With the falling petals, they brush her collar.
She cuts silk in the shape of their wings,          (5)
Adding a touch of gold!
```

# "Mist on the Willows" (*Liu han yen*), Four Lyrics

## [1]

```
Willows line the Sui Embankment.                     (3)
They edge the banks of the Pien.                     (3)
Mile upon mile, green shadow covers the shores.      (6)
The wood of the imperial boats and barges is fragrant. (7)
The silk sails are all unfurled.                     (3)

I dream about the beautiful spring south of the river. (7)
We sail as though screened by feathery tassels.      (6)
The unfinished song of the pipes rises like a riptide, (7)
Enveloping the sorrow of spring!                     (3)
```

[2]

Willows stand beside the bridge.
They overrun the spring scenery.
Mirrored in water, misted, they brush the road.
Often their branches are cut to give to the travelers.
In secret, their spirits grieve.

The song that is heard is an air for the bamboo flute.
The pain of parting is throbbing at every note.
Better to transfer the willows nearer the palace gate,
Near the emperor's loving grace!

[3]

Willows thrive along Chang-t'ai.
Their branches are like banners.
They dip low, grazing the hats of the visitors.
The shimmering beauty of springtime fills the capital.
Lovely shaded mists drift about.

These willows have parted from roadside and riverside.
They escape being pulled away by the travelers.
And they are so much envied by the fine-browed ladies,
When their leaves are so dainty!

[4]

Willows fill the imperial canal.
They overrun the spring scenery.
Gracefully, they trail across the palace walls.
Sometimes, their watery image is like the finest silk,
Waves of pale yellow surging up.

Yesterday when the emperor's carriage toured the park,
The wind pressed their waists, pliant and soft.
These willows have a good place, very near the palace,
Thick with a lovely shaded mist!

# "Drunk Among the Flowers" (*Tsui hua-chien*), Two Lyrics

[1]

Don't ask any questions!                                        (3)
I'm afraid of questions!                                        (3)

```
Questions add all the more to my suffering.            (5)
The waters of spring are flooding the pond.            (5)
Mandarin ducks still seek each other there.            (5)

Last night, the rains fell in an icy sleet.           (5)
At a time near dawn, it was extremely cold.            (5)
I think of him in the frontier guard tower.            (5)
No news has come for such a very long time.            (5)
```

[2]

```
I think of him so often!
I oughtn't think at all!
Thinking adds all the more to my suffering.
The Milky Way forms an impermeable barrier,
A barrier that divides us from one another.

Dewdrops are spilling into the golden pans.⁴
Along the river, the elm flowers are white.
The wind tosses the tinkling jade pendants.
This night, what special night could it be?
```

## "Sand of Silk-Washing Stream" (*Huan-ch'i sha*), Two Lyrics

[1]

```
Rippling waves of spring water drench the green moss.        (7)
The purple sandalwood blossoms across P'i-p'a Island.        (7)
Under a clear sky, mandarin ducks sleep on the sands.        (7)
They snuggle to keep nice and warm.                          (3)

The dust stirring at their feet, the goddesses go by.        (7)
They come upon a man beside the Pearl-Sporting River.        (7)
A heady scent of musk rises as they undo their belts.        (7)
Returning home slips from his mind.                          (3)
```

---

⁴ The Emperor Wu (*r.* 140–86) of the Han dynasty was obsessed with the desire to become an immortal. He set up pans to be held by bronze statues of immortals to catch the dew for use in the elixir of immortality.

## [2]

```
[Variation]
Each year on the seventh night, they are always true.⁵      (7)
The bright Milky Way runs shallow in a wisp of cloud.        (7)
In the moonlight a shrike flies by the Magpie Bridge.        (7)

I hate the fleeting cicada and pity the Waiting-Maid.⁶       (7)
I am touched with envy as I sit and work at the loom.        (7)
Limitless love will fill their meeting on this night.       (7)
```

# "Spring in the Moon Palace" (*Yüeh-kung ch'un*), One Lyric

## [1]

```
Within the crystal palace, the cassia is in flower.         (7)
The immortals often come to look.                           (5)
Double petals decorate the gold-hearted red blooms.         (7)
Toasts are drunk from agate cups.                           (5)

The jade rabbit and silver toad vie to be on guard.         (7)
The goddesses Ch'ang O and Ch'a Nü frolic together.         (7)
Heavenly music can be heard in the distance.                (6)
The Jade Emperor has come to see.                           (5)
```

# "A Deep Love" (*Lien-ch'ing shen*), Two Lyrics

## [1]

```
Drop by drop, the water clock drips sadly in the cold.      (7)
I was drunk in the moonlit red tower.                       (4)
As the feast was ending, we met together in the quilt.      (7)
My heart knew reckless desire.                              (3)
```

⁵ The seventh night of the seventh month is the night when the Herd Boy and the Weaving Maiden cross the Milky Way and come together.

⁶ The "fleeting cicada" is the *hui-ku*, described in the *Chuang-tzu*, "The morning mushroom knows nothing of twilight and dawn; the summer cicada knows nothing of spring and autumn. They are short-lived." See Burton Watson, *The Complete Works of Chuang-tzu* (New York: Columbia University Press, 1968), p. 30.

The "Waiting Maid" is a star in the constellation Aquarius, north of the Weaving Maiden star.

Now the dawn light is peeking under the pearl screens.          (7)
The chatter of orioles comes from the grove.                    (5)
Languorously, I get up and pull open the curtains.              (6)
My feeling of love is so deep!                                  (3)


## [2]


The flowers by the jade hall shine in the rich spring.
The goddesses are all together there.
Their gold-threaded silk skirts whisper on the ground.
The melodic strains are clear.

When wine and music are done, we feel heavy and sated.
Just one smile from her can sway your heart.
Forever, I want to be as close as a mandarin duck.
My feeling of love is so deep!


# "Speaking of Love" (*Su chung-ch'ing*), Two Lyrics

## [1]

Peach blossoms are adrift on rippling tides of water.          (7)
Rosy clouds brighten the spring day.                           (5)
Gentleman Liu has gone.                                        (3)
Gentleman Juan is gone.                                        (3)
Sad regrets make it hard to be calm.                           (5)

Grieving, I sit by the cloud screen,                           (5)
Calculating his return.                                        (3)
When will I again hold his hands to welcome him home?          (7)
I tell him my feelings!                                        (3)


## [2]


Their plumage soft and bright, mandarin ducks cuddle,
By a pond filled with scented lotus.
They snuggle the grass.
They shine on the bank.
They wash in duckweed wet with rain.

But I am lost in my uneasy thoughts,
Thoughts of the border.
When will I again untie my sash and close the screen?
I tell him my feelings!

# "Echoing Heaven's Everlastingness" (*Ying t'ien-ch'ang*), One Lyric

## [1]

| | |
|---|---|
| Mandarin ducks ooze in the warmth of the quiet river. | (7) |
| Two by two, fishing boats return to the distant bank. | (7) |
| At evening, wind and rain blow over the islet rushes. | (7) |
| Great snow-white egrets fly up from the sandy shoals. | (7) |

| | |
|---|---|
| The boat lamps are a glow on the far shore. | (5) |
| But in what place does his boat stop the night? | (6) |
| Her silken sleeves gently ripple in the breeze. | (6) |
| The girl picking lotus is deeply sorrowful. | (5) |

# "Song of Ho Man-tzu" (*Ho Man-tzu*),[7] One Lyric

## [1]

| | |
|---|---|
| The moon shines in front of the red tower. | (6) |
| Orioles cry outside the green silk window. | (6) |
| She lies awake, wanting news of Liao-yang. | (6) |
| How can she bear to be in her lonely room? | (6) |
| She hates the time the flowers will bloom. | (6) |
| Oh Prince, the grass grows lush and green![8] | (6) |

# "A Stretch of Cloud over Mount Wu" (*Wu-shan i-tuan yün*), One Lyric

## [1]

| | |
|---|---|
| The rains have cleared above Wu Mountain. | (5) |
| Wispy clouds set off the bright blue sky. | (5) |
| Once scattered by the wind, they come together again. | (7) |
| At evening, in front of the twelve peaks,[9] | (5) |
| They enfold the trees where monkeys wail. | (5) |
| They mist the tops of the drifting boats. | (5) |
| By day and by night near the banks of the Ch'u River, | (7) |
| How often does that fair goddess descend? | (5) |

---

[7] The title of this song, *Ho Man-tzu*, is the name of a singer who lived in the eighth century.
[8] This is an allusion to the *"Chao yin-shih"* in the *Ch'u-tz'u* anthology, see ch. 1, n. 1, p. 46.
[9] The twelve peaks refer to the twelve peaks of Wu Mountain.

## "Immortal at the River" (*Lin-chiang hsien*), One Lyric

### [1]

```
The cry of the cicada dies away with the setting sun.    (7)
The Hsiao and Hsiang glow with silvered moonlight.       (6)
The waters rush endlessly near the Huang-ling Shrine.    (7)
Crimson trees cover the Ch'u mountains.                  (4)
Mist and rain screen the Kao-t'ang Pavilion.            (5)

The lights on the moored boats flicker with the wind.    (7)
The white duckweed spreads far its fragrant scent.       (6)
The goddesses play the se in clear and sweet harmony,¹⁰  (7)
Scarlet strings, sorrowful and restive!                  (4)
Clouds scatter, unveiling the limitless sky.             (5)
```

# Niu Hsi-chi (*c.* A.D. 930)

## "Immortal at the River" (*Lin-chiang hsien*), Seven Lyrics

### [1]

```
Jagged cliffs overhang the soaring peaks of Mount Wu.    (7)
Chill mist and icy trees ascend level after level.       (6)
The palace of Yao Chi remains but an ethereal vision.    (7)
A golden censer within beaded curtains,                  (4)
Its spicy smoke rises thickest in the day.               (5)

Since the king of Ch'u awoke suddenly from his dream,    (7)
There has been no pathway on earth to the goddess.       (6)
Even today clouds and rain are a melancholy presence.    (7)
Above the river, the moon slowly sinks.                  (4)
The boat sets forth with the morning bell.               (5)
```

### [2]

```
The home of the goddess Hsieh is in the cloudy peaks.¹¹
Twisting creepers cast dark shadows on the ground.
```

---

¹⁰ The goddesses are the goddesses of the Hsiang River. This line alludes to a line in the "*Yüan-yu*" in the *Ch'u-tz'u* anthology, "I made the Hsiang goddesses play on their zithers." See David Hawkes, *Songs of the South* (Boston: Beacon Press, 1962), p. 86.

¹¹ There seems to be some doubt as to which immortal is the topic of this lyric. Hua Lien-p'u in the *Hua-chien chi chu* suggests that it is Hsieh Nü who received the Way at Hsieh-nü hsia, also known as Hsieh-nü ao. However, Hsiao Chi-tsung in the *Hua-chien chi* believes that the goddess is Hsieh Tzu-jan, mentioned in chapter 66 of the *T'ai-p'ing kuang-chi*, who upon her ascent into heaven left behind her earthly clothing and ornaments. *T'ai-p'ing kuang-chi*, comp. Li Fang and others A.D. 978 (Peking: *Chung-hua shu-chü*, 1961), ch. 66, pp. 408–13.

Deep within the white clouds, the grotto stands open.
At this time, in the alchemist's stove,
A single pellet is changed to yellow gold.

A gossamer gown of rose falls across the rocky ledge.
Wind wails in the pines like the cry of the ch'in.
Often the trumpet of the crane rises from the forest.
They are feasting on the Magic Islands.
But is there a place where I can find you?


## [3]

Wasted trees line the palace wall by the Wei Parapet.[12]
Cheerless and alone, I sadly climb the jade tower.
In silence, I contain my feelings and play the pipes.
The clear melody is mixed with anguish.
It whirls on the winds to the far horizon.

Why is the one riding the dragon suddenly descending?[13]
It is as if he sensed my deep need crying for him.
If he guides me, the road to the immortals isn't far.
This world is very like a large screen,
Emblazed with the most beguiling pictures!


## [4]

By the river in spring, Huang-ling remains abandoned.
Only the orioles can be found singing their songs.
The garden is filled with layers of thick green moss.
The dark clouds are aimlessly drifting.
They scatter and go back to the mountains.

Pipes and drums seldom play, and the incense is cold.
The goddess of the moon is a resplendent crescent.
Everyone agrees that I am the most romantic creature.
You know even the passionate Ch'ü Yüan,
Was quite willing to risk all just for me![14]

---

[12] The Wei Parapet was a guard tower overlooking the Wei River. The palace wall of the capital of the ancient state of Ch'in was located near this watchtower.

[13] Nung Yü, p. 211.

[14] This poem is written in the persona of one of the goddesses of the Hsiang River, the Hsiang fu-jen, who is also one of the goddesses to whom the Huang-ling Shrine is dedicated. Ch'ü Yüan is the fourth century B.C. poet from the state of Ch'u to whom is traditionally attributed the authorship of the *Nine Songs* of the *Ch'u-tz'u* anthology. One of these songs is in honor of the Hsiang fu-jen, in which the poet expresses his devotion by saying, "I can hear my beloved calling to me: / I will ride aloft and race beside her." See David Hawkes, *The Songs of the South*, p. 39.

## [5]

Rippling waves cross the Lo River in glorious spring.
A lovely woman seems to rise up out of the depths.
She skims the waters as though wearing sheerest silk.
Folds of mist hold back the bright sun.
A pearl and azure crown is dimly glimpsed.

Her gown billows in the winds as if she were dancing.
Phoenixes circle and soar, and I watch breathless.
But well I know that such intimacy can never be mine.
Ts'ao Chih's tribute to the Lo goddess,[15]
In a thousand years will still be honored!

## [6]

Wind blows the willows on the banks of the Han River.
Wild grasses compete for a place along the shores.
Fresh ripples trail the splash of the mandarin ducks.
Those alluring goddesses of the pearls,[16]
Smile with just a hint of what is to come.

Their softly rolled hair sways with each dainty step.
Breezes toss their silk skirts in a whirl of dust.
Can their sojourn in the crystal palace be so futile?
In vain they suffer their tender hands,
To loosen their belts as gifts for lovers!

## [7]

The waves of Lake Tung-t'ing churn under a clear sky.
Chün Mountain is covered by a cloud of heavy mist.
There lies the true border between men and immortals.
There, jade towers and jeweled palaces,
Shine on one another by the circling moon.

For endless miles the lake is the cold hue of autumn.
The bright light of the stars mingles in its flow.
Oranges in the frosty groves seem redder and fresher.
At the very foot of the Lo-fu Mountain,
Lies a path where we could meet in secret!

---

[15] "Lo-shen *fu*," p. 210.
[16] Pearl-Sporting River, p. 212.

# "Song of the Wine Spring" (*Chiu-ch'üan tzu*), One Lyric

## [1]

| | |
|---|---|
| She stirs on the pillow and cold mat. | (4) |
| At dawn, a faraway bell breaks her fading dream. | (6) |
| Slanted moonbeams grow pale. | (3) |
| Curtains shimmer in shadows. | (3) |
| Sweet incense still lingers. | (3) |

| | |
|---|---|
| In her dreams, they spoke of their love for one another. | (7) |
| Her delicate hands wipe the welling tears. | (5) |
| The letters from a year ago, | (3) |
| The things remembered today, | (3) |
| All attend her broken heart. | (3) |

# "Mountain Hawthorns" (*Sheng-ch'a-tzu*), One Lyric

## [1]

| | |
|---|---|
| Mist dissolves above the mountains in spring. | (5) |
| Bare pinpoints of stars dot the tranquil sky. | (5) |
| The fading moonlight falls across her cheeks. | (5) |
| She wept sad tears of parting until the dawn. | (5) |

| | |
|---|---|
| They have already said so much, | (3) |
| But their love is not yet done. | (3) |
| She turns round to him to say one thing more, | (5) |
| "Please keep in memory this green silk skirt, | (5) |
| Wherever you go cherish the blossoming grass!" | (5) |

# "Joy at Renewal" (*Chung-hsing le*), One Lyric

## [1]

| | |
|---|---|
| The warm green pond is flooded with radiant sunlight. | (7) |
| Willow catkins whirl like sprays of fine rain. | (6) |
| The red flowers have withered. | (4) |
| And my drunken dreams are few. | (4) |

| | |
|---|---|
| Only the wild geese come on the spring clouds. | (6) |
| The curtains hang loose. | (3) |
| The east wind is a bleak sigh. | (4) |
| I despise the man who left me. | (4) |
| The tears dampen my silk robe. | (4) |

## "Paying Homage at the Golden Gate" (*Yeh chin-men*), One Lyric

### [1]

```
It was already late autumn.                                    (3)
A zigzag of mountain roads went in all directions.             (6)
His horse gave a cry, he used the whip, and off he went.       (7)
At dawn, birds filled the frost—covered trees.                 (5)

Her dream is broken by the palace bells and drums.             (6)
Numberless tears have stained the fragrant pillow,             (6)
A lone patch of crimson aswirl in the thin morning mist.       (7)
The lovely woman grieves, but says not a word.                 (5)
```

# Ou-yang Chiung (896–971)

## "Sand of Silk-Washing Stream" (*Huan-ch'i sha*), Three Lyrics

### [1]

```
The catkins fall and the orioles' cries fade at sundown.       (7)
Her jade face is like a sleepy flower flushed with wine.       (7)
Bamboos etch the window, and smoke rises from a brazier.       (7)

She draws the screens, and in solitary silence, grieves.       (7)
She pulls the pillow close, her hair spills to the side.       (7)
At this time, beside whom does her heart so closely lie?       (7)
```

### [2]

```
Her gown of bright azure silk gently brushes the ground.
On this occasion, her new robe is especially enchanting.
Soft winds dance in the folds, revealing her sweet skin.

She sits alone, and in solitary plaint, plays the pipes.
She walks in the garden, and plucks a blossoming branch.
What can she do when she is hopelessly smitten with him!
```

### [3]

```
They see one another, and tears take the place of words.
Done with drinking, he shares with her the joys of love.
A phoenix screen and mandarin duck quilt shield the bed.
```

In a mist of musk and orchid, he listens to her breathe.
Through the sheerest film of silk, he looks at her body.
Does she hate him now for being such a no—account lover?

## "A Song in Three Characters" (*San-tzu ling*), One Lyric

### [1]

Spring is coming to an end.                                   (3)
The days go by more slowly.                                   (3)
Peonies have come to bloom.                                   (3)
The silk curtain is raised.                                   (3)
The azure screen is closed.                                   (3)
She holds his sweet letter.                                   (3)
Tears mark her pretty face.                                   (3)
They are one in their love.                                   (3)

He has yet to come in view.                                   (3)
Only the swallows reappear.                                   (3)
He scorns to keep his date.                                   (3)
The fragrant incense fades.                                   (3)
She slumps over the pillow.                                   (3)
The moon is shining bright.                                   (3)
The flowers are dimly pale.                                   (3)
It rankles to think of him!                                   (3)

# CHAPTER SIX

## Ou-yang Chiung (896–971)

### "Song of the Southern Country" (*Nan-hsiang tzu*), Eight Lyrics

#### [1]

| | |
|---|---|
| The budding grass is like a soft mist. | (4) |
| The pomegranates come to flower beneath the southern sky. | (7) |
| At sunset by a river tower, spring shimmers on the water. | (7) |
| Mandarin ducks dip in the waves. | (3) |
| I can't see enough of the far-flung rivers and mountains! | (7) |

#### [2]

[Variation]
The oars pull up on the painted barge.
Beyond the hibiscus hedge, bamboo criss-cross the bridge.
As voyagers bob on the water, girls watch from the beach.
They turn and look around, (2)
And laughingly point to the banana grove where they live!

#### [3]

[Variation]
The sand is flat on the distant shore.
Rosy clouds at sunset brightly glow on our homeward road.
A peacock preens the gold and azure feathers of his tail.
He is very near the water, (2)
But being used to travelers, he doesn't rise up in alarm!

#### [4]

Whose dwelling lies within the grotto?
The magnolia boat is tied and moored with magnolia lines.
A woman in ruby sleeves leads one of the gentlemen aside.
Strolling beside the south bank,
They laugh in the spring wind as they have a little chat!

[5]

She is sixteen and the sweetest thing.
Her breast shines white as snow, and her face is a lotus.
Her gold-hooped earrings are set with drops of turquoise.
Her rosy-hued gown fits closely.
Smiling, she comes to the river to welcome the travelers!


[6]

Our travels take us through Nan-chung.
The leaves of the palms shade the red-blooming smartweed.
After a scattering of rain, everyone comes to the shores.
They are plucking the red beans.[1]
Beneath a tree, she gracefully reaches out her pale hand!


[7]

Her rolled up sleeves are of shagreen.
Gathering herbs in the grotto, she smiles to welcome him.
A gourd of new wine hangs on top of a vine-covered staff.
The sunflower mat is spread out.
The setting sun is a shimmer among the blossoming nutmeg!


[8]

The wild ducks are a shiny blue-green.
The sandy spit lies covered with fragrant white duckweed.
On the island the autumn rain is a dark and somber shade.
It pounds away the reed flowers.
Where will those fishing boats find harbor for the night?


## "Offering Deep Affection" (*Hsien chung-hsin*), One Lyric

[1]

She looks closely at the color of the flowers,                     (5)
As they try to laugh at the east winds.                            (4)
Across her two lovely cheeks,                                      (3)
Her make-up is that same hue.                                      (3)

---

[1] The red bean is a token of love.

She shuts herself deep within the small tower.                    (5)
The spring scene is too heavy and full.                           (4)
At evening, on the fifteenth,                                     (3)
She feels nothing but sorrow,                                     (3)
In the moon's brilliant glow.                                     (3)

Her love is not yet finished.                                     (3)
She has written him a letter.                                     (3)
Her gown is tinted with the fragrant red of her tears.           (7)
Her pain is no match for those mated swallows.                   (5)
They soar and fly as one by the window.                          (4)
Spring is drawing to a close.                                     (3)
The catkins have fallen away.                                     (3)
The willow branches are bare.                                     (3)

## "Offering Congratulations to the Enlightened Reign" (*Ho ming-ch'ao*), Two Lyrics

### [1]

I remember the day when we first met among the flowers.          (7)
I lifted my red sleeve to hide my face,                           (4)
And so frivolously turned my head away.                           (4)
I played with the sash on my red skirt,                           (4)
And quite deliberately with my slender,                          (4)
Jadelike fingers, I began to pick away,                          (4)
A pair of phoenixes stitched with gold.                          (4)

The green wu-t'ung trees are locked deep in the garden.          (7)
Who could know how much we would love one another?               (5)
Will there be a time when we can be forever close?               (5)
I envy the mated swallows that come in the spring.               (5)
Flying, they descend to the jade tower,                          (4)
Where day and night, they are together!                          (4)

### [2]

I remember the time after we had met among the flowers.
I could only depend upon my frail hand,
And secretly throw to you the red bean.
With you, I could find no explanations,
No clever words to tell you how I felt.
And since you've gone, it is as it was,
But I have no joy in these spring days.

The gold thread is matted on the green silk of my gown.
I look well at the design of mated mandarin ducks.
In vain, the splashing tears soak through my robe.
I think youth's splendid bloom will not last long.
And in the end, it will all be for you,
That I am quietly growing so very thin!


## "Song of the River City" (*Chiang-ch'eng tzu*), One Lyric

### [1]

Grasses on Chin-ling's shores lie still in the evening sun.    (7)
The rosy clouds of sunset are bright.                          (3)
The water moves in a relentless flow.                          (3)
The pomp and splendor of the Six Dynasties,                    (4)
Quietly, inexorably, pass in the sound of the waves.           (5)
In vain, does the moon still rise above the Ku-su Pavilion.    (7)
But just like the lovely Hsi Shih's mirror,                    (4)
It glows in beauty on the river city.                          (3)


## "Spring in the Phoenix Tower" (*Feng-lou ch'un*), One Lyric

### [1]

Her upswept hair is like a thick green cloud,                  (5)
Deep in the fastness of slatted blinds.                        (4)
She has written an elegant letter.                             (3)
In her dream she sees him, but waking, she feels wearied.      (7)
She wipes the tears on her cheeks.                             (3)
The pearly drops melt on her face.                             (3)
Then she wonders where that handsome man might have gone,      (7)
And with whom does he savor the fine scenery?                  (5)

In the confines of her tower room,                             (3)
Her thoughts of love are without limit.                        (4)
By the railing, her eyes gaze far away.                        (4)
Secretly, she is beset by sad thoughts.                        (4)
The willow blossoms are swept high by the east wind.           (6)
The setting sun is aglow in the window.                        (4)
The scented chill of the curtains fills the empty screen.      (7)
Flowers of the cherry-apple are fading,                        (4)
Orioles chatter in their falling bloom.                        (4)

# Ho Ning (898–955)

## "Manifold Little Hills" (*Hsiao ch'ung shan*), Two Lyrics

### [1]

When spring arrives, blossoming trees cover the capital.    (7)
In the imperial arbor, orioles sing sweetly.    (5)
Butterflies race madly about.    (3)
The dawn flowers holding the dew seem to weep with envy.    (7)
Sunlight glistens all around.    (3)
In gentle breezes, the flowers are fragrant.    (5)

Mist screens the long silky willow branches.    (5)
The crystal blue water in the palace drains,    (5)
Swirls as it enters the pond.    (3)
From time to time, a drizzle of rain bathes the scenery.    (7)
The royal road stretches far,    (3)
And everywhere, the reed—pipes can be heard!    (5)

### [2]

It is just the time the capital is bright and sparkling.
The assembled immortals first come to pluck,
Branches of the cassia trees.[2]
Their hairpins of horn, and robes of hemp are befitting.
Their spirits roam very free.
On the paths, sleeves and whips swing loose.

Willows unfold like brows arched with grief.
A melody of pipes and strings fills the air,
As we go to seek the flowers.
Time seems to stop by the banks of the Ch'ü—chiang Pond.
The lucky winners are posted,
The names pass through the palace courtyard!

## "Immortal at the River" (*Lin-chiang hsien*), Two Lyrics

### [1]

On the river late in spring, the cherry-apple is fragrant.    (7)
By the tower, a silken fog veils the delicate rain.    (6)
In a feathered cap of azure, she emerges from the screens.    (7)
Her musky aura and phoenix belt stir the blowing duckweed.    (7)

[2] "To pluck the cassia" means to achieve the third, and highest, level in the examination system, the *chin-shih* degree.

Gilt birds flutter with every tremble of her jade hairpin.     (7)
Her snowy skin and cloudlike hair seem to evanesce.            (6)
Calmly she points far off, to the east of the green waves,     (7)
Where the king of Yüeh's palaces lie in the red smartweed.     (7)


## [2]

Her long red robe of palace silk trails across the ground.
The warbling of the orioles is the faintest murmur.
Her blue silken cap is fastened with a clasp made of horn.
With each tiny step, gold phoenixes prance on her hairpin.

The skin of her delicate cheeks is like softened red jade.
Her eyes betray the passion that lies in her heart.
Bashful and shy, she is reluctant to slip into the quilts.
By the light of the burning candle, we are deeply in love.

# "Deva-like Barbarian" (*P'u-sa man*), One Lyric

## [1]

The budding plums of Yüeh are bursting open in the chill.      (7)
A cold frosty mist still envelops the deep indigo waters.      (7)
The apricots, sensing new warmth, blush red.                   (5)
The spiders' webs sway madly with the winds.                   (5)

Green sedges line the path around the steps.                   (5)
Her distant dreams still bear love's burden.                   (5)
She again greets spring in grief at parting.                   (5)
So hard the endless entreaties of her heart!                   (5)

# "Mountain Flowers" (*Shan-hua tzu*), Two Lyrics

## [1]

Orioles trim her fragrant robe, thin as a cicada's wing.       (7)
Dawn mists swirl the gossamer as she passes the flowers.       (7)
Gilt birds waver on her hairpin, and red claws dip down.       (7)
A dark cloud of hair falls loose.                              (3)

She smiles, and dimples on her cheeks hug her rosy face.       (7)
The lining of her gold-sewn apron is washed with silver.       (7)
Her spring thoughts are mixing with the budding grasses,       (7)
As they burgeon so rich and lush!                              (3)

[2]

The sound of the chill pipes ends with a lingering wail.
The silver—striped mats and the painted screen are cold.
A golden circlet is an icy weight on her jadelike wrist.[3]
She hurries through her toilette.

Many times her hands are warmed over the incense burner.
Drinking some wine, her red lips take on a bright gleam.
She makes up a game to play with a flossy red fly whisk.
She whisks it over the gentleman!

## "Song of Ho Man-tzu" (*Ho Man-tzu*),[4] Two Lyrics

### [1]

| | |
|---|---:|
| She has just reached sixteen, the age for marriage. | (6) |
| Her frustrated feelings stir everyone's indulgence. | (6) |
| She is like a peach or pear, but with a parrot's tongue. | (7) |
| It is too bad that she must spend the nights alone. | (6) |
| How I begrudge that lovely blue silk skirt of hers. | (6) |
| I envy it for always staying so close to her waist! | (6) |

### [2]

[Variation]
I have written to her countless numberless letters.
She is like a flower locked in spring's brilliance.
No use to look for the clouds and rain of Mount Wu.                    (6)
That only causes my fading dreams to run on and on.
How I begrudge that little duckling incense burner.
I envy it for always being so close in her screens!

## "The Unfortunate Woman" (*Po-ming nü*), One Lyric

### [1]

| | |
|---|---:|
| It is almost the hour of dawn. | (3) |
| The sound of the water clock winds around the flowers. | (7) |

---

[3] The fourth character in this line is missing so it is impossible to determine what image the poet intended for the gold bracelet on her arm. I have arbitrarily chosen to continue the sense of the cold begun in the first and second lines, and have described the bracelet as an "icy weight."

[4] The title of this song, *Ho Man-tzu,* is the name of a singer who lived in the eighth century.

In the window, the light of the stars is dim.                (5)
The cold mist's chill seeps in above the curtains.           (6)
The fading moonlight slips from the tree branches.           (6)
Her dream breaks to an empty stillness in the curtain.       (7)
She struggles to rise, her sad brows so tiny.                (5)

# "Viewing the Plum-Blossoms" (*Wang mei-hua*), One Lyric

## [1]

The grasses of spring remain hidden from view.              (6)
They still lie under a residue of winter snow.              (6)
Fragrance bursts from the chill plum–blossom branches.      (7)
Coldly lovely, the rare blooms move the heart.              (6)
How is it the Lady Shou–yang cannot be anywhere found?      (7)
Who plays a song to the blossoms on the flute?              (6)

# "Heaven's Immortal" (*T'ien-hsien tzu*), Two Lyrics

## [1]

Her robe, willow tinted, is stitched with a gold phoenix.   (7)
With delicate fingers, she casually toys with a red bean.   (7)
The barest hint of emotion plays on her brows and cheeks.   (7)
Within the peach–blossom grotto,                            (3)
She dreams about the jade tower.[5]                         (3)
With whom can she share even one slip of spring's sorrow?   (7)

## [2]

At the grotto's entry, spring's blooms whirl in the wind.
Sadness clings to the somber green brows of the immortal.
Why is it the Gentleman Juan has not yet returned to her?
She only dallies at her alchemy,
And dawdles over her scriptures.
In vain the peach blossom drifts to and fro in the water!

---

[5] The jade tower here is a reference to the Yao-t'ai where Chien Ti, the ancestress of the Shang dynasty (second millennium B.C.) was shut away. Ti K'u, the first ancestor of the Shang people, sent her a swallow, and she became pregnant by swallowing its egg.

## "The Beautiful Spring Scene" (*Ch'un-kuang hao*),[6] Two Lyrics

### [1]

| | |
|---|---|
| It is warm at the silk window. | (3) |
| It is quiet within the screen. | (3) |
| A cloud of hair tumbles loose. | (3) |
| She gets up, and her body feels heavy and weak, | (6) |
| In the idleness of mid—spring. | (3) |

| | |
|---|---|
| Her jade fingers cut silk patches for her face. | (6) |
| Bits of sweet cake are spread on a golden dish. | (6) |
| Peeping at Sung Yü is a matter causing endless regret.[7] | (7) |
| Her tiny brows bend and curve. | (3) |

### [2]

[Variation]
The duckweed leaves are silky.
The apricot blooms are bright.
The painted boats are buoyant.
A pair of mandarin ducks rise dripping on to the bank.                    (7)
The boatmen chant their songs.

The spring waters have neither winds nor waves.
The spring sky is part drizzly, and part sunny.
At evening, lovely women stroll on the southern shore.
How tender the loving emotion!

## "Gathering the Mulberry" (*Ts'ai-sang tzu*), One Lyric

### [1]

| | |
|---|---|
| A necklace of beads loops round her white throat. | (7) |
| The silken ties are hanging loose. | (4) |
| To fill time in her fragrant room, | (4) |
| They throw the dice, risking all for lichee nuts. | (7) |
| Her slippers are topped with flossy red pom—poms. | (7) |

[6] "Spring scene," *Ch'un-kuang*, in the title of this poem can also mean an illicit affair.

[7] This line is a reference to the "Teng-t'u tzu *hao-se fu*," "The Lechery of Master Teng-t'u *fu*," attributed to the third century B.C. poet Sung Yü. In it Sung Yü plays the leading role. Defending himself against a charge of being licentious, Sung Yü describes the beauty of a neighbor girl and says, "For three years this lady has been climbing the garden wall and peeping at me, yet I have never succumbed." Arthur Waley, *One Hundred and Seventy Chinese Poems* (London: Constable, 1962), p. 14.

```
A golden fringe borders her skirt.                        (4)
Languorously, she begins to frown.                        (4)
As spring thoughts stir, mama becomes suspicious.         (7)
```

## "The Willow Branches" (*Liu-chih*), Three Lyrics

### [1]

```
Lissome and green, I bow in the mist as if in parting.    (7)
Brightly blooming, I shelter the frowning azure brows.    (7)
Leaves dark green, I make a trysting place for lovers.    (7)
A golden gossamer, I await the Lo goddess in the wind!    (7)
```

### [2]

```
Her turquoise silk skirt is banded with a golden sash.
She ignores the smudged curves of her blackened brows.
Drunkenly, she chews away the beauty mark at her lips.
Pulling her lover to her, she acts the perfect wanton!
```

### [3]

```
The Magpie Bridge has begun to straddle the Milky Way.
But this night, the transcendent lover is known as Ho.[8]
If I hadn't clambered up that cassia tree on the moon,
Then how could I ever have found the Lady of the Moon!
```

## "The Fisherman" (*Yü-fu*), One Lyric

### [1]

```
Egrets poise among the white iris on the cold bank.       (7)
Winds over the duckweed lightly snip away the foam.       (7)
The mist falls like a veil.                               (3)
The sun sets a slow course.                               (3)
The perfume of the lotus pulls at my hook and line.       (7)
```

[8] The night is the seventh night of the seventh month when the Weaving Maiden and the Herd Boy come together for their yearly reunion. The poet, Ho Ning, fancies that this time he will take the Herd Boy's place and traverse the heavens.

# Ku Hsiung (*c.* A.D. 933)

## "The Beautiful Lady Yü" (*Yü mei-jen*), Six Lyrics

### [1]

| | |
|---|---|
| The chatter of the dawn orioles breaks her dream of love. | (7) |
| A gilt phoenix covers the rolled curtain. | (5) |
| Her evening's make-up untouched, her reeling head sobers. | (7) |
| Idly she fixes an azure hairpin, and turns to the screen. | (7) |
| She moves with gentle elegance. | (3) |
| | |
| Fragrant red and delicate tints brush her peachlike face. | (7) |
| She gracefully arranges her silk sleeves. | (5) |
| Good times must be hated for they are hard to find again. | (7) |
| The garden is a tangle of green, dimly shaded by willows. | (7) |
| She resents her spring feeling! | (3) |

### [2]

The Ching-yang Bell rings in the wind rushing the screen.
Flower sprays trim a mandarin duck quilt.
At dawn, the curtain is raised on the chilled thick mist.
Capped with azure, powdered and painted, she is adorable.
Her idle thoughts are alluring.

Without a word, she gets up and does her morning make-up.
Her beauty shines in the precious mirror.
Clusters of bright green lotus cover the top of the pond.
Dew bathes the pillow and mats, and lotus scents the air.
Her regrets go in the distance!

### [3]

The azure screen loosely conceals a trailing pearl blind.
A fine rain covers the pond and pavilion.
Dew holds fast to the red lotus, quenching their perfume.
The beautiful woman is the perfection of charm and grace.
Her make-up has just been done.

A slight wisp of smoke rises from the golden duck burner.
Her hair is piled atop the glossy pillow.
Her pale brows softly frown, light powder veils her face.

Past happiness so often comes with a start in her dreams.
She repents such deep emotions!


## [4]

Wu–t'ung trees are a silhouette in the window at evening.
Orioles cry lazily in the fallen flowers.
The small screen is twisted, covering the mountain scene.
By a blue curtain, her powder is sweet, the burner chill.
Her brows are drawn in a frown.

That silly boy so foolishly departed to go his merry way.
He was most thankless for the springtime.
Her teardrops splash the red silk of her painted sleeves.
Her heart breaks, and quietly she leans against the door.
Soon, the twilight will arrive!


## [5]

Deep in her room, the spring scene stirs earnest thought.
Her regrets are like the entangled vines.
The singing orioles pay lovesick court to the lush grass.
Apricot branches, as if painted, yield to the thin mists,
And stand poised at her window.

Sorrowfully she leans on the railing, her brows so frail.
The willows cast shadows along the steps.
Her handsome young gentleman still hasn't come back home.
This makes her dream she is pursuing the willow blossoms,
Winding around the far horizon!


## [6]

Her youthful beauty is more radiant than bright red jade.
Dawn and dusk, she departs Three Islands.
A hairpin holds her lotus cap, her tiny comb hangs askew.
Wind ripples her silk sleeves, clouds of hair drift free.
A picture could not be so fair.

She turns ever so slowly, her waist slender and delicate.
A patch of azure rests between her brows.
Wind gusts round the altar, the apricot blooms are sweet.
Now she very much regrets she cannot drive the phoenixes,
And seek out the Gentleman Liu!

KU HSIUNG

# "River Messages" (*Ho ch'uan*), Three Lyrics

## [1]

Swallows reel in the winds.                                          (2)
The landscape is cloudless.                                          (2)
By the little window, the screen is warm.                           (4)
The mandarin ducks entwine their throats.                           (4)
Her mirror is shut away, and though her chignon is awry,            (7)
She is too lazy to redo it.                                         (2)
The cherry-apple is a shadow on the screen.                         (5)

No longer does the gold duck burner perfume the curtain.           (7)
There has been no word or news.                                    (3)
The memory of their love comes all in vain.                        (5)
She draws toward the east wind.                                    (3)
Spring has just come to flower.                                 - (3)
Her face is grief-stricken.                                        (2)
Teardrops stain her robe, one upon another!                        (5)

## [2]

[Variation]
The bannister winds around.
The time is late in spring.
Tiny rippling waves wash across the pond.
The willow branches grow tender and soft.
Dewdrops wet the fresh flowers.                                    (3)
Apricot branches come to bloom.                                    (3)
Orioles warble their songs.
The wild grass lies flat as if it were cut.

To tell the truth, this world is just as good as Heaven,
And can be roamed for pleasure.
My intoxicated eyes take it for a painting.
Lingering in front of the pond,
I am moved by these good times.
My heart has broken in two.
Because of the flowers, we must pursue joy!

## [3]

[Variation]
The oars lift in the water.
The boat journeys on ahead.
The flashing waves reach in the distance.

I don't at all know where we are passing.
Flowery banks and grassy beaches extend ever farther on.
There is a fine misty rain.
Soaring partridges chase after one another.

At world's end, parting's ache sobs in the river's flow,
Rails from the monkey's shriek.
But with whom can I express these thoughts?
I lean against the orchid oars.
I am overcome by my sorrow.                                (2)
My soul seems to melt away.
The fragrant incense will soon burn to ash!

## "Song of Kan-chou" (*Kan-chou tzu*), Five Lyrics

### [1]

| | |
|---|---|
| Ambergris and musk rise from the burner by the curtain. | (7) |
| Light flickers across the screen. | (3) |
| The candle is a shimmer of flame. | (3) |
| The tower gong sounds the hour, happily it is not late. | (7) |
| Silk mats are stitched with mandarin ducks. | (5) |
| On top of the stone-block pillow. | (3) |
| Her sweet lips whisper such intimate words. | (5) |

### [2]

Whenever I encounter a fine evening and a good morning,
I get a sense of wistful longing.
I find my feelings are very hurt.
In a welter of clouds, the waters bar me from my lover.
I am alone and desolate on the silken mats.
On top of the stone-block pillow,
There are many drops of fresh-fallen tears.

### [3]

Like Liu and Juan, I, too, seek out the fair immortals.
And with a lovely grotto dweller,
Now at last I keep my rendezvous,
When the banquet is done, we lie together in the quilt.
Filled with love, I see her beautiful face.
On top of the stone-block pillow,
She rests ever fearful of the morning bell.

[4]

Among the dewy peach blossoms deep in that small tower,
I hold fast to the jade wine cup,
And listen to the precious ch'in.
Drunk, I go back to the room and crawl into the quilts.
Gleaming moonlight falls across her bodice.
On top of the stone-block pillow,
A tiny dot of azure lies between her brows.

[5]

In the night I tipsily play the pipes in the red tower.
At the places to tap the rhythms,
Her slender fingers sound softly.
On the screen is an ancient picture of low-lying banks.
Mist and moonlight fill the deserted court.
On top of the stone-block pillow,
Her eyes are bright waves in the lamplight.

## "Song of the Jade Tower in Spring" (*Yü-lou ch'un*), Four Lyrics

[1]

Moonlight shines on the jade tower as spring rushes by.            (7)
On the courtyard steps, bamboo tremble in the sad wind.           (7)
Her dream shaken, she wakes in her mandarin duck quilt.           (7)
Where are those occasional bursts of music coming from?           (7)

It is a sorrow that the gentleman had his fun and left.           (7)
On the pillow, her dainty green brows gather and frown.           (7)
Over the screen, dawn orioles chat on flowery branches.          (7)
Behind the curtains, the red candle flickers and burns.          (7)

[2]

Shining willows stand by the jade tower in late spring.
The rain is fine, the wind airy, the grass softly hazy.
In the painted hall, parrots talk in their carved cage.
The screen brushed with spun gold is still half closed.

As the fragrance dies, she is desolate by the curtains.
She leans on a railing, her quiet sad thoughts far off.
She hates him, and asks where did he go to play around?
It is for him she is tearful, her face so very unhappy.

[3]

Sparkling dewdrops glow on the window in the moonlight.
A wind—blown scent of chrysanthemums daubs her sleeves.
The clay burner is cold, only a trace of aloes is left.
She grieves in her room, the door is shut all day long.

She slowly unrolls the quilt as tears are rushing down.
At the mirror, she blushes to put the pins in her hair.
For no reason at all, he ended their nights of delight.
She can't figure out a way to manage that wild playboy.

[4]

A pair of swallows flies to and fro skimming the water.
Mountains weave in and out on the panels of the screen.
She frowns as spring's grief absorbs her every thought.
She idly tunes the ch'in on its cushion of red brocade.

When she said good—bye, emotion made her voice tremble.
Traces of teardrops still smear her pink—powdered face.
For a long time she stands alone, until it is twilight.
She dreads the ceaseless dreaming in the night to come.

# CHAPTER SEVEN

## Ku Hsiung (*c.* A.D. 933)

### "Sand of Silk-Washing Stream" (*Huan-ch'i sha*), Eight Lyrics

[1]

| | |
|---|---|
| In the lure of the spring scene, she hates his being away. | (7) |
| How can she bear that he has not yet returned home to her? | (7) |
| Soft breezes and a light dew cover over the pear blossoms. | (7) |
| | |
| Beyond the curtain, two lovesick swallows dip in the wind. | (7) |
| In front of the railing, tender green willows fall aslant. | (7) |
| By the screen, her rapturous dreams reach the far horizon. | (7) |

[2]

Red lotus lie coldly sweet on the flat green of the islet.
Moonlight enfolds the empty pavilion while crickets chirp.
Wild geese startle her dream, tugging at her love for him.

In the burner by the curtains, the fading musk is chilled.
She is heedless of the dust smudging her gold—sewn skirts.
The solitary candle in the window is awash in waxen tears.

[3]

The fragrance of the lotus in the wind scents the curtain.
Ducks splash in the pond, their feathers a silken brocade.
A screen enfolds an antique scene of the Hsiao and Hsiang.

She hates to enter the empty hangings, a solitary phoenix.
Tears cling to her cheeks like bright lilies on an island.
She regrets she thinks so much of that cold—hearted youth.

[4]

He has felt a heavy sadness in the year since he left her.
A moonlit window and a flowery garden make a pretty scene.
In his constant yearning, his heart has broken with grief.

The Bluebird has not delivered any words of love from her.
In what fragrant chamber is the goddess Yao Chi concealed?
How can he endure the pain that she is ever gone from him?

## [5]

Chrysanthemums fly in courtyard breezes, the dew is thick.
A hidden cricket chirps in the cold sedge round the steps.
In the splendor of this evening, when will he come to her?

Winds blow on the curtain, and the red candle drips tears.
The fragrance and warmth of the quilts suffuses her dream.
Waking, she lies on the pillow afraid of the morning bell.

## [6]

Clouds pale in the high winds, and leaves scatter and fly.
In the courtyard, chill rains drench the silky green moss.
Deep in her room, she quietly closes screens and curtains.

The lovely woman grieves unseen on the gold-banded pillow.
Mandarin ducks circle round the painted silk of her skirt.
How can she bear the ingratitude of his failure to return?

## [7]

Wild geese cry in the far sky as a jade clock rings clear.
Beyond the small silken window, the glistening moon rises.
The smoke from the gold burner lies still on the curtains.

Where has he gone that he cannot return nor send any word?
The splendor of this night will rouse my unsettled dreams.
In the chill of the mat and pillow, emotion overwhelms me.

## [8]

The dew is white in glowing moonlight, autumn comes again.
Those times of our secret meetings are forever lost to us.
When will my love for you no longer struggle in my dreams?

I remember how lovable you are when you crinkle your brow.
I have no words to speak as I pause within my small study.
My hidden thoughts are of the past, sadness overwhelms me.

# "Song of the Wine Spring" (*Chiu-ch'üan tzu*), Seven Lyrics

## [1]

| | |
|---|---|
| The willows are dancing in the wind, | (4) |
| Softly roused by the spring mist and sprinkling rain. | (6) |
| The apricot blossom grieves. | (3) |
| The orioles start to jabber, | (3) |
| East from the painted tower. | (3) |

| | |
|---|---|
| By the brocade screen, her lonely thoughts have no limit. | (7) |
| She still has not received any word or news from him. | (6) |
| Dust is covering her mirror. | (3) |
| Pearl teardrops are falling, | (3) |
| Spoiling her beautiful face. | (3) |

## [2]

[Variation]

Her silk sash is stitched with gold.
In a mist of orchid and musk, her heavy heart breaks.
The painted screen is aside.
Her hair falls in confusion.
Her regrets so hard to bear!

| | |
|---|---|
| Often her falling tears spill on the mandarin duck quilt. | |
| Where could that cold-hearted man have gone? | (5) |
| Moonlight fills the windows. | |
| Flowers spread on the trees. | |
| All news has come to an end. | |

## [3]

[Variation]

| | |
|---|---|
| The sun sets over the small railing. | (4) |
| Winds pass the green window as she grows sad and anxious. | (7) |
| Phoenixes dance in the loose folds of the azure curtains. | (7) |
| The old incense has chilled. | (3) |

| | |
|---|---|
| It is so hard to break the bonds of her parting emotions. | (7) |
| Her beautiful face seems to have become old. | (5) |
| Blurred traces of tears are intermingled with her powder. | (7) |
| In secret, her heart breaks. | (3) |

[4]

[Variation]
Her brows are black, her cheeks red.
Her upswept hair shines like a dark iridescent cloud.
Mandarin ducks on a hairpin,
Gold kingfishers on a clasp,
Paired, they suit the heart.

She has no place to send her secret thoughts in a letter.
Swallows come to the orchid hall, and spring passes away.        (7)
It is a year since he wrote.
Countless tears have fallen.
Her regrets so hard to bear!

[5]

[Variation]
She closes and puts away the mirror.
She packs the azure patches for they have no further use.        (7)
Gilt insect and jade swallow clasps,                             (4)
She locks in a scented case.
She is so weary with regret.

Her hair is falling loose, but she is too numb to fix it.
Her pillow is drenched with splashing tears.                     (5)
By a silver lamp within the curtains, she is fast asleep.        (7)
Wild geese are flying south.

[6]

[Variation]
A clear wind is on the green waters.
Light aromas from the glossy red lotus pass the railings.        (7)
Her azure brows are softly furrowed.                             (4)
Her regret is beyond bounds.
A small screen leans aslant.

She really detests that bounder for not coming back home.
Deceitfully, he left her a silken love-knot.                     (5)
Deep in the curtains, thick sweet smoke rings the pillow.        (7)
He is heedless of her youth.

[7]

[Variation]
Her brows are sad, her face flushed.
The painted hall is dazzling in the last light of spring.          (7)
Fine rains soak the falling flowers.                               (4)
Isolated in the green tower,
Her thoughts wander far off.

She can see that the blossoming time will soon fade away.
Desolate, with no one to talk to, she murmurs to herself.          (7)
The fine silk of her jacket,
Is moist with powder stains.
She is overcome with sorrow.


## "Willow Branches" (*Yang-liu chih*), One Lyric

[1]

In her room on an autumn night, her thoughts are lonely.          (7)
A distant water clock sounds.                                      (3)
The fragrance fades from the silk curtains and hangings.          (7)
Light flickers from a candle.                                      (3)

She thinks of that handsome gentleman gone away for fun.          (7)
No place for her to find him!                                      (3)
Even more she hears the sighing rain beyond the screens.          (7)
Tiny drops splash the banana.                                      (3)


## "Hatred of Distant Places" (*Hsia-fang yüan*), One Lyric

[1]

The screens are in dim shadows.                                    (3)
The striped silk mats lie flat.                                    (3)
Chiffon sleeves envelop her jade fingers.                          (5)
Her light fan is silk stitched with gold.                         (5)
Her tender red cheeks are like two shining flowers.               (7)
Her brows are darkly shaded like distant mountains.               (7)

The phoenix pipes play no more.                                    (3)
The mirror is coated with dust.                                    (3)
All news from the frontier is broken off.                         (5)
She is suddenly startled from her dreams.                          (5)

Over the years, that gentleman has been ungrateful.        (7)
How could she not have come to hate his cold heart?        (7)


## "Offering Deep Affection" (*Hsien chung-hsin*), One Lyric

### [1]

She:
It is warm within the mandarin duck curtains.              (5)
The screen painted with peacocks leans askew.             (5)
I wait in the utter stillness,                            (3)
In the brightness of the moon.                            (3)
I remember the happiness and joy of the past,            (5)
And I bitterly regret our present separation.            (5)
By the light of a silver lamp,                           (3)
The water clock is relentless.                           (3)
But our happy times have gone!                           (3)


He:
A light fragrance rises from the burner.                 (4)
The curtains are loose in my empty room.                 (4)
There are so many stirrings in my heart,                 (4)
As I ponder these my so secret thoughts.                 (4)
I am bound fast by your loveliness and charm.            (5)
My dreams are a kind of mindless doting.                 (4)
Right now in your golden room,                           (3)
Your head at rest on a pillow,                           (3)
You should begin to know this!                          (3)


## "Echoing Heaven's Everlastingness" (*Ying t'ien-ch'ang*), One Lyric

### [1]

Her gold embroidered silken skirts softly rustle.        (7)
Her painted trousers are of sheer yellow chiffon.        (7)
Her sash trails down loose.                              (3)
Parrots twine in its folds.                              (3)
A curling azure crown dips with each dainty step.        (7)

Her back to me, she is rouging her lips.                 (5)
Slowly turning, she takes a quick peek at me.            (6)
Her brows so somber, she quietly comes to me.            (6)
She leans by the screen, lazy and still.                (5)

# "Speaking of Love" (*Su chung-ch'ing*), Two Lyrics

## [1]

| | |
|---|---|
| Fragrance fades from the screens, spring rushes ever on. | (7) |
| She smooths a mandarin duck quilt. | (3) |
| Around the silk folds of her sash, | (3) |
| Coil a pair of phoenixes sewn with bright gold. | (5) |
| Outside the window, the bright moon draws near. | (5) |
| So still and silent! | (2) |
| Her heart breaks, but nowhere can she find him. | (5) |
| He cares not for her loving heart! | (3) |

## [2]

| | |
|---|---|
| [Variation] | |
| In the endless night, where is he that he scorns her so? | (7) |
| The news from him no longer comes. | (3) |
| Her fragrant rooms are all closed. | (3) |
| She frowns so sadly! | (2) |
| Soon the moon will be on the wane. | (3) |
| How can she bear his not coming to be with her? | (5) |
| She hates lying in an empty quilt. | (3) |
| If he could take her heart in place of his own, | (5) |
| Then he would come to know the depth of memory! | (5) |

# "Lotus Leaf Cup" (*Ho-yeh pei*), Nine Lyrics

## [1]

| | |
|---|---|
| Spring is over, and flowers fall in the small court. | (6) |
| Oh so desolate! | (2) |
| Leaning on the railing, her brow is furrowed. | (5) |
| It is he who made her feel so ill, with only her memories. | (7) |
| Do you know it or not? | (3) |
| Do you know it or not? | (3) |

## [2]

From whose house comes the medley of music and song?
Sound so clear!
Her regret at their parting now reaches afar.
The lamp is behind the curtains, the moon above the tower.
Am I suffering or not?
Am I suffering or not?

## [3]

The delicate willows and pretty flowers are falling.
Path so bright!
A handsome young man is standing right there.
I catch a strong whiff of his heady orchid and musk scent.
Am I going mad or not?
Am I going mad or not?

## [4]

I do remember that time when we met with each other.
Oh so skittish!
Your hair was mussed, your limbs softly weak.
You, gentle lady, were silent and wouldn't lift your head.
Were you timid or not?
Were you timid or not?

## [5]

Through the long night, the music is a grievous sob.
Oh moon so dim!
A light dew lies on the chill chrysanthemums.
Gradually the dampness drenches the gold silk of her robe.
Can you return or not?
Can you return or not?

## [6]

I suffered much to write that poem in memory of you.
Do you know it?
Each and every word concerns my love for you.
The red notepaper on which I wrote shows my deep feelings.
Do you read it or not?
Do you read it or not?

## [7]

Fragrance from the gold duck burner fills the quilt.
Shining pillow!
Her tiny chignon is set with flowery patches.
Her waist is like a slim willow, her face is like a lotus.
Do you love me or not?
Do you love me or not?

## [8]

On the winding steps, butterflies soar in warm mist.
Mid—springtime!
Buds flower, and willow branches trail loose.
Her cheeks are like flowers, her waist is like the willow.
Is she elegant or not?
Is she elegant or not?

## [9]

You went your way, and once again there was no news.
Spring is over!
The lush green moss has overgrown the garden.
I twist the sash of my skirt as I walk confused and alone.
Are you coming or not?
Are you coming or not?

## "Song of the Fisherman" (*Yü-ko tzu*), One Lyric

### [1]

| | |
|---|---|
| The dawn breezes are clear. | (3) |
| The deserted pond is green. | (3) |
| I go to the railing and watch the rare birds splashing. | (7) |
| The painted blind is loose. | (3) |
| The azure screen is aslant. | (3) |
| My sleeves fill with the lovely scent of the lotus. | (6) |
| | |
| Oh to let free my feelings! | (3) |
| To behold everything fully! | (3) |
| I am relaxed, my heart is calm, I am content with life. | (7) |
| My wine—cup is always full. | (3) |
| Time is racing ever onward. | (3) |
| I haven't the heart to compete for fame and wealth! | (6) |

## "Immortal at the River" (*Lin-chiang hsien*), Three Lyrics

### [1]

| | |
|---|---|
| The sky is washed with blue, the pond is like a mirror. | (7) |
| I watch by the tower with a heart full of feeling. | (6) |
| My robe is heavy with the clear scent of the red lotus. | (7) |
| The bed is ivory, the mats rare and fine. | (4) |
| The landscape screen is closed. | (3) |
| The jade ch'in rests crosswise. | (3) |

Secretly I think of the joy and pleasure of other days.        (7)
But now today, my life is one of profound sadness.             (6)
The clay burner is warm, a thin wisp of smoke is light.        (7)
No voice is heard but the cicada's chirp.                      (4)
The fading sun begins to slant.                                (3)
The small window shines bright.                                (3)


## [2]

[Variation]
By the railing in my secluded rooms, it is late spring.
Lush willows, pale flowers, but few orioles there!
I think of past joys, and they still seem as they were.
I find I am frowning with a serious look.
All the day long, the bloom goes from by face.                 (5)

Why hasn't there been any message from that crazy fool?
He can't compare with the swallows who yet return.
A fine musky smoke drifts deep within the painted hall.
The screen is empty, the pillow is chill.
A light drizzling rain falls in the soft wind.                 (5)


## [3]

[Variation]
Moonlight pierces the curtain, wind rustles the bamboo.
As she leans toward the screen, her brows are sad.
By the steps, the heavy dew on the blossoming branches,
Resembles the tears of grief on her face.
Her beauty is ruined by the pain in her heart.                 (5)

The incense fades, and the gold duck burner grows cold.
How can she bear that he failed to keep his tryst?
Her embroidered jacket is rumpled, her hair disheveled.
She is filled with so much lonely sorrow.
Her love has gone to the far-reaching horizon.                 (5)


# "The Drunken Gentleman" (*Tsui-kung tzu*), Two Lyrics

## [1]

Wispy clouds drift in the boundless autumn sky.                (5)
A scent of the red lotus floats on the railing.                (5)
Her pillow is next to a small landscape screen.                (5)
At evening, the door is bolted with a gold bar.                (5)

```
She wakes up, and her eyes have a languid look.      (5)
Alone, she watches afar with unceasing emotion.      (5)
In the fading willows, the stray cicada chirps.      (5)
Her heart is breaking just as it did last year!     (5)
```

[2]

```
Gold branches overflow the willows on the bank.
The rain clears, and orioles warble in harmony.
Her dwelling is next to the green willow trees.
There are many young men who come and go there.

A horse is heard crying in the distant grasses.
In the high tower, she half raises the screens.
She smooths her sleeves with a hint of a frown.
Encounters like this are always very difficult!
```

## "Song of the Water Clock at Night" (*Keng-lou tzu*), One Lyric

[1]

```
All the old familiar happiness!                      (3)
All the new despair and sorrow!                      (3)
In the tower, she covers her face to stifle the tears. (6)
The blooming willows are azure.                      (3)
The few evening clouds are red.                      (3)
The sea—swallows touch wings as they fly along.      (5)

The curtains are partly raised.                      (3)
The screen closes on the slant.                      (3)
The unevenness of the faraway peaks confounds the eye. (6)
Strains of music fill her ears.                      (3)
Flowing wine runs from her cup.                      (3)
"Don't say a word about the wrongs of the past!"     (5)
```

# Sun Kuang-hsien (898?–968)

## "Sand of Silk-Washing Stream" (*Huan-ch'i sha*), Nine Lyrics

[1]

```
On the bank deep in smartweed, oranges perfume the winds. (7)
At river's edge, the far sky of Ch'u unfolds in a glance. (7)
A boat on the hazy horizon is a solitary splash of light. (7)
```

My eyes follow the wild geese flying off in the distance.      (7)
My thoughts join with the water rushing in endless space.      (7)
Red orchids atop azure waves recall the Hsiao and Hsiang!      (7)


## [2]

Peach and apricot scent the wind, the screens fall loose.
A garland of flowers fastens the door of her lovely home.
The early swallows chat secretly among the painted beams.

Scrolls penned with verse hang on the walls of her rooms.
On a pillow by the dawn screen, she sobers from the wine.
But she suspects that she is adrift in a world of dreams!


## [3]

The flowers are slowly scattered in the unbearable winds.
Curtains hang to the ground in the empty hall at evening.
Fallen red petals sadly swirl over the moss by the steps.

On her smooth powdered face, a golden patch comes undone.
A touch of fragrance lingers in the warmth of the burner.
The sweetness in her heart has no place to join with him!


## [4]

As she silently holds the mirror, tears well in her eyes.
In the grip of emotion, she is too weary to fix her hair.
The fine rain in the court is steeped in spring's sorrow.

Only the willows can know the hurtful sadness of parting.
The apricot blooms ought to understand her ruined beauty.
The tears fall, her heart suffers the pain of separation!


## [5]

She steps lightly as her long apron winds along the path.
At night, she has a good view through the slatted blinds.
At these times, she so regrets the seclusion of her life.

Already her heart breaks in the shadow of a dying candle.
Even more sadly she hears the music of pipes and strings.
He sends no word from afar, so why has she such feelings?

## [6]

Her hair just washed in scent, she stands by the railing.
The warm winds and the glow of the late sun dry her hair.
Like a moist cloud, her hair, yet uncoiffed, floats free.

Her azure sleeves partly screen the beauty of her breast.
Her exquisite hairpin nearly falls to her sweet shoulder.
At this time, her captivating ways make her so endearing!

## [7]

The fading fragrance from the curtains blows on the wind.
A gold-sewn phoenix in a round nest sways back and forth.
I grieve with the falling flowers and the drizzling rain.

Wherever could this rotten scoundrel be passing his time?
He pretends he is drunk and greatly needs to go to sleep.
How can I not have misgivings, thinking he loves another?

## [8]

Her angry strumming tumbles mud from the swallows' nests.
She breaks the strings, and hangs the zither in the hall.
The cock, at his ease, cries the dawn from atop the wall.

The bamboo shoots are just opening, making a new pathway.
Their red bloom faded, peach buds fall in their old lane.
She can't bear to be shut up in these rooms all day long.

## [9]

His black hat is cocked, the insignia at his belt hidden.
He steals the quiet streets seeking the immortal's house.
He is recognized and admitted with one knock on the door.

When she is about to receive a guest, she gets a bit shy.
And if someone shows love for her, she grows more remote.
Timidly she looks down, asking about the letter he wrote!

# "River Messages" (*Ho ch'uan*), Four Lyrics

## [1]

The peaceful times of Emperor Yang![1]                    (4)
Times of leisurely jaunts and play!                       (4)
His canal goes on, mile after mile.                       (4)
The willows are like silk,                                (3)
As they embrace the rippling green waters of spring.      (6)
The wind is calm over the far-reaching Huai.              (5)

The three thousand women in attendance are like flowers,[2]  (7)
Vying for clouds and rain.                                (3)
But where is there joy enough to detain him?              (5)
Wind billows in the sails.                                (3)
The horizon is a red haze,                                (3)
Like a fire in the sky!                                   (2)
The Ta-yeh reign period was lost in a dream![3]           (5)

## [2]

[Variation]
Willows trail with golden branches,
Veiled in mist and screened by fog.
Catkins fall in the drizzling rain.
Beautiful women of Ch'u are aboard the phoenix boat.      (6)
Gracefully, they dance.                                   (2)
The drums sound like thunder over the waves.

Dragons and tigers lock in battle to divide up the land.
The people have no leader.
He fords the river at T'ao-yeh, going south.
He has splendid notepaper,
And exquisite inspiration.
He finishes off a poem,
And shows it around to all his royal ladies.

## [3]

[Variation]
The flowers drift away.                                   (2)
The mist is a gossamer.                                   (2)

---

[1] Emperor Yang of the Sui dynasty (*r.* 604–618).
[2] See ch. 3, n. 1, p. 67.
[3] Ta-yeh was the reign title of Emperor Yang of the Sui dynasty. It lasted from 604 to 618.

Among the lush ponds and pavilions,                                      (4)
It is so lonely in the late spring.                          .            (4)
She softly frowns, her mind lost in the deepest thought.                 (7)
Tears bathe her collar.                                                   (2)
No one can know what lies deep in her heart.                             (5)


The scent goes from the burner, ashes lie cold as frost.
A curtain shadows the bed.
The swallows come back to the rosy apricots.
Night has come to the sky.
There is only a stillness!
She sleeps in solitude.
Her cloudlike hair trails across the pillow.


# [4]


[Variation]
The wind is blustering,                                                   (2)
The waves are rippling.                                                   (2)
The lotus leaves flash and sparkle.                                       (4)
The drops of dew spill like pearls.                                       (4)
Sailing along in the magnolia boat,                                       (4)
Wherever have all these alluring beauties come from?                      (6)
Their faces glow with the shining red lotus.                              (5)


The "Ta-t'i" song maddens the traveler from Hsiang-yang.
The mist covers the waves.
The boundless lake is a brilliancy of white.
My body has made a return.
My heart has not returned.
The setting sun slants.
Waterfowl rise up from the distant sand bar.

# CHAPTER EIGHT

## Sun Kuang-hsien (898?–968)

### "Deva-like Barbarian" (*P'u-sa man*), Five Lyrics

#### [1]

| | |
|---|---|
| Bright moonlight floods the steps like a cascade of water. | (7) |
| The golden knocker clatters when the door is being closed. | (7) |
| Chill shadows fall from the topmost eaves. | (5) |
| The curtain is trailing loose on its hook. | (5) |
| | |
| A smoky mist of azure softly curls around. | (5) |
| The red candle flame shakes with laughter. | (5) |
| So this is what Kao-t'ang is really about. | (5) |
| The screen conceals her long autumn dream. | (5) |

#### [2]

The wings of the cock beat a hurried tattoo atop the wall.
A pale white light from the east is shining in the window.
Beyond the gate, the dawn orioles chatter.
Behind the tower, the setting moon gleams.

The faint chill conceals her tipsy manner.
Her powder is as splendidly white as ever.
She takes his hand to say good-bye to him,
Her gold robe trailing halfway behind her.

#### [3]

No one has swept away the flowers fallen in the courtyard.
The feeble east wind consigns the fragrance to the ground.
It is late in spring and there is no news.
At world's end, wherever can she find him?

A six-panel screen opens in the dawn hall.
Her furrowed brow is like Hsiang Mountain.[1]
How can she bear the pain of this parting?
Her tormented heart suffers more each day.

[1] Hsiang Mountain, *see* Chün Mountain, p. 206.

[4]

The morning rain bathes the blue grotto on the dark cliff.
Over the flowers they call each other to the south stream.
They set sail in a skiff of magnolia wood.
The calm waves flow onward to the horizon.

A tap on the boat fuddles the kingfishers.
The beautiful lady lifts her fragrant arm.
The rosy sun is about to sink in the west.
In the mist, he opens his ivory–tied belt.

[5]

Clusters of cotton blossoms shine around the small shrine.
The birds of Yüeh cry the coming dawn in the spring scene.
Brass drums pulsate to the southern songs.
People of the south kneel to many spirits.

The boat speeds along in the gusting wind.
Her sleeves coral, she stands by the mast.
She keeps turning back to the distant bay.
Endless sorrow rises from the misty waves.

## "Spirit of the Yellow River" (*Ho-tu shen*), Two Lyrics

[1]

| | |
|---|---|
| The green water of the Fen flows on and on. | (5) |
| Scattered leaves fly up among the twilight clouds. | (6) |
| She left trailing azure plumes, giving no date of return. | (7) |
| The gate to the shrine is shut to the setting sun. | (6) |
| | |
| In the eerie gloom, ancient paintings cling to the walls. | (7) |
| Even then, her feathered chariot was jade–wheeled. | (6) |
| A silent chill darkness descends on the sanctuary. | (6) |
| A tiny flame in the silver lamp flickers and dies. | (6) |

[2]

The grass on the river bank is fresh green.
It is late spring by the shrine of the Hsiang–fei.[2]

---

[2] Hsiang-fei, *see* Hsiang River, p. 207.

The southern sky of Ch'u is a pale-colored strip of blue.
The wild geese soar across in slanting formations.

Alone I lean on a vermilion railing, my feelings endless.
My heart is breaking with memory all the day long.
There is no sign of oars bringing a boat this way.
Wild ducks hover in the air on a distant sand bar.

## "The Beautiful Lady Yü" (*Yü mei-jen*), Two Lyrics

### [1]

| | |
|---|---|
| It is lonely by the red window with no one to talk to. | (7) |
| Rain wets the pear blooms in quiet darkness. | (5) |
| Her silk gown ripples the ground, her make-up is done. | (7) |
| The rich aroma in the clay burner is just fading away. | (7) |
| Her heart is breaking! | (3) |

| | |
|---|---|
| Since he went to the horizon, no news has come of him. | (7) |
| All the day, her thoughts are only with him. | (5) |
| When will these constant memories ever come to an end. | (7) |
| She cannot bear to be dashed against parting's sorrow. | (7) |
| Her tears are falling! | (3) |

### [2]

The splendid wind lightly fans the billowing curtains.
Gold-winged phoenixes are blown to the side.
She hears the nestlings softly cry in the azure eaves.
At this time, a charming manner conceals her emotions.
Hard to be calm alone!

In vain, the painted hall obscures the flowing waters.
The charred incense scatters and burns away.
There is no place she can send on her thoughts to him.
Flowers drifted on the lush grass, but he didn't come.
No one at all knew it!

## "The Flowers in the Rear Garden" (*Hou-t'ing hua*), Two Lyrics

### [1]

| | |
|---|---|
| Palace orioles warble with the ringing Ching-yang Bell. | (7) |
| The dew is chill in the golden hall. | (4) |

Pale yellow hydrangea blooms blow in the rising breeze.          (7)
The leaves seem to be cut from jade.                             (4)

Night comes to the high reaches of the tower.                   (5)
The pearl screens are rolled.                                    (3)
She looks at a thousand sweet fallen flowers.                   (5)
Beautiful women ride in the splendid imperial carriage.         (7)
The feast begins in the rear garden.                            (4)

[2]

[Variation]
Shih-t'ou is as it was, an abandoned city by the river.
Old palaces lie in the spring scene.
The Lady Chang's long lustrous hair is now silky grass.[3]
Beauty such as hers is hard to find.

The jade blooms have all withered and fallen.
Is there someone who would remember?                            (4)
The wild pear twine as though woven.                            (4)
This only adds all the more to the pain of my thoughts.
My sorrow and despair have no limit.

## "Mountain Hawthorns" (*Sheng-ch'a-tzu*), Three Lyrics

### [1]

Sad and lonely, she shuts the vermilion door.                   (5)
It is a moment ready for the arrival of dusk.                   (5)
The hidden silence fills the small courtyard.                   (5)
Drops of rain splash from the wu-t'ung trees.                   (5)

She labors at her embroidery,                                    (3)
Her feelings in every stitch.                                    (3)
Her thread entwines a pair of mandarin ducks.                   (5)
She waits for the time when no one is around,                   (5)
And tells her most intimate thoughts to them.                   (5)

[3] The Lady Chang is Chang Kuei-fei (Chang Li-hua) who was the favorite of Ch'en Hou-chu (Ch'en Shu-pao), the last emperor of the Ch'en dynasty (r. 583–589). She was noted for having extremely long shining black hair. *Nan-shih*, 6 vols., compiled by Li Yen-shou and completed in A.D. 659 (Peking: Chung-hua shu-chü, 1975), ch. 12, pp. 347–48.

## [2]

[Variation]
He rides his fine horse in the warm sunlight.
Loosening the reins, he pads the willow path.
A dark green mist blends in the lush grasses.
The white catkins fall whirling in the winds.

Whose splendid carriage is coming across the flowers?          (7)
The fair immortal is not quite clear in view,
And so he most recklessly uses his jade whip.
Just a step or two keeps him from her beauty!

## [3]

Tall wu–t'ung trees brush by the golden well.
Slanting moonbeams fall across the jade hall.
The palace paths are lonely, no one is there.
She frowns, the grief she bears so very deep.

A jade burner has grown cold.
The fragrance has faded away.
It has been long since he gave her his favor.
The imperial carriage still has not returned.
With whom can she talk of this hidden sorrow?

## "Immortal at the River" (*Lin-chiang hsien*), Two Lyrics

### [1]

Frost hits the wu–t'ung by the well, the dry leaves fall.          (7)
It is cold by the blue curtain and carved railing.               (6)
Her pale make–up just suits the flowered cap on her head.        (7)
Silently she holds back her emotions.                            (4)
For a long time she leans on the bannister.                      (5)

Where was his carriage going as it went so far, far away?        (7)
Many griefs and many sorrows come with separation.               (6)
She can't bear the tangled feelings binding up her heart.        (7)
The mirror and case are long covered.                            (4)
She has no wish to view a solitary phoenix.                      (5)

[2]

The evening rain is melancholy deep in the closed garden.
Brooding, she sits by the lamp at the first watch.[4]
Her jade hairpin presses down, crushing her tumbled hair.
The silk curtain hangs halfway loose.
It is shimmering in the bright candlelight.

All along, her wish is to surrender the celestial pearls,[5]
She lowers her head, and can only tune the zither.
Paired swallows and phoenixes rouse her deepest emotions.
There is yet the sadness of the dawn,
When he will seek after the clouds of Ch'u.

## "Song of the Wine Spring" (*Chiu-ch'üan tzu*), Three Lyrics

[1]

| | |
|---|---|
| The empty sands spread out without limit. | (4) |
| The road to Yang Pass stretches for endless miles. | (6) |
| The horses whine and whinny. | (3) |
| The men are going on and on. | (3) |
| Gloomy clouds lie over Lung. | (3) |
| | |
| My furs and fighting clothes are old and much too small. | (7) |
| Mile after mile, the Mongolian frost is white. | (5) |
| I recall beauty left behind, | (3) |
| Separated even in my dreams. | (3) |
| I go up into the high tower. | (3) |

[2]

A bannister winds around the small tower.
Orioles and flowers have come in the second month.
Her thoughts are in despair.
She will soon die of sorrow.
Pain lies deep in her heart.

She faces the Hsiao and the Hsiang on the opened screen.
The endless myriad miles pass before her eyes.
Tears stain her rosy cheeks.

---

[4] The first watch is between 7:00 and 9:00 P.M.
[5] See Pearl-Sporting River, p. 212.

Her brows gather in a frown.
Her regrets are so profound.

### [3]

Her brow furrows as she is at the window.
The soft feathers of her hairpin curl on her neck.
The swallows have all mated.
The phoenixes shine by twos.
They have found new friends.

Her delicate hands lightly brush her tiny arching brows.
She sighs with the form sighing in the mirror.
Her azure brows softly bend.
A pale red mists her cheeks.
She puts on morning make-up.

## "Pure Serene Music" (*Ch'ing-p'ing yüeh*), Two Lyrics

### [1]

Her grieving heart is about to break.                           (4)
It is just the flowering time of mid-spring.                    (5)
She is like a fallen branch or a phoenix without a mate,        (7)
As once again they have had to part from one another.          (6)

She covers the mirror and in silence lowers her head.          (6)
Her thoughts become as one with the thick lush grass.          (6)
She depends on the east wind to carry him her dreams,          (6)
And to be with him the day through, wherever he goes!          (6)

### [2]

Silently, listlessly, she is waiting.
What can she do to be free of spring regret?
In the end, she couldn't keep that playboy from leaving.
Where are the flowers so dark, and the willows thick?

Day and night, she is in despair with a broken heart.
Fading sunbeams slant through the windows at evening.
Her grief deepens by the red door in a twilight haze.
In vain does he return on his silken-saddled charger.

# "Song of the Water Clock at Night" (*Keng-lou tzu*), Two Lyrics

## [1]

| | |
|---|---|
| A clock strikes in the cold. | (3) |
| She hears the distant geese. | (3) |
| At midnight the pretty lady is deep in the garden. | (6) |
| She closes the ornate doors. | (3) |
| She looses the pearl screen. | (3) |
| The garden is bathed with bright moonlight. | (5) |

| | |
|---|---|
| She is speechless and still. | (3) |
| Her fragrant rooms are cold. | (3) |
| A red curtain half conceals her freshness of form. | (6) |
| Her manner is most alluring. | (3) |
| Her heart is pure and sweet. | (3) |
| Her love is as deep as the rivers and seas. | (5) |

## [2]

This night we came together.
When we have to say goodbye,
We look at each other and my heart can only break.
I have to turn my head away.
I fiddle with my hairclasps.
I say nothing, but the tears wet my collar.

The silver arrow is falling.
The shining frost is fading.
Beyond the wall a cock cries the approaching dawn.
I attend your parting words.
But I feel so very dreadful,
I grieve that we must go our separate ways.

# "The Taoist Nun" (*Nü-kuan tzu*), Two Lyrics

## [1]

| | |
|---|---|
| The wind is fragrant, the dew is sweet. | (4) |
| The fading scents lightly fall across the altar, | (6) |
| Within the Jui-chu Palace. | (3) |
| Bright bits of round green moss lie scattered. | (5) |
| The red peach petals lie trampled and crushed. | (5) |

Her fame reaches way beyond the Wu—hsia Gorge.                    (5)
Her name is recorded in the palace of Tzu—wei.                    (5)
The immortals are gathered at the Yung-ch'eng.                    (5)
In dreams, she goes there.                                        (3)


                              [2]


She is a pale blossom, fragile as jade.
Her gown makes her seem like a heavenly goddess.
Red jade adorns her waist.
By night, she collects the elixirs of the dew.
By day, she burns the subtly fragrant incense.[6]

An azure mist surrounds her staff of divinity.
A yellow and lavender hat binds her rich hair.
"Don't play on the flute when you are with me,
I am not so easily misled!"


# "Song of a Dandy" (*Feng-liu tzu*), Three Lyrics

## [1]

A grass hut fenced with hibiscus is by a winding stream.         (6)
The sounds of chickens and dogs can be heard everywhere.         (6)
The watery grasses grow long.                                    (3)
The wild greens are in bloom.                                    (3)
Outside the gate, the spring waves rise in a green tide.         (6)
The loom clatters,                                               (2)
Its noise hurried.                                               (2)
"Ya, ya," it cries, as the shuttle moves back and forth.         (6)


## [2]

In the coming dusk the tower stands near the crossroads.
I glimpse a woman, a worthy companion for the immortals.
She lightly powders her face.
She elegantly combs her hair.
She is poised in the light where the curtain has opened.
Without any words,
Without invention,
Her silk skirt trailing after her, she slowly withdraws.

[6] The dew and the incense are essences important to self-purification in the Taoist regimen.

[3]

His horse with golden reins and a jade bit softly cries.
He tethers it within the shade of the green willow tree.
The red door has been closed.
The brocade screens are down.
Water runs through the winding garden, and flowers fall.
The party is over,
And he turns away.
In the deep of night, he makes his way back to the town.

## "Pacifying the Western Barbarians" (*Ting hsi-fan*), Two Lyrics

[1]

He is galloping his horse past the Chi—lu Mountain.      (6)
The border grasses are white.                            (3)
The north sky is very bright.                            (3)
The horse's hooves are light.                            (3)

He removes a beautifully crafted bow from its case.      (6)
He pulls it back into a near perfect orb.                (5)
The whistling arrow goes its way beyond the clouds.      (6)
The dawn geese rise startled.                            (3)

[2]

Exiled, she lies on her pillow in the autumn night.
A chill frost fills the tent.
The moon is radiantly bright.
It is just the midnight hour.

From a watch tower somewhere, a flute coldly wails.
She wakes from a dream and hears its cry.
She thinks of home so many thousands of miles away.
The tears rush down her face.

## "Song of Ho Man-tzu" (*Ho Man-tzu*),[7] One Lyric

[1]

His hat and sword went along with him, she did not.      (6)
Her love for him runs as deep as the deepest river.      (6)

[7] The title of this song, *Ho Man-tzu*, is the name of a singer who lived in the eighth century.

The sleeve of her singing gown half hides her sad brows.    (7)
The teardrops splash full on the front of her robe.         (6)
She hates to grieve the clouds and lament the rain.         (6)
Her heart has broken, but where could she seek him?         (6)

## "Jade Butterflies" (*Yü hu-tieh*), One Lyric

### [1]

Spring is almost at an end.                                 (3)
The scene is yet luxuriant.                                 (3)
The flowers filling the garden are still yellow.            (5)
A pair of powdery wings gambols in the distance.            (5)
A butterfly whirls and whisks over the low wall.            (5)

In the warmth of the winds,                                 (3)
It finds itself a playmate.                                 (3)
They dart away, hovering over the fading growth.            (5)
The woman speaks not a word as she watches them.            (5)
Her dancing skirt is heavy with a scent of musk.           (5)

## "Eight-Beat Barbarian Tune" (*Pa-p'ai man*), One Lyric

### [1]

The peacock's golden-threaded tail fans out behind him.     (7)
He is timid of people and flies up into the clove tree.     (7)
The Yüeh women strive to get his feathers on the beach.     (7)
Calling to each other, they go home in the setting sun.     (7)

## "Song of the Bamboo Branches" (*Chu-chih*), Two Lyrics

### [1]

Spring waters flow by the gate.                             (4)
Bamboo branches!                                            (2)
The duckweed is in flower.                                  (3)
Young daughters!                                            (2)
The shores are empty of people.                             (4)
Bamboo branches!                                            (2)
The small skiff is aslant.                                  (3)
Young daughters!                                            (2)
The lady is gently drifting by.                             (4)

Bamboo branches!                                                              (2)
Dusk is nearing the river.                                                    (3)
Young daughters!                                                              (2)
She throws some crumbs of food,                                              (4)
Bamboo branches!                                                              (2)
Feeding the blessed ducks!                                                    (3)
Young daughters!                                                              (2)


[2]


Like the tangled knotted ropes,
Bamboo branches!
Just so her deep feelings.
Young daughters!
Of the many yards of Yüeh silk,
Bamboo branches!
Her gown takes eight feet.
Young daughters!
Willows brush against her body.
Bamboo branches!
Falling round her reverie.
Young daughters!
The lotus blossoms have fallen,
Bamboo branches!
Exposing the inner hearts!
Young daughters!


## "Thoughts of Paradise" (*Ssu ti-hsiang*), One Lyric

[1]

What can be done?                                                             (2)
Repressing her feelings is making them greater!                              (5)
The curtains hang down all day long in the water hall.                       (6)
Her brow wrinkles with shame.                                                 (3)
The folds of her silken skirt rustle along the ground.                       (6)
Daintily she steps, her train like a blue wave.                              (5)
She has seen all she wants of rain splashing the pond,                       (6)
Patting down the round lotus!                                                 (3)


## "A Toast to the Traveler" (*Shang hsing pei*), Two Lyrics

[1]

Galloping away from the pavilion in a great haste,                           (6)
He took to the distant road, far from where we parted.                       (7)

Over the myriad miles of north, east, west, and south,     (7)
Don't ever refuse to get drunk!                            (4)
The wild pear is in bloom.                                 (3)
The river grasses are wet.                                 (3)
I stand quite still.                                       (2)
The tears rush down.                                       (2)
He rides the fastest of horses!                            (4)

## [2]

[Variation]
The boat pulls back in readiness to get under way.
At the very edge of the water, old friends take leave,
One leaves, one stays, our feelings can't be the same.
The gold goblet is in my hands.
The silk-clad women mourn.
The pipes and strings sob.
I turn in a goodbye.
The sail passes from view.                                 (3)
Waves fill the river like snow!

# "Paying Homage at the Golden Gate" (*Yeh chin-men*), One Lyric

## [1]

I couldn't make him stay!                                  (3)
Even if I could make him stay, it wouldn't be good!        (6)
His spring robe made of sacking shone white as the snow,   (7)
The day he was about to go from Yang-chou.                 (5)

He so lightly took leave.                                  (3)
Willingly he deserted me.                                  (3)
The river was filled with sails in the rising wind.        (6)
Now he covets those pretty palace ducks in bright array.   (7)
But I, solitary phoenix, am still but one.                 (5)

# "Thoughts of the Yüeh Beauty" (*Ssu Yüeh-jen*), Two Lyrics

## [1]

The ancient pavilion is in ruins.                          (3)
The green grasses reach far away.                          (3)
Outside the Kuan-wa Palace, it is late spring.             (6)
The legacy of her azure brows was an unending regret.      (7)
Wherever could I go to find some trace of her?             (6)

The beautiful silken gowns she wore are all vanished.                (7)
Her tears have turned to dewdrops on a flower.                       (6)
I mourn as the clear waters spill across the horizon.               (7)
Mandarin ducks, pair after pair, soar and fly.                     (6)


## [2]

Lotus on the island are withered.
The palace trees look so ancient.
The ruined park of Ch'ang-chou stands forlorn.
I imagine the beautiful woman in this deserted place.
In the moonlight, I stand alone on the bridge.

After the spring, Wu fell in the rising autumn winds.
Red and green orchids have perished of sorrow.
The romance of this place will only break your heart.
As my soul melts, I cease hoping for Hsi Shih.


# "Willow Branches" (*Yang-liu chih*), Four Lyrics

## [1]

In the warm wind by the Ch'ang Gate, dry catkins fall.             (7)
They cross the river city like a kind of melting snow.             (7)
With the coming of evening, near the inn by the river,            (7)
Like so many idlers, willows loll across red railings.            (7)


## [2]

Rain showers the willows near the ponds and pavilions.
The moisture assures that they will long be nourished.
They look just like soldiers all ready for inspection.
Lined up, and at attention, they face the spring wind!


## [3]

Although the willow roots grow beside the muddy river,
The songs of the sheng sound around them all day long.
What could compare with their exquisite gold branches?
Even the yellow orioles are no match for their beauty!

[4]

Countless withered willows lament the fall of the Sui.
Their branches dip low as if to solace the Wu palaces.
But at least in the resplendent moonlight at Huai-yin,
In the taverns, flutes still play for them their song.[8]

## "Viewing the Plum-Blossoms" (*Wang mei-hua*), One Lyric

[1]

| | |
|---|---|
| A few flowery branches are just skimming the low wall. | (7) |
| The red blooms shine against green sepals in the snow. | (7) |
| Someone is roused by them to thoughts of the frontier. | (7) |
| Beyond the screens, it is almost midnight. | (5) |
| In the moonlight, a wailing flute cuts her with grief. | (7) |
| She only hears the sobbing from the river. | (5) |

## "Song of the Fisherman" (*Yü-ko tzu*), Two Lyrics

[1]

| | |
|---|---|
| The rich grass is flourishing. | (3) |
| The churning waves are rising. | (3) |
| At the lake's edge, the water flows green with grass. | (7) |
| I pass along smartweed shores. | (3) |
| I pull in at the maple island. | (3) |
| The jade wheel of the moon rises on the horizon. | (6) |

| | |
|---|---|
| Drumming the gunwales, I sing. | (3) |
| I look afar into the distance. | (3) |
| The oars creak, could they know where we are heading? | (7) |
| The yellow snow-geese cry out. | (3) |
| The white seagulls are asleep. | (3) |
| Who other than I is free to travel far and wide? | (6) |

[2]

The fireflies flit all around.
Shiny sparks flash on and off.
On a cold night, icy waters pass vast eastern shores.

---

[8] The flutes are, of course, playing the "Willow Branch Song."

Winds sweep into the distance.
A flute sobs in the emptiness.
The gold wave of the moon shines over the miles.

Pollia blossoms on the island.
Its scent is dainty and sweet.
Wild geese at roost cry out it is time for the frost.
I cruised along the Cha River.
I crossed over the Sung River.
All of this is mine to enjoy day in and day out!

# Wei Ch'eng-pan (c. A.D. 910)

## "Deva-like Barbarian" (*P'u-sa man*), Two Lyrics

### [1]

Her sheer silken skirt is the color of the autumn waves.     (7)
Her eyebrows are painted dots like the tiniest of hills.     (7)
When we see one another at the feasting,     (5)
We know the depth of our hidden emotion.     (5)

The azure plume on her hairpin trembles,     (5)
And frowning, she plays the gold zither.     (5)
The feast done, we go to her sweet room,     (5)
Where I may untie her jade—trimmed sash.     (5)

### [2]

A mist of gold leaf lightly shimmers on her silken gown.
For a splendid gathering, she sings in the autumn night.
The music throbs, her gaze is so pretty.
Azure feathers curl in her upswept hair.

The wine gives her face a soft red glow.
Her brows are like a far hill in autumn.
The plush curtains are redolent of musk.
Who can know what is deep in our hearts?

# CHAPTER NINE

## Wei Ch'eng-pan (*c.* A.D. 910)

### "Flowers Fill the Palace" (*Man-kung hua*), One Lyric

[1]

| | |
|---|---|
| The snow is a piercing sleet. | (3) |
| The wind is cutting and cold. | (3) |
| Where could that man have gone to revel and carouse? | (6) |
| When he is drunk, he wallows in every romantic pleasure, | (7) |
| That the perfumed curtains and quilts have to offer. | (6) |

| | |
|---|---|
| Spring and autumn, dawn and dusk, I think always of him. | (7) |
| I sorrow at the pillow, solitary within the screens. | (6) |
| Why has he turned from the love once first in his heart? | (7) |
| Tears flow across the gold embroidery on my sleeves. | (6) |

### "The Magnolia Flower" (*Mu-lan hua*), One Lyric

[1]

| | |
|---|---|
| The hibiscus come to tiny bloom. | (3) |
| Their scent flutters on the air. | (3) |
| In the jade hall, her feelings are like the deepest water. | (7) |
| She shuts away her make-up case. | (3) |
| She closes fast the golden door. | (3) |
| By the screen, her sleeves trail loose in her dazed grief. | (7) |

| | |
|---|---|
| Across the scene, mists linger over the beautiful flowers. | (7) |
| On a winding islet, mandarin ducks doze in brocaded wings. | (7) |
| She mournfully stares far away, her quiet thoughts of him. | (7) |
| The flowery patches on her cheeks crumple with her sorrow. | (7) |

### "Song of the Jade Tower in Spring" (*Yü-lou ch'un*), Two Lyrics

[1]

| | |
|---|---|
| In the desolate painted hall, swallows fly in the beams. | (7) |
| An azure curtain, rolled high, slants across the window. | (7) |
| The spring scene in the garden is a sad reproach to her. | (7) |
| Red petals from falling flowers pile deep on the ground. | (7) |

By the screen, her snowy white face bends low in sorrow.        (7)
Teardrops fall on the golden stitchery of her silk robe.        (7)
After the good days, the cold moon has broken her heart.        (7)
Why is it such a long time since he has come to see her?        (7)

## [2]

Her darkened brows softly frown, her teeth shine bright.
Orioles are singing in the shadow of a flowering branch.
The clear melodies rise up, halting the floating clouds.
In the quiet hall, the song swirls over the dusty beams.

Her jade wine-cup is filled, her emotions not yet spent.
But that gentleman sitting so close beside her is drunk.
Spring breezes drift across the mats, song follows song.
The beautiful women are extremely graceful and alluring.

# "Speaking of Love" (*Su chung-ch'ing*), Five Lyrics

## [1]

The music and feasting are done, the moon is just full.        (7)
The songs of love have stirred her sorrows.                     (5)
The mist and dew are chill.                                     (3)
The water is a gentle flow.                                     (3)
Her thoughts make it so hard to find sleep.                     (5)

Incense curls round the hem of the curtain.                     (5)
Regrets come without cease.                                     (3)
She thinks of him, and helplessly, she lies wide awake.         (7)
Many walls keep them apart!                                     (3)

## [2]

In late spring, flowers cluster around the small tower.
A gust of wind blows open the silk curtain.
She wakes up from drowsing,
And descends from the dais.
The mark of the pillow is on her red cheek.

A gold hairpin falls from her tangled hair.
She talks with her darling.
When he must go, they clasp hands, swearing their love,
Again and again they swear!

## [3]

Clouds pass from the Milky Way, the jade clock runs on.
The soft chirp of a cricket fills the hall.
The bamboo mats are frosty.
The green windows are cold.
The red candle splashes its perfumed tears.

A chilled light seeps from the bright moon.
It cuts at one's own heart.
How can I bear to be so alone and walk beside the pond,
And see the mandarin ducks!

## [4]

A golden autumn wind gently fans the green silk window.
The flame in the silver lamp blazes aslant.
His head rests on a pillow.
Why has he so many regrets?
Mountains on the screen shield rosy clouds.

In clouds and rain, he left the lady of Wu.
He recalls her pretty face.
In his dreams, he goes round and round the far horizon,
To get to where she dwells!

## [5]

Spring was in her eyes, the red on her cheeks was soft.
Her jealous airs begged for my forgiveness.
Tiny buds were on her face.
Jade eardrops faintly rang.
Often we drank together on spring mornings.

After we parted, I recalled her slim waist.
I am worn by my sad dreams.
And now today, the wind whines desolately in the trees.
My regret reaches far away!

# Mountain Hawthorns" (*Sheng-ch'a-tzu*), Two Lyrics

## [1]

At night, the skies clear of mist and rain.                (5)
The falling flowers have no words to speak.                (5)

It is hard to talk of what is in the heart.                                    (5)
Mated swallows in the beams fly to and fro.                                     (5)


I play the ch'in in the warmth of the wind.                                     (5)
I feel regret coming together with my love.                                     (5)
The strings snap free, and my heart breaks.                                     (5)
Tears rush down on my golden-threaded robe.                                     (5)


[2]

It is desolate in the solitude of the hall.
Late at night, the silk curtain hangs down.
The lamp is dark, and the screen is aslant.
The moon is cold, and the pearl blind thin.


Sorrow and regret make it so hard to sleep.
Where is he so greedy for joy and pleasure?
I see that spring has come back once again.
But I must still remain so very much alone.


## "Melody in C" (*Huang-chung yüeh*),[1] One Lyric

### [1]

There is a warm mist by the pond, and the grass is lush.                       (7)
She is sad and regretful in the idleness of night.                             (6)
Sorrowfully she sits, her thoughts a confusion.                                 (5)
She thinks about the man who loved her, now so far away.                        (7)
Her isolation is like the isolation of the Peach Spring.[2]                     (7)


She recalls their pleasure when the autumn moon was low.                        (7)
Outside on the flowering path, they spoke of love.                              (6)
They drank together, and in secret, held hands.                                 (5)
Why has she not seen him since the coming of the spring?                        (7)
In her dreams, she is carried west of the Brocade River.                        (7)


---

[1] *Huang-chung* in the title is the ancient name of a note on the Chinese musical scale corresponding to the note C on the western scale.

[2] This is an allusion to "The Peach Blossom Spring" by T'ao Ch'ien (365–427) in which a fisherman stumbles by chance upon a grove of peach trees and thence discovers a group of people living in a happy utopia with no contact nor knowledge of the outside world. See James Robert Hightower, *The Poetry of T'ao Ch'ien* (Oxford: Clarendon Press, 1970), pp. 254–58.

## "Song of the Fisherman" (*Yü-ko tzu*), One Lyric

### [1]

| | |
|---|---|
| Her eyebrows are like willows. | (3) |
| Her hair resembles the clouds. | (3) |
| Gauzy silks and sheer chiffons cover her snow—white body. | (7) |
| Suddenly she wakes from sleep. | (3) |
| The clock runs down to a stop. | (3) |
| Dawn orioles and a fading moon lie beyond the window. | (6) |

| | |
|---|---|
| Her feelings run so very deep. | (3) |
| Nowhere can she speak of them. | (3) |
| Flowers fall and catkins soar at the time of ch'ing—ming. | (7) |
| That handsome young gentleman, | (3) |
| How casually he said good—bye. | (3) |
| Once he had gone, he never sent a single word to her! | (6) |

# Lu Ch'ien-i (*c.* A.D. 940)

## "Immortal at the River" (*Lin-chiang hsien*), Two Lyrics

### [1]

| | |
|---|---|
| The ruined park is quiet behind serried doors of gold. | (7) |
| The silk window sorrowfully faces the empty autumn. | (6) |
| The imperial banners have vanished, without any trace. | (7) |
| Music and song once filled the jade tower. | (4) |
| Now ended, the melodies are lost to the winds. | (5) |

| | |
|---|---|
| The misty moon is unaware of changes in man's affairs. | (7) |
| Late at night, its light shines deep in the palace. | (6) |
| The lotus blooms face each other in the deserted pond. | (7) |
| In secret mourning for the fallen kingdom, | (4) |
| Clear dewdrops stream across the fragrant red. | (5) |

### [2]

The feckless dawn orioles startle her from her dreams.
When she rises, she is just sobering from the wine.
Misted willows are a dark green shimmer at the window.
The azure curtains are casually rolled up.
Apricot petals are scattered across the steps.

Ever since the time the gentleman went to play around,
She has seemed a fading lotus or the saddened moon.
In the evening, a drizzling rain sprinkles the garden.
Her hands crumple the sash from her skirt.
Without a word, she leans on the cloud screen.

## "The Taoist Nun" (*Nü-kuan tzu*), Two Lyrics

### [1]

White jade trees line the phoenix tower. (4)
When the Gentleman Liu left, I felt a deep sorrow. (6)
It is now late in the spring. (3)
Within the grotto, my sadness is all in vain. (5)
I can't expect constancy in the world of men. (5)

The shrine is far away in the distant bamboo. (5)
The altar stands dark within the dense pines. (5)
By the clouds, I lower my head and look down. (5)
You know what is in my heart! (3)

### [2]

[Variation]
She chants a Taoist litany at the altar.
Her magic staff and rainbow flag are face to face,
Summoning the immortals to her presence. (4)
The jade at her waist sways in the moonlight.
A musky smoke curls around the golden burner.

The heavy dew runs across the frosted tablet.
A sudden wind blows aside her feathered robe.
She wishes to stay, but it is hard to remain.
She has to go back to Heaven!

## "Thoughts of the Yüeh Beauty" (*Ssu Yüeh-jen*), One Lyric

### [1]

An azure screen is pulled aside. (3)
A silver candle burns behind it. (3)
A water clock is a distant echo in the clear night. (6)
Two bands of embroidered blossoms twine around her mat. (7)
Tears wet the flowers, and the hidden perfume dies. (6)

```
The coral pillow is glossy, her hair falls in a tangle.      (7)
Her slender hands feel too lazy even to use a comb.          (6)
If he were once again to come to see her in her dreams,      (7)
Her heart would surely break a thousand times more!          (6)
```

## "The Beautiful Lady Yü" (*Yü mei-jen*), One Lyric

### [1]

```
The lotus buds softly perfume the mist—covered island.       (7)
The tender green leaves lift to the rain.                    (5)
A clear dawn breeze blows through the latticed window.       (7)
A pale chill light crosses the ivory bed and the mats.       (7)
Silver—striped mats lie flat.                                (3)

The Chiu—i Mountain runs black along a slanted screen.       (7)
She frowns as she rests against a pillow.                    (5)
She won't hope for him, because it would make her ill.       (7)
Her hairpin dips low, tears flow on her powdered face.       (7)
She is helpless with emotion.                                (3)
```

# Yen Hsüan (*c*. A.D. 940)

## "The Beautiful Lady Yü" (*Yü mei-jen*), Two Lyrics

### [1]

```
Bright red blossoms burst from the ripened lotus pods.       (7)
Her shining eyes wander slowly over them.                    (5)
Held in the jaws of a tiny fish, her hairpin dips low.       (7)
A rich red color suffuses the sheer silk of her skirt,       (7)
And she looks so captivating.                                (3)

Secretly, they met where waves bathe the hidden lotus.       (7)
They moved in a dream of clouds and rain.                    (5)
The sweet red traces of her bite were left on his arm.       (7)
She lies awake in late autumn as the clock slows down.       (7)
Her thoughts are only of him!                                (3)
```

### [2]

```
Her waist is slim, her throat white, her skin so soft.
Her hair is piled up in deep dark layers.
```

As she smiles, her brows are moons and her eyes stars.
She is more beautiful than either the willow or peach.
Her make-up is prettily done.

Silver-striped mats shine on the green silken curtain.
Her eyes are veiled by the gossamer mist.
At rest, she is a flowering, if a bit tipsy, hibiscus.
On this marvelous night, she is unable to come to him.
Her heart rushes with sorrow!


## "Immortal at the River" (*Lin-chiang hsien*), Two Lyrics

### [1]

| | |
|---|---|
| The rain stops, and a scent of lotus lingers in the air. | (7) |
| On the banks, cicadas chirp from arching willows. | (6) |
| In vain does this marvelous scene surround the old pond. | (7) |
| He has not encountered any immortals. | (4) |
| Where was it that King Hsiang had his dream?[3] | (5) |
| | |
| The splendid mats lie side by side, the pillow is chill. | (7) |
| The gathering dust makes it seem cold and lonely. | (6) |
| He leans on a winding railing, his regrets far-reaching. | (7) |
| The dewdrops are pearls on the lotus. | (4) |
| Just like little beads of sweat on her face! | (5) |

### [2]

The twelve peaks of Mount Wu reach to the chill horizon.
The tips of the bamboo branches caress the altar.
Richly robed, she sweeps along the clouds with the rain.
Curtains hang deep within the temple.
The incense grows cold in the sinking winds.

She wishes to ask where it is the king of Ch'u has gone.[4]
The azure screen still conceals a golden phoenix.
The monkeys cry, and the moon is bright on the sand bar.
A lonely boat is bringing a traveler.
To be suddenly wakened from a dream is hard!

[3] See Kao-t'ang, p. 209. See also p. 26.
[4] See Kao-t'ang, p. 209.

# "Sand of Silk-Washing Stream" (*Huan-ch'i sha*), One Lyric

## [1]

| | |
|---|---|
| It is lonely in the tasseled curtains, the mats are chill. | (7) |
| A pillow close by the screen is tinged with fragrant dust. | (7) |
| In a small garden, flowers weep dew at the peak of spring. | (7) |

| | |
|---|---|
| Liu and Juan have never been to visit this magical grotto. | (7) |
| After all, Ch'ang O is a goddess who lives up on the moon. | (7) |
| This life has no path to seek even a neighbor in the east.[5] | (7) |

# "Eight-Beat Barbarian Tune" (*Pa-p'ai man*), Two Lyrics

## [1]

| | |
|---|---|
| The delicate yellow willows are enfolded in cloudy mist. | (7) |
| The red plum blossoms begin to fade in the blowing wind. | (7) |
| The scene does not ease her grief all alone in her room. | (7) |
| She paces, she sits, she paces again, her brow furrowed. | (7) |

## [2]

Sorrow crosses her brows like a sad and melancholy mist.
Tears stream down her red cheeks, her powder is stained.
She is wretched with grief, but doesn't know the reason.
When she meets someone, she says she is upset by spring.

# "River Messages" (*Ho ch'uan*), One Lyric

## [1]

| | |
|---|---|
| The autumn rain! | (2) |
| The autumn rain! | (2) |
| Through the day, through the night, | (4) |
| It falls in constant driving drops. | (4) |
| She grieves at parting by a dark lamp and chill mats. | (7) |
| The lovely lady! | (2) |
| Sorrow has overwhelmed her! | (3) |

---

[5] A reference to the "Teng-t'u tzu *hao-se fu*" by Sung Yü, in which Sung Yü is spied upon with amorous intent by his lovely neighbor to the east. See ch. 6, n. 7, p. 124.

The west wind gusts, and bamboo rattle at the window.          (7)
The sound stops and starts.                                     (3)
Two jade tears cling to her shining face.                       (5)
He promised to meet her when the wild geese returned.           (7)
He did not come!                                                (2)
The wild geese came back, but he did not!                       (5)

# Yin O (*c.* A.D. 920)

## "Immortal at the River" (*Lin-chiang hsien*), Two Lyrics

### [1]

Clusters of water chestnuts are blooming on the pond.           (7)
The wind carries their scent over the balcony.                  (6)
In times past, she had been his companion right here.           (7)
They stood so very close together.                              (4)
Movingly, they spoke of their deep love.                        (5)

She smiled, and her manner was incomparably graceful.           (7)
She was like a lotus bud bursting into flower.                  (6)
Since they parted, her mind is a confusion of memory.           (7)
The past returns in idle snatches.                              (4)
A gold lock holds the door to her rooms.                        (5)

### [2]

The Milky Way is calm on a cold night in late autumn.
Moonlight shines over the garden in the court.
Very often she dreams of her love by the west window,
But when she suddenly comes awake,
It is really hard to control her sorrow.

A low flame is burning in the half-gutted red candle.
A silver screen shines in the dark behind her.
But near the pillow, what is the most painful of all?
Across the leaves of the wu-t'ung,
Drop by drop, the dew drips like pearls!

## "Flowers Fill the Palace" (*Man-kung hua*), One Lyric

### [1]

The moon is a still presence.                                   (3)
Not one human voice is heard.                                   (3)

```
A fragrant incense winds around the back garden.          (6)
That handsome prince of romance still has not returned.   (7)
She is too idle to sweep the petals on the path.          (6)

Her parting regrets are many.                             (3)
Their meetings were only few.                             (3)
In what fairyland does he lie drunk and fuddled?          (6)
A clock rings clear, a cuckoo cries from a palace tree.   (7)
Sorrow presses at the window in the spring dawn.          (6)
```

## "Apricot Garden in Blossom" (*Hsing-yüan fang*), One Lyric

### [1]

```
Her make-up is perfect, her face is a bright flower.      (6)
When I glimpse her, I can think only of my feelings.      (6)
Shyly she takes a step, her gown of the sheerest Yüeh silk. (7)
She is beautiful and delicate.                            (3)

All the day long, I wait and watch very near her apartment. (7)
But it is as though we were separated by many walls.      (6)
When will I ever stop dreaming of coming together with her? (7)
And entering the cloud screen!                            (3)
```

## "The Drunken Gentleman" (*Tsui-kung tzu*), One Lyric

### [1]

```
The twilight mist spreads along the damp moss.            (5)
But the gate to the mansion still stands open.            (5)
All the day, he drank and searched for spring.            (5)
On his way back, he is covered with moonlight.            (5)

He slips from the saddle, and dallies a while.            (5)
His flower-festooned turban is dangling askew.            (5)
What will really make his beautiful one angry,            (5)
Are those fresh splashes of wine on his robes!            (5)
```

## "Deva-like Barbarian" (*P'u-sa man*), One Lyric

### [1]

```
The clouds at the border are white in a pale autumn sky.  (7)
She sits alone by the window looking at the misty paths.  (7)
```

The watch horn is sounding in the tower.                    (5)
Just at twilight, he returns very drunk.                    (5)

It is hard to talk to this crazy person.                    (5)
But he still will say farewell tomorrow.                    (5)
When he is on his horse and ready to go,                    (5)
I will refuse to hand him his gold whip!                    (5)


# Mao Hsi-chen (*c.* A.D. 940)

## "Sand of Silk-Washing Stream" (*Huan-ch'i sha*), Seven Lyrics

### [1]

In late spring, the orioles are flying round the steps.     (7)
The crystal curtain is like a cascade of sparkling dew.     (7)
Clouds glow in the evening sky like rose-colored silks.     (7)

Willow branches hang loose like countless azure sashes.     (7)
Crushed red petals form a sweet filigree on the ground.     (7)
An orchid-scented breeze blows aside the delicate mist.     (7)


### [2]

The fragrant red of the fallen flowers is a misty blur.
Luxuriant grasses fill the garden, very lush and green.
A gold bar holds the door, and silk curtains hang down.

A pair of swallows talk to one another with easy grace.
A scene of Mount Wu at evening covers the azure screen.
Her heart breaks as she drinks alone in her empty room.


### [3]

By evening in her red room, she is a little less tipsy.
Curling golden feathers are caught in her tangled hair.
Perfumed snow and talking flowers could not be as fair.

As if she were just about to give herself to her lover,
Her slender fingers move quickly along her silken sash.
Her roused spring feelings soon become lonely feelings.

[4]

Her hairpin is dangling askew from her upswept chignon.
She dozes upon a splendid mat, much too lazy to get up.
Her tight-fitting bodice is of embroidered red brocade.

Her fine brows gather in a shy frown, her heart breaks.
Confused and silent, her thoughts are still all of him.
Blue mountains in a cloudy sky sweep across the screen.

[5]

A long sash holds the gossamer folds of her silk skirt.
A fresh mixture of sweet fragrance rises from her body.
Slanted azure patches glow on her plum blossom make-up.

She pretends not to see him, and acts a little bit shy.
It would be much too forward to laugh or talk with him,
But she risks ruffling him by stealing some tiny looks.

[6]

A swallow hairpin softly brushes her cap of green jade.
Clasping her breast, she quietly goes toward the steps.
She walks slowly in little bow-shaped slippers of silk.[6]

Secretly she thinks how best to get her heart's desire.
How can she bear that he so often fails to come to her?
The sun rises above the garden, her thoughts go astray.

[7]

Half-drunk and dazed with emotion, she lies on her mat.
Heavy and weary, she is too weak to take off her skirt.
She is tired of the sound of the parrots in their cage.

She is too numb even to fix her gold and azure hairpin.
Her ivory comb holds her hair like the moon in a cloud.
Smoky musk scents the brocade screen and silk curtains.

[6] Footbinding is believed to have begun in China during the tenth century. One tradition associates it with the court of Li Yü (r. 961-975), the last ruler of the Southern T'ang dynasty. Its earliest connection was with shoes worn by dancers, and apparently it was only slightly constricting, in contrast to the tight and crippling bindings used in later dynasties. See Howard S. Levy, *Chinese Footbinding* (New York: Walton Rawls, 1966), pp. 38–41.

## "Immortal at the River" (*Lin-chiang hsien*), Two Lyrics

### [1]

The emperor of the Southern Ch'i favored one lovely lady.[7]    (7)
There were three thousand women in the royal palace,            (6)
But the grace and beauty of Lady P'an surpassed them all.       (7)
Within a pepper and orchid-scented grotto,                      (4)
She was a divine goddess amid clouds and rain.                  (5)

Yet dalliance and pleasure were not enough for her heart.       (7)
Her air of romance was really alluring in her prime.            (6)
She danced on the golden lotus, her waist lithe and slim.       (7)
She charmed the ruler, and lost the state.                      (4)
Since then, this story so often has been told!                  (5)

### [2]

Near dawn, she listens to the orioles from her dark room.
The moon is a dim shimmering glow at the red window.
The fallen flowers are rustling in hurried gusts of wind.
A fading candle is veiled by the curtains.
Its light flickers across the screen and harp.

In silken covers and brocade mats, her jade skin is warm.
Thin wisps of perfumed smoke slant and swirl around.
Her pale brows shyly frown as her feelings overwhelm her.
Her thoughts a secret, she dreams at will.
Where can she go to pursue the floating cloud?

## "Song of the Water Clock at Night" (*Keng-lou tzu*), Two Lyrics

### [1]

The clear autumn scene is fresh.                                (3)
The Milky Way is a pale shimmer.                                (3)

---

[7] The emperor was Hsiao Pao-chüan (*r.* 498–501) who was killed by Liang Wu-ti (*r.* 502–520), the founder of the Liang dynasty. (Hsiao Pao-chüan was reduced in rank posthumously and given the title, Marquis of Tung-hun.) According to tradition, Hsiao Pao-chüan had constructed a lotus made of gold, and then had his favorite, the Lady P'an, walk on top of the structure. He said admiringly that lotuses sprang from her every step. The "golden lotus," which became a term for bound feet, derived from this and was originally a special platform on which dancers performed. See Howard S. Levy, *Chinese Footbinding* (New York: Walton Rawls, 1966), p. 39.

It is dark in her room, the gutted candle has grown cold.        (6)
The turquoise curtains are silk.                                  (3)
The crimson coverlet is brocade.                                 (3)
Sweet fragrance rises from the incense burner.                   (5)

The water clock is a choked sob.                                 (3)
The crickets make hurried cries.                                 (3)
Bright frost fills the garden, shining white as the snow.        (6)
A new moon sits high in the sky.                                 (3)
The thin clouds gather together,                                 (3)
Like a bright curtain clinging to a jade hook.                   (5)

[2]

Mist covers over the chill moon.
A hush lies on the autumn night.
Its sound lengthening, the clock turns in a golden basin.
The silken curtains trail loose.
The brocade screen stands empty.
The flame of the candle smolders to fiery ash.

No human voices are to be heard.
There is never an end to sorrow.
She is alone in her dreams, and can't know what he feels.
For so very long, she remembers.
When she came together with him,
They talked so intimately when they made love.

## "The Taoist Nun" (Nü-kuan tzu), Two Lyrics

[1]

The green peaches and red apricots!                              (4)
They are shimmering in the late afternoon sunlight,             (6)
Deep within iridescent clouds.                                  (3)
Orioles chatter in the fragrant warm grasses.                   (5)
The cry of the crane rises on the clear wind.                   (5)

A cap of jade leaves sits atop her dark hair.                   (5)
Her rainbow sleeves brush the lute she holds.                   (5)
She should play with the master of the flute.[8]               (5)
Secretly, she seeks after him!                                  (3)

[8] Hsiao Shih, see Nung Yü, p. 211.

[2]

Delicate brows brush her soft face.
She says not a word, her lips the smallest red dot.
Her hair is like a small hill.
Her chignon trails loose in a cloud of green.
The silk of her gown is the palest of yellow.

Sadness overtakes her deep within the garden.
Slowly, she walks beside the falling flowers.
With slender fingers, she very gently places,
More incense in a jade burner!


## "Pure Serene Music" (*Ch'ing-p'ing yüeh*), One Lyric

[1]

It is almost the end of spring.                                    (4)
It is desolate and empty in the house.                            (5)
Pair by pair, pretty butterflies dance across the railings.       (7)
The screens are up, and a fine rain fills the night sky.          (6)

Alone by the curtains in her room, she silently grieves.          (6)
The incense has burned down, only a faint scent lingers.          (6)
Just at that very moment when her heart begins to break,          (6)
The east wind whirls in the trees, the flowers fly away.          (6)


## "A Southern Song" (*Nan-ko tzu*), Two Lyrics

[1]

Her sad brows are the green of a far mountain.                    (5)
Her eyes shine brightly on her beautiful face.                    (5)
A gown of sheerest red silk covers her fragrant rosy body.        (7)
It is quiet in the evening hall deep in the garden.               (6)
She is playing a silver harp.                                      (3)

Her hair trembles with the shimmer of a cloud.                    (5)
Her skirt muffles the little taps of her feet.                    (5)
She shyly asks her lover to explain the names in the song.        (7)
It is the time willows and apricots come to flower,               (6)
And she has so many emotions.                                      (3)

## [2]

Regret rises up, only to rise again and again.
Her churning emotions make her broken-hearted.
Dazed with feelings she is like a still branch of flowers.
Her beauty glows on the curtain as she idly stands.
Her robe of silk is fragrant.

Secretly, she thinks she is the cloud goddess.
She ought to feel pity for that elegant dandy.
When evening comes, she walks gracefully out of her rooms.
Her hairpin falls in a languid slant from her hair.
Her desire is without bounds!

# CHAPTER TEN

## Mao Hsi-chen (*c.* A.D. 940)

### "Song of Ho Man-tzu" (*Ho Man-tzu*),[1] Two Lyrics

#### [1]

```
She is disconsolate that her youth is slipping away.      (6)
The years pass with the startling speed of an arrow.      (6)
She thinks of lost joys, so much rushes back to memory.   (7)
Her ever-rising desire makes it hard to remain calm.      (6)
Golden willow branches trail over a winding railing.      (6)
A silver zither, strings broken, lies by the window.      (6)

Only chattering swallows are heard in the courtyard.      (6)
The falling flowers lightly drift across the garden.      (6)
She can't stop her thoughts of him, not for one moment.   (7)
How can she bear that he fills her days with sorrow?      (6)
But who can see her lonely dreams through the night,      (6)
Or her heart that so utterly breaks when she awakes!      (6)
```

#### [2]

```
She does not speak, her make-up is smudged and thin.
She is shyly timid, her sleeves hang light and easy.
How often in her fragrant rooms has he slept past dawn?
The morning sun is a pale glow at the silken window.
Within iridescent curtains, they secretly made love.
Now he suddenly wakes, his head on a crystal pillow.

Her smiling face is soft like a fresh picked flower.
But her azure brows are caught in a sorrowful frown.
She looks at him, and her suffering grows even greater.
As she does her hair, he sees her rose jade fingers.
She stands alone, languidly leaning on the red door.
Who could know his parting would bring such emotion?
```

[1] Ho Man-tzu is the name of a singer who lived during the eighth century.

# "Manifold Little Hills" (*Hsiao ch'ung shan*), One Lyric

## [1]

| | |
|---|---|
| Paired swallows from the eaves fly in front of her rooms. | (7) |
| Sorrowful and desolate, she feels so much regret. | (5) |
| She hates to sleep all alone. | (3) |
| In her quiet seclusion, she thinks of the man she adores. | (7) |
| The curtains are of red silk. | (3) |
| The gold duck burner is cold, its fragrance gone. | (5) |

| | |
|---|---|
| Who would believe her loveliness is being ruined? | (5) |
| By the screen, jade tears stream down her cheeks, | (5) |
| And splash the flowered dots. | (3) |
| She is too weak and listless even to get up on the swing. | (7) |
| All the blossoms are falling. | (3) |
| She grieves as a dazzling sky spreads before her. | (5) |

# "Pacifying the Western Barbarians" (*Ting hsi-fan*), One Lyric

## [1]

| | |
|---|---|
| The garden is covered in thick shadows of deepest green. | (6) |
| Orioles jabber away at her. | (3) |
| Butterflies fly around her. | (3) |
| They play with a fair rose. | (3) |

| | |
|---|---|
| She leans on a railing in a soft breeze as the sun sets. | (6) |
| A lingering fragrance clings to her silken gown. | (5) |
| She has not yet received any news from her handsome man. | (6) |
| When will he return to her? | (3) |

# "The Magnolia Flower" (*Mu-lan hua*), One Lyric

## [1]

| | |
|---|---|
| She shuts fast the red door. | (3) |
| She hooks the azure screens. | (3) |
| The orioles' cries fill the garden in the lonely spring. | (7) |
| Rubbing tears from her face, | (3) |
| She hates that handsome man. | (3) |
| He hasn't come back yet, and once more the flowers fall. | (7) |

She faces the bright sunset,                                                    (3)
Leaning beside a small door.                                                    (3)
How can she bear to recall the past over and over again?                       (7)
Her pillow of gold is chill.                                                    (3)
The painted screen is bleak.                                                    (3)
She is too weary even to mist the curtains with perfume.                        (7)

# "The Flowers in the Rear Garden" (*Hou-t'ing hua*), Three Lyrics

## [1]

The orioles sing, swallows chatter, and the grass is lush.                     (7)
Flowers are in bloom in the rear garden.                                        (4)
There were banquets in the past, and music filled the air.                     (7)
The pipes and strings played very clear.                                       (4)

But since the change of dynasty, this happy time is ended.[2]                   (7)
The painted beams stand black with dust.                                        (4)
The heart shatters like a tiny crescent moon made of jade.                     (7)
She is shut away deep within the palace.                                        (4)

## [2]

Lissome and graceful, the dancers are so very captivating.
Every new-powdered face rivals the rest.
Softly frowning they step, pearl and azure hairpins asway.
Their glossy hair is like tinted clouds.

Their red lips slowly part as they begin to sing the song.
Their brocade robes are fastened aslant.
With dainty hands they frequently brush their rosy cheeks,
And laughingly toy with the golden dots.

## [3]

Her freshly scented crimson sleeves are made of Yüeh silk.
So lightly they veil her gold bracelets.
Silently leaning on a railing, she spreads her dainty fan,
Concealing the loveliness of her cheeks.

---

[2] The song, "*Hou-t'ing hua*," is believed to have been originally composed by the last ruler of the Ch'en dynasty, Ch'en Shu-pao (*r*. 583–588). The allusion is specifically to the fall of the Ch'en dynasty, but it would apply equally well to the times in which Mao Hsi-chen himself lived.

Spring fades in the warm sun, the orioles take their ease.
The fallen petals cover over the garden.
Why haven't we been able to come together for a long time,
Deep in the garden, in the painted hall?


## "Song of the Wine Spring" (*Chiu-ch'üan tzu*), Two Lyrics

### [1]

| | |
|---|---|
| She idly rests within silken curtains. | (4) |
| Lazily, she thinks about all the many kinds of love. | (6) |
| Her little red lips are pursed. | (3) |
| Her feathered hairpin is heavy. | (3) |
| Her dark hair lies to one side. | (3) |

| | |
|---|---|
| On the screen at twilight, the spring mountains are green. | (7) |
| They are shimmering in a fragrant misty haze. | (5) |
| Her sweetly affectionate heart, | (3) |
| Is taken captive by her dreams. | (3) |
| Her softly curving brows frown. | (3) |

### [2]

A phoenix prances atop the mirror box.
Red cheeks and azure brows shimmer over the surface.
Her moon comb rests on a slant.
Her rich dark hair is lustrous.
Her fragrant powder is chilled.

Her breath warms the sweetest dawn bud to put in her hair.
Golden swallows fall softly from her hairpin.
The sun is starting to come up.
The screens are only half open.
She looks at her faded make-up.


## "Deva-like Barbarian" (*P'u-sa man*), Three Lyrics

### [1]

| | |
|---|---|
| Pear blossoms drift through the garden like fragrant snow. | (7) |
| High in the tower on a quiet night, wind strums the cheng. | (7) |
| Slanting moonbeams shine on the curtains. | (5) |
| She thinks of him, her dreams are fitful. | (5) |

The lamp flickers behind the tiny window.                    (5)
The noisy swallows break her gloomy mood.                     (5)
The screen is closed, the fragrance gone.                     (5)
Floating clouds go back to the mountains.                     (5)


[2]


She rolls a silken screen high, and gazes across the pond.
Raindrops splash from the lotus just like tumbling pearls.
It is late summer, the nights grow chill.
A light wind crosses the fragrant waters.

Cheerless and alone, she mourns the past.
How can she bear this feeling of anguish?
All unseen, time hurries by so very fast.
Idly, she waits for autumn to come again.


[3]


The pale blue of the sky harmonizes with the spring scene.
Not a word has arrived from that pleasure-seeking gallant.
All the day long, the red door is closed.
Parting's grief quietly breaks her heart.

Orioles cry in the warmth of green trees.
Swallows dip wings over the flooded pond.
Desolate, she faces the landscape screen.
She thinks of him in a wine-filled dream.


# Li Hsün (855?–930?)

## "Sand of Silk-Washing Stream" (*Huan-ch'i sha*), Four Lyrics

[1]

The daintiness of her attire is especially nice in summer.    (7)
Her Yüeh silk gown is light yellow, the color of turmeric.    (7)
Azure patches and crimson lips enhance her beautiful face.    (7)

She says nothing of her bitterness when they are together.    (7)
But every time they part, she thinks of him over and over.    (7)
By a moonlit window, the path smells sweet, she dreams on.    (7)

## [2]

She goes to the garden at evening to see the cherry–apple.
Her captivating look is in imitation of the palace ladies.
A tiny hairpin pulls aside a little sprig of flowery buds.

A comb carved from jade sits aslant a sleek cloud of hair.
Her sweet snowy skin shows through her gold–threaded gown.
What are her inner thoughts in the light of the dying sun?

## [3]

He seeks his old love, parting's grief breaking his heart.
There is no way to meet that lady in the jade tower again.
Raindrops carve designs along the dust of the busy street.

For a long time he has not met with the Wu Mountain dream.
How can he bear to waste the springtime by the Chin River?
"If wine is there among the flowers, don't rush to say no!"

## [4]

The fragrance of the red lotus brings him to the railings.
How can he bear to remember the lady as sweet as a flower?
Old pleasures are like a dream that leave behind no trace.

Mountains on the folds of an azure screen are in darkness.
The bed is chill, the striped mat is like rippling silver.
His heart breaks as he hears the cry of the autumn cicada.

## "Song of the Fisherman" (*Yü-ko tzu*), Four Lyrics

## [1]

| | |
|---|---|
| The mountains of Ch'u are dark green. | (3) |
| The Hsiang waters are cold and fresh. | (3) |
| I can't ever see quite enough of the soft spring breezes. | (7) |
| The grasses flourish, heavy and lush. | (3) |
| The flowers bloom, abundant and rich. | (3) |
| The fishermen at the oars harmonize without any stop. | (6) |

The boats bob freely among the waves.                                    (3)
They sail ahead without restrictions.                                    (3)
The fishermen return in the moonlight to the curving bay.                 (7)
The deep cups are spilling with wine.                                    (3)
A cloudy mist spreads along the room,                                    (3)
And no one can distinguish the wealthy from the poor!                    (6)


[2]


Rushes come to full flower in autumn.
Evening crosses the Hsiao and Hsiang.
The fine scene on Orange Island is like a painted screen.
Within the green swirls of the mists,
Beneath the brilliantly shining moon,
The lines hanging from the small boats are pulled in.

The water is my one true native land.
A cabin of reeds is my own true home.
Fish broth together with some rice are what I always eat.
There is lots of wine to fill my cup.
My shelves are piled high with books.
My mind cannot brood over matters of fame and wealth!


[3]


Silken willow branches softly tumble.
Flowery blooms spread over the trees.
Orioles cry, and dusk fills the spring mountains of Ch'u.
The oars move the light boat forward.
It forges on through the deep inlets.
It moves to the slow chants of the "Fisherman's Song."

The trawling lines are all pulled in.
There is still the fine wine to come.
We make straight for a secluded village hidden in clouds.
We come downstream from the sand bar.
We reach to the shallows of the ford.
Startled egrets fly in a flurry, one after the other!


[4]


Around the slopes of Chiu-i Mountain,
Out across the flowing Hsiang waters,
The rush flowers are in bloom, and the autumn wind rises.
Within the swirling water and clouds,

By the moonlight above the mountains,
The boat frolics through a welter of light and cloud.

I play the ch'in, its tones so clear.
I drink to the full of the fine wine.
Aboard the tiny skiff, my mind can be happy and carefree.
I can go where I want, east and west.
Whenever I want I can come to a stop.
And I don't have to worry whether I'm sober or drunk!

## "A Stretch of Cloud over Mount Wu" (*Wu-shan i-tuan yün*), Two Lyrics

### [1]

| | |
|---|---|
| A traveler journeys through the Wu-hsia Gorge. | (5) |
| He brings his boat to a stop beside the shore. | (5) |
| Once the king of Ch'u dreamed of the goddess Yao Chi, | (7) |
| But this divine tryst was a dream of long ago. | (5) |
| | |
| Dust has darkened the rolled-up pearl screens. | (5) |
| The perfume has faded from the azure curtains. | (5) |
| He turns into the west wind and grief overwhelms him. | (7) |
| The rain at dusk splashes the deserted shrine. | (5) |

### [2]

An ancient temple sits in the green mountains.
The blue waters flow round the imperial lodge.
The sound and the color envelop the women's pavilion.
For a long time, I can think only of the past.

The morning clouds and rain return at evening.
Like mist on a flower, spring turns to autumn.
Why must the monkeys wail so close to my lonely boat?
Hasn't this traveler enough sorrow of his own?

## "Immortal at the River" (*Lin-chiang hsien*), Two Lyrics

### [1]

| | |
|---|---|
| A pavilion is empty on the pond, its screens rolled up. | (7) |
| In a moment of coolness, she slowly strolls about. | (6) |

The lotus have been crushed and scattered by the rains.        (7)
Trailing willow branches brush the bank.                       (4)
A cicada is chirping in the lingering sunset.                  (5)

Silently she lowers her head, her thoughts so far away.        (7)
A pair of fish hang down from her slanted hairpin.            (6)
Many times, she has read in secret the letter he wrote.       (7)
Her emotion at parting is a deep regret.                       (4)
She can't do anything about their separation!                 (5)

[2]

Orioles jabber by the curtain, the warm sun shines red.
The dying incense in the jade burner is yet heavy.
When she gets up, her thoughts are sleepy and confused.
She mourns the loss of her spring dream,
But who can know her joy at seeing him there!

She forces herself to put on her make-up in the mirror.
She is a blossoming lotus gleaming on a tiny pool.
Nowhere can she find any reminder of her old happiness,
Still she makes herself turn for a look.
The Chiu-i Mountain spreads along the screen!

# "Song of the Southern Country" (*Nan-hsiang tzu*), Ten Lyrics

[1]

The mist stretches without end.                               (3)
The rain pours biting and cold.                                (3)
Flowers fall along the banks, and the partridges cry out.     (7)
A distant voyager in a tiny skiff nears an outlying ford.     (7)
He thinks of his true homeland.                                (3)
The waters calm at ebb tide, dusk darkens spring's scene!     (7)

[2]

The fragrant oars rise up high.
Ripples start across the water.
We all race to carry the straw baskets for picking lotus.
We see one another as we circle the hollows of the banks,
And everyone is asked to feast.
After downing a cup of wine, a red glow is on our cheeks!

## [3]

As we close upon the road home,
We knock the gunwales and sing.
The place we seek for pearls has a lot of wind and water.
A bridge spans curved banks, the moon rims the mountains,
All hidden within a misty veil.
The flowering nutmeg falls in thousands of tiny clusters!

## [4]

We get aboard the painted boat.
We sail beside the lotus banks.
The boatman's song wakes the mandarin ducks with a start.
A lady decked with flowers laughingly hugs her companion.
She is so lovely and appealing.
We pick lotus leaves to use as shades in the evening sun!

## [5]

We drink deep of the fine wine,
The cups filled to overflowing.
As we laze, we ask the ladies to play the pipes and sing.
To avoid the heat, we let the boat bob in the soft waves.
It tumbles about free and easy.
The lichee blooming on the shores shine red in the water!

## [6]

The clouds are heavy with rain.
The waves go to meet the winds.
An old fisherman sails round the green waters of the bay.
The spring wine is sweet and mellow, the perch is superb.
But who will get drunk with me?
I tie up my tiny skiff, and doze off under a rattan sail!

## [7]

A still moon is over the sands.
A light mist covers the waters.
Amid the scented lotus, the boat sails through the night.
Who is that girl with the shiny hair and the rosy cheeks?
I turn and gaze back from afar.
The boatman's song is a slow chant as she leaves the bay!

## [8]

The fish vendors have all gone.
Only a few boats sail the ford.
In Annam, cloud—capped trees grow mistier as one watches.
The traveler waits for the tide as dusk comes to the sky.
They say farewell on the banks.
Sadly he hears the monkeys cry in the pestilential rains!

## [9]

She dresses her soft dark hair.
A comb of bone is fixed behind.
Her crimson robe shimmers against the green of her skirt.
Warm spring breezes drift below King Chao T'o's pavilion.
The flowers overflow the banks.
When she takes a stroll, her neighbor ladies go with her!

## [10]

At the place we see each other,
The sky grows clear at evening.
Hai—t'ung trees dip in front of King Chao T'o's pavilion.
All unseen, her eyes look at me with the deepest feeling.
She gives me two blue feathers.
Riding an elephant, she is first to cross over the water!

## "The Taoist Nun" (*Nü-kuan tzu*), Two Lyrics

### [1]

| | |
|---|---|
| Stars rise on high as the moon crests. | (4) |
| I wait deep within the red cassias and the green pines. | (6) |
| The service at the altar begins. | (3) |
| A golden bell sounds with clear dulcet tones. | (5) |
| A pearl banner stands poised in verdant moss. | (5) |
| | |
| The Taoist litany is chanted in a low murmur. | (5) |
| Fanciful thoughts rush to and fro in my mind. | (5) |
| When dawn comes, she will return by the road, | (5) |
| That leads to faraway P'eng—lai! | (3) |

[2]

Night is calm in the spring mountains.
Sadly she hears scattered chimes in the sacred grottos.
The jade hall is standing empty.
Light mist falls from the pearls on her sash.
A fine haze tugs the edge of her azure skirt.

She faces the flowers and her desire deepens.
She slowly strolls about, gazing at the moon.
Where are the handsome Liu and Juan this day?
Not one letter has she received!

# "Song of the Wine-Spring" (*Chiu-ch'üan tzu*), Four Lyrics

[1]

It is lonely within the green tower.                        (4)
Wind gusts the screen, trembling the pearls and azure.      (7)
The moon is a dim and hazy glow.                            (3)
The flowers pale in the shadows.                            (3)
Spring's grief enfolds them all.                            (3)

She seeks to recall the past in her flickering dreams.      (7)
Tears run on her cheeks like dew over a crimson peach.      (7)
Her rolled hair is pulled aside.                            (3)
A phoenix dips from her hairpin.                            (3)
Her thoughts go to the distance!                            (3)

[2]

The rains drench the fallen flowers.
Perfumes fade from bits of red strewn beside the pond.
Her grief at separation runs on.
The spring song comes to an end.
She closes up the silver screen.

Day and night, solitary sails depart the land of Ch'u.
She idly tunes the gilt zither, her pain so very deep.
Emotion overflows in the melody.
Words pour out from the strings.
She can't bear to hear any more!

[3]

[Variation]
The autumn rain falls without cease.
The sounds are scattered among the withered lotus.          (6)
How can she bear to listen on her pillow in the night?      (7)
Her fuddled head clears of wine.

Her melancholy thoughts race on with the endless rain.
It is near dawn, the candle is dark, the incense cold.
The mist spreads filmy and fine.
The rains beat bitter and chill.
They seep in through the screen!

[4]

[Variation]
The autumn moon is of rare splendor.
It shines pure white beyond the green silk window.          (6)
In the hushed cold, it dazzles the flowers and bamboo.      (7)
Its rays are a seal on the pond.

The dewdrops lie cool and thick.                            (3)
A cricket chirps from the steps.                            (3)
The moon wakes the lovely lady, her dreams fading.          (6)
Deep in the night, its light slants beside the pillow.      (7)
Dark shadows flicker to and fro!                            (3)

# "Gazing After the Distant Traveler" (*Wang yüan-hsing*), Two Lyrics

[1]

The spring day is slowly ending, her thoughts are lonely.   (7)
The traveler is far away, off on some mountain road.        (6)
She often hears orioles chattering at the lattice window.   (7)
One by one, the silken willow branches tug at her sorrow.   (7)

She has done with her embroidery.                           (3)
She no longer plays on the pipes.                           (3)
She looks like a flower languishing away all unseen.        (6)
The love-knot is still tied to the sash of her old skirt.   (7)
She bears the solitude of the night in the wind and moon.   (7)

[2]

Dewdrops cover the darkened courtyard as the leaves fall.
The brows of the lovely woman are gathered in grief.
As soon as he left, he forgot their happy times together.
Clouds and water rush far away, letters are slow to come.
The screen stands halfway closed.
The pillow is pulled to the side.
A candle quietly drips tears, two drops splash down.
Crickets chirp from time to time, the clock moves faster.
The gleaming moon at the window peers in at the curtains.

## "The Deva-like Barbarian" (*P'u-sa man*), Three Lyrics

[1]

Across the winding pond, rising winds ripple the waters.        (7)
Among the hai-t'ung trees, the door slants halfway open.        (7)
The setting sun shines over the flat grass.                     (5)
Pair by pair, the partridges are flying by.                     (5)

Where has the far voyager gone in his boat?                     (5)
They saw each other, but had to stay apart.                     (5)
Silently, her heart is just about to break.                     (5)
She gazes at the distant water in the mist.                     (5)

[2]

I wait in idleness while the springtime is passing away.
The curtains cast flickering shadows on the green steps.
The setting sun slants across the railings.
The cuckoo's cry mourns the fallen flowers.

I so hated the indifference of your manner,
When you went away to the Hsiao and Hsiang.
Lost in thought, I lean against the screen.
Tears fall, splashing the red of my cheeks.

[3]

Two swallows fly in the misty rain outside the curtains.
Petals fall over the steps in piles of crimson and pink.
She strums a melody on the precious zither.
Her heart goes after that boat so far away.

```
The road runs out beyond Ch'u's cloudy sky.
If he follows it, he'll be gone for a year.
The fragrance fades deep within the screen.
Where can she again find her old happiness?
```

## "Song of the West Stream" (*Hsi-ch'i tzu*), One Lyric

### [1]

```
A gilt and azure hairpin sways back and forth.          (6)
Make-up done, she ponders a dream by a window.          (6)
The sun is high in the sky,                             (3)
But spring is soon to pass,                             (3)
And he hasn't yet returned!³                            (3)
She feels too lazy to sweep the fallen petals.          (6)
Silently, she stands by a small screen,                 (5)
Weeping for the fading red!                             (3)
```

## "The Beautiful Lady Yü" (*Yü mei-jen*), One Lyric

### [1]

```
In a golden cage, the parrots announce the coming dawn.  (7)
With a quick flutter of wings, they fly apart.           (6)
That night, she had met in secret tryst with her lover.  (7)
She felt so ecstatic, only slowly did she become sober,  (7)
And he was late to leave for home.                       (3)

Flowers hide her from the moonlight as she sees him go.   (7)
A phoenix dips to the side of her glossy hair.            (6)
She turns, and with graceful steps, goes into her room.   (7)
She stands by the screen, quietly toying with her comb.   (7)
Her azure brows gather in a frown.                        (3)
```

## "River Messages" (*Ho ch'uan*), Two Lyrics

### [1]

```
Ever onward I go!                                          (2)
Where is it I go?                                          (2)
```

---

³ *Lai*, "to come," makes little sense in this line, and I have followed the suggestion of Hsiao Chi-tsung and changed it to *wei*, "not yet." Hsiao Chi-tsung, *Hua-chien chi* (Taipei: Hsüeh-sheng shu-chü, 1977), p. 532.

The land of Ch'u is so far and vast.                        (4)
Mountains and waters twine together,                        (4)
In morning clouds and evening rains.                        (4)
As ever, in front of the twelve peaks of Mount Wu,          (6)
The cries of the monkeys reach to the boat.                 (5)

Isn't my heart in tiny knots like the budding lilacs,       (7)
Because we had to say farewell!                             (3)
All news of my homeland has come to an end.                 (5)
I think of my lovely one among the flowers,                 (5)
Facing the bright moon in the spring winds.                 (5)
Her sorrow ought to be as mine!                             (3)

[2]

[Variation]
Spring is ending!
The rain is fine!
I said goodbye at the southern bank.
Sadness pressed heavily at my brows.
Everywhere, the flowers are falling.
Caroling birds seemed to sing a melody of parting.
Red teardrops ran along my powdered cheeks.

Close by the river, once again we tied the love-knot,
And I sobbed with deep emotion.
Whenever will we be able to meet once more?
I couldn't bear to turn around and look after you.         (6)
Already the sand bar lay between us.                        (4)
The splashing oars go far away!

# Biographical Notes
## (in alphabetical order)

Chang Pi 張泌 (Tzu-ch'eng; *c.* A.D. 961)

Chang Pi was a native of Huai-nan in Anhui Province. He served Li Hou-chu (*r.* 961–975), the last ruler of the Southern T'ang who was renowned as the most famous *tz'u* writer of the Five Dynasties. When Li Hou-chu surrendered to the Sung dynasty in A.D. 975, Chang Pi served the Sung government in the Institute of History, and later as an official in Honan Province. After Li Hou-chu's death in A.D. 978, Chang Pi would go to his grave on the occasion of the Cold Food Festival, and carry out the rites of mourning for his former ruler.

However, since *Among the Flowers* was compiled by A.D. 940, and Chang Pi's *tz'u* are included rather early in the collection, Hu Shih suggests that the Chang Pi represented in *Among the Flowers* is not the same Chang Pi who served in the court of Li Hou-chu. For one thing, Chang Pi is given the official title, "*she-jen*," or "Grand Secretary" in *Among the Flowers*, a title he would not have held until A.D. 961 when Li Hou-chu ascended the throne. Hu Shih believes the Chang Pi in *Among the Flowers* is an earlier figure, possibly an official in the state of Shu, about whom nothing is known. (Hu Shih, ed. *Tz'u-hsüan* [1927; reprint ed., Taipei: Commercial Press, 1959], p. 20.) There is no evidence to prove the case one way or the other, and most scholars accept the Chang Pi in *Among the Flowers* as the same Chang Pi who served in the court of Li Hou-chu. Twenty-seven of his *tz'u* are included in *Among the Flowers*.

Ho Ning 和凝 (Ch'eng-chi; 898–955)

Ho Ning was a native of Hsü-ch'ang in Shantung Province. He received his *chin-shih* degree under the Later Liang dynasty (907–923) which maintained the T'ang examination system for all but three of its sixteen years. Ho Ning successively served all five of the northern dynasties during the period of the Five Dynasties (907–960), the Later Liang, the Later T'ang (923–936), the Later Chin (936–947), the Later Han (947–951), and the Later Chou (951–960). He achieved special prominence during the Later Chin when he served as Chief Minister, and tutor to the heir-apparent. Twenty of his *tz'u* are included in *Among the Flowers*.

## Hsüeh Chao-yün 薛昭蘊 (courtesy name unknown; *c.* 900–932)

Hsüeh Chao-yün was a native of Ho-tung in Shansi Province. He served the Earlier Shu dynasty (907–925) as a Vice-Minister on the Board of Rites. He is said to have had a high opinion of his ability, and was conceited and insolent. He was very fond of the tune "Sand of Silk-Washing Stream," and sang it whenever possible, even in the course of his official duties. Nineteen of his *tz'u* are included in *Among the Flowers*.

## Huang-fu Sung 皇甫松 (Tzu-ch'i; *c.* A.D. 859)

Huang-fu Sung was a native of Hsin-an in Chekiang Province. He was the son of Huang-fu Shih (*c.* A.D. 810), a disciple of the famous T'ang writer Han Yü (768–824). It is believed that Huang-fu Sung's official career was blocked because he incurred the enmity of the powerful official, Niu Seng-ju (779–847). The title, "*hsien-pei*," ascribed to Huang-fu Sung in *Among the Flowers* is simply an honorary term meaning "the elder." Twelve of his *tz'u* are included in *Among the Flowers*.

## Ku Hsiung 顧敻 (courtesy name unknown; *c.* A.D. 933)

Ku Hsiung served the Earlier Shu dynasty (907–925) and was appointed Prefect of Mao-chou in Szechuan Province. Afterwards, he served Meng Chih-hsiang (*r.* 934–935), the founder of the Later Shu dynasty (934–965), rising to the post of Grand Marshal. Fifty-five of his *tz'u* are included in *Among the Flowers*.

## Li Hsün 李珣 (Te-jun; 855?–930?)

Li Hsün was of Persian ancestry, and his family home was in Tzu-chou in Szechuan Province. He served in the court of Wang Yen (*r.* 918–925), the last ruler of the Earlier Shu dynasty, where he was renowned for his literary ability. Li Hsün's younger sister, Li Shun-hsien, was a palace lady of the second rank in Wang Yen's court, and she was also noted for the composition of *tz'u*. After the fall of the Earlier Shu dynasty, Li Hsün did not again enter public life. Thirty-seven of his *tz'u* are included in *Among the Flowers*.

## Lu Ch'ien-i 鹿虔扆 (courtesy name unknown; *c.* A.D. 940)

Lu Ch'ien-i received his *chin-shih* degree during the Later Shu dynasty (934–965). He continued in the service of that dynasty, rising to the post of Grand Protector. Six of his *tz'u* are included in *Among the Flowers*.

## Mao Hsi-chen 毛熙震 (courtesy name unknown; *c.* A.D. 940)

Mao Hsi-chen was a native of Szechuan Province. He served in the court of the Later Shu dynasty (934–965) as a Director of the Imperial Library. Twenty-nine of his *tz'u* are included in *Among the Flowers*.

Mao Wen-hsi 毛文錫 (P'ing-kuei; c. A.D. 930)

Mao Wen-hsi was a native of Kao-yang in Shantung Province. After receiving his *chin-shih* degree, he entered the service of the Earlier Shu dynasty (907–925) where he rose to the post of Director of Instruction. Afterwards, he served in the court of the Later Shu dynasty (934–965). Thirty-one of his *tz'u* are included in *Among the Flowers*.

Niu Chiao 牛嶠 (Sung-ch'ing; 850?–920?)

Niu Chiao was a native of Lung-hsi in Kansu Province. He was a grandson of the famous and powerful T'ang minister, Niu Seng-ju (779–847). Niu Chiao received his *chin-shih* degree in A.D. 878, and served in the Imperial Library. He went to Szechuan to serve Wang Chien, who was then military Governor of Shu. When Wang Chien proclaimed himself Emperor of the Earlier Shu dynasty (907–925), Niu Chiao was appointed a Grand Counselor in the Imperial Chancellery of the Shu government. Thirty-two of his *tz'u* are included in *Among the Flowers*.

Niu Hsi-chi 牛希濟 (courtesy name unknown; c. A.D. 930)

Niu Hsi-chi was a native of Lung-hsi in Kansu Province. He was a nephew of Niu Chiao (850?–920?) whose *tz'u* are also included in *Among the Flowers*. He served the Earlier Shu dynasty both as a Han-lin academician, and as President of the Board of Censors. When the Earlier Shu dynasty fell to the Later T'ang dynasty (923–936), Niu Hsi-chi then entered the service of the new dynasty. He was appointed Assistant Military Governor of the area around Ch'ang-an. Eleven of his *tz'u* are included in *Among the Flowers*.

Ou-yang Chiung 歐陽烔 (courtesy name unknown; 896–971)

Ou-yang Chiung was a native of Hua-yang in Szechuan Province. As a young man, he entered the service of Wang Yen (r. 918–925), the second and last ruler of the Earlier Shu dynasty (907–925). Ou-yang served as a Grand Secretary in the Imperial Secretariat. After Shu fell to the Later T'ang (923–936), Ou-yang followed Wang Yen to Lo-yang. When Meng Chih-hsiang (r. 934–935), the founder of the Later Shu dynasty (934–965), took control of Shu, Ou-yang returned to Szechuan and served both Meng Chih-hsiang and his son Meng Ch'ang (r. 935–965). When Meng Ch'ang surrendered to the Sung dynasty, Ou-yang was made a Grand Counselor to the Emperor in the Sung government. Ou-yang Chiung is the author of the preface to *Among the Flowers*, and together with Lu Ch'ien-i, Yen Hsüan, Mao Wen-hsi, and Han Ts'ung (not included in *Among the Flowers*) formed a coterie of poets in the Later Shu court known as the "Five Ghosts." Seventeen of his *tz'u* are included in *Among the Flowers*.

Sun Kuang-hsien 孫光憲 (Meng-wen; 898?–968)

Sun Kuang-hsien was from Kuei-p'ing in Szechuan Province. He rose to high rank in the service of the Southern P'ing dynasty (907–963), which ruled in Hupei and eastern Szechuan and was the smallest and weakest of the ten southern kingdoms during the period of the Five Dynasties (907–960). Sun Kuang-hsien served the Southern P'ing as Assistant Military Governor, and as Honorary Director of the Imperial Library. Later Sun Kuang-hsien persuaded the Southern P'ing ruler to surrender to the Sung. He was rewarded by the Sung emperor with the post of Censor in Huang-chou, but he died before being able to take up the post. Sixty-one of his *tz'u* are included in *Among the Flowers*.

## Wei Ch'eng-pan 魏承班 (courtesy name unknown; *c.* A.D. 910)

Wei Ch'eng-pan's father was Wei Hung-fu, who was an adopted son of Wang Chien (*r.* 907–918), the founder of the Earlier Shu dynasty. Because of this, Wei Hung-fu was allowed to use the name Wang Tsung-pi and was enfeoffed as Prince of Ch'i. His son, Wei Ch'eng-pan, served the Earlier Shu court as an Officer of Surveillance, rising to the post of Grand Marshal. Fifteen of his *tz'u* are included in *Among the Flowers*.

## Wei Chuang 韋莊 (Tuan-chi; 836–910)

Wei Chuang was from Tu-ling in Shensi Province. When the rebel leader Huang Ch'ao entered Ch'ang-an in A.D. 880, Wei Chuang was there, and he endured great suffering until he was able to escape in 882. For the next ten years he traveled extensively through south-central China, returning to Ch'ang-an in 893. He then took and passed the *chin-shih* examination, and in 896 he was assigned to a post in Szechuan. While there, he purchased and renovated the home of the poet Tu Fu (712–770), whom he much admired. Wei Chuang was instrumental in persuading Wang Chien to proclaim himself emperor of the Earlier Shu dynasty (907–925) after the fall of the T'ang. He then served Wang Chien as his Chief Minister. Wei Chuang, like Wen T'ing-yün, was as famous for his *shih* poetry as he was for his *tz'u* compositions. Forty-eight of his *tz'u* are included in *Among the Flowers*.

## Wen T'ing-yün 溫庭筠 (Fei-ch'ing; 812–870)

Wen T'ing-yün was a native of T'ai-yüan in Shansi Province. Very little is known with any certainty of the life of Wen T'ing-yün. When he was young, he exhibited great literary talent; however, as he grew older, he displayed an equal talent for the enjoyment of wine, women, and song as a frequent habitué of the cabarets and bordellos. He developed a reputation for eccentric behavior, and although he sat for the civil-service examinations, he was unsuccessful, and therefore occupied only minor posts of little distinction. He was noted as an accomplished musician, and he is the first poet to write extensively in the *tz'u* form. He was equally adept in the writing of *shih* poems which resemble his *tz'u* with regard to choice of theme and concentration of mood. Sixty-six of his *tz'u* are included in *Among the Flowers*.

Yen Hsüan 閻選 (courtesy name unknown; *c.* A.D. 940)

Yen Hsüan was apparently a man of humble origins who lived during the time of the Later Shu dynasty (934–965). He is listed in *Among the Flowers* simply as a *ch'u-shih* or "retired scholar." Eight of his *tz'u* are included in *Among the Flowers*.

Yin O 尹鶚 (courtesy name unknown; *c.* A.D. 920)

Yin O was a native of Ch'eng-tu in Szechuan Province. He served in the court of Wang Yen (*r.* 918–925) of the Earlier Shu dynasty, rising to the rank of Counselor. Yin O and Li Hsün (855?–930?) were good friends, and Yin O was noted for writing playful poems to make fun of Li Hsün. Six of his *tz'u* are included in *Among the Flowers*.

# Glossary

Apricot Garden (Hsing-yüan 杏園) was a garden in Ch'ang-an that was part of the pleasure complex built around the area of the Ch'ü-chiang Pond. During the T'ang dynasty (618–907), it was the custom for the successful degree candidates to come to this garden to feast in celebration of their advancement.

Bluebird (*ch'ing-niao* 青鳥) is one of the three bird messengers (*san ch'ing-niao*) who attend the goddess, the Queen Mother of the West.

Bridge of Stars (*hsing-ch'iao* 星橋) is the Milky Way. See Magpie Bridge.

Brocade City (Chin-kuan ch'eng 錦官城) is the city of Ch'eng-tu in Szechuan. It was known as the "City of the Brocade Officer" or the "Brocade City," because it was famous for the fine brocade materials produced there. See Brocade River.

Brocade River (Chin-p'u 錦浦) is the name of a river in Ch'eng-tu in Szechuan. It was said to have water that was excellent for the washing of silk, hence the fame of Ch'eng-tu silks. There is a legend that a lady took pity on a Buddhist monk who had fallen into a ditch. She washed his clothes for him in the river, and a hundred flowers miraculously appeared on the water. As a result, this river is also known as the "Flower-Washing Stream" or the "Hundred Flowers Water." See Brocade City.

Cassia Tree (*kuei-shu* 桂樹) is frequently used as an image for the moon, because it was believed in popular folklore that a cassia tree grew on the moon. "To pluck the cassia" also meant to achieve the third and highest level in the examination system, the *chin-shih* degree.

Cha River (Cha-shui 霅水) is a river in Chekiang Province in the prefecture of Wu-hsing.

Ch'a Nü (姹女) or Ho-shang ch'a-nü (河上姹女) is "the elegant girl by the riverside," a Taoist alchemical term for mercury.

Chang Hsü (張緒) was a romantic figure who lived during the reign of Emperor Wu (*r.* 484–494) of the Southern Ch'i dynasty. It is said that one day Emperor Wu planted willows in front of the Ling-ho Palace and compared their beauty to the handsome Chang Hsü.

Chang-hua Palace (Chang-hua t'ai 章華臺) was a palace of the ancient kings of Ch'u. It was noted for the willows that grew there.

Chang-t'ai (章臺) originally was the name of a street in Ch'ang-an during the Han dynasty. Chang-t'ai became a term used for a brothel, and *chang-t'ai liu*, "*chang-t'ai* willow*,*" became an expression referring to prostitutes.

Ch'ang-an (長安) is located northwest of Sian in present-day Shensi Province. It was known as the "western capital" in contrast to Lo-yang which was known as the "eastern capital." Ch'ang-an was built during the reign of the Han emperor Hui (*r.* 194–187) and it was the capital of the Former or Western Han dynasty. After the short-lived Hsin dynasty of the usurper Wang Mang (*r.* 8–23), the capital was moved to Lo-yang by Emperor Kuang-wu (*r.* 25–57), who established the Eastern or Latter Han dynasty. After the downfall of the Han in A.D. 220, Ch'ang-an remained an important imperial center, and once again rose to cosmopolitan glory as the capital of the T'ang dynasty. At that time, it was a city of possibly more than a million inhabitants. It was laid out in checkerboard fashion and covered an area of slightly more than five by six miles.

Ch'ang-chou (長洲) was the name of a park in Kiangsu Province southwest of the prefecture of Wu.

Ch'ang Gate (Ch'ang-men 閶門) was a gate in the city of Soochow.

Ch'ang-men Palace (Ch'ang-men kung 長門宮) is the name of a palace in Ch'ang-an built by Emperor Wu (*r.* 140–86) of the Han dynasty for the empress and her attendants. It was here that Empress Ch'en, consort of Emperor Wu, paid the poet Ssu-ma Hsiang-ju (179–117) to write the poem "Ch'ang-men *fu*" in her honor so that she might regain favor with the emperor.

Ch'ang O (嫦娥 or Heng O 姮娥) is the Wife of I the Archer who obtained the elixir of immortality from the Queen Mother of the West. Ch'ang O stole the elixir and fled with it to the moon where she was changed into a toad. She is the Lady of the Moon or the Goddess of the Moon.

Chao-chün is Wang Chao-chün (王昭君), the court lady who in 33 B.C. was married to the king of the Hsiung-nu. According to legend, she failed to bribe the court painter with the result that he drew an unflattering picture of her. It was only after she had been promised in marriage to the Hsiung-nu ruler that the emperor saw her and realized what a beautiful woman he was losing. According to early legend, she had a son who succeeded his father, and in accordance with the custom of the Huns, he married her along with his father's other wives and had sons by her. A later version of the legend says that she poisoned herself rather than submit to incest. Her grave near Kuei-sui in Sui-yüan Province is said to be the only patch of green in a brown wasteland. Her name became associated very early with the Chinese *p'i-p'a*, a musical instrument resembling a guitar imported to China during the Han dynasty. She is often depicted as holding a *p'i-p'a*, and is a popular subject for poets and musicians.

Chao T'o (Chao T'o wang 趙佗王) was recognized by Han Kao-tsu (*r.* 206–194) as the king of Southern Yüeh (Annam, Vietnam) in 196 B.C. King Chao T'o's capital was in the area of present-day Canton. The pavilion he constructed was on the Yüeh-hsiu Mountain in Kuangtung Province.

Chao-yang Palace (Chao-yang kung 昭陽宮) is the name of the palace of the empress and her attendants built in Ch'ang-an by Emperor Ch'eng (*r.* 32–6) of the Han dynasty.

*Cheng* (箏) is a twelve- or thirteen-stringed musical instrument similar to the zither.

Chi-lu Mountain (Chi-lu shan 鷄祿山) was a mountain near the Chi-lu Pass in Yü-hun prefecture in Mongolia.

Chiang-tu (江都) is also known as Yang-chou (揚洲) and is in the present-day district of Chiang-tu in Kiangsu Province. It was a major terminal city on the canal system constructed by Emperor Yang of the Sui dynasty (*r.* 604–618) which extended as far south as the Hangchow area.

Chin-ling (金陵) is another name for the present-day city of Nanking.

Chin River, see Brocade River

*Ch'in* (琴) is a seven-stringed musical instrument resembling a zither.

Ching-yang Tower (Ching-yang lou 景陽樓) was the name of a tower in present-day Kiangsu Province north of the district of Chiang-ning. Emperor Wu of the Southern Ch'i dynasty (*r.* 484–494) had a special bell made for this tower to awaken the palace ladies at an early hour.

Ch'ing Gate (Ch'ing-men 青門) was a gate southeast of the city of Ch'ang-an during the Han dynasty (202 B.C.–A.D. 220).

*Ch'ing-ming* (清明) is a festival in early spring during which the Chinese visit and care for their family graves. It is also known as Tomb-Sweeping Day.

Chiu-i Mountain (Chiu-i shan 九疑山) is a mountain in Hunan Province south of the district of Ning-yüan. The Hsiang River rises near Chiu-i Mountain, and it was believed to have been the burial place of the sage-emperor Shun, whose wives were honored as the goddesses of the Hsiang River, the Hsiang-fei.

Ch'u (楚) is the name of an ancient feudal state believed to be originally of "barbarian" origin in the Yangtze valley in the south. Ch'u occupied the middle Yangtze area and the valley of the Han River. By the eighth century B.C., it was already a great power and remained a formidable force until its defeat by the Ch'in and consolidation into the empire in the second century B.C. Ch'u was the home state of the poets Ch'ü Yüan and Sung Yü, and the state in which was located the Wu Mountain and the Hsiao and Hsiang rivers. Many of the mountain and river goddesses in the *Hua-chien chi* derive from Ch'u legend and folklore, most particularly from the *Ch'u-tz'u*, an anthology of poetry in the Ch'u style utilizing themes and images common to the state of Ch'u.

Ch'u River (Ch'u-chiang 楚江) flows from the district of Sung-p'an in Szechuan Province into Lake Tung-t'ing in Hunan.

Ch'ü-chiang Pond (Ch'ü-chiang ch'ih 曲江池) was a pond southeast of Ch'ang-an. Apricot Garden was just to the west of it. During the T'ang dynasty a feast was held in a pavilion named after this lake to honor the successful degree candidates announced in the spring.

Ch'ü-t'ang (瞿唐) is the westernmost of the three famous gorges of the Yangtze River. The rocky configurations make these gorges very hazardous to shipping, especially during the monsoon season. Ch'ü-t'ang rises above the river and just below the walls of K'uei-chou. The other two gorges, the Wu-hsia Gorge and the Hsi-ling Gorge are further downstream.

Ch'ü Yüan (屈原) was a fourth century B.C. poet from the state of Ch'u. He is most famous for his poem, the "*Li-sao*," "Encountering Sorrow," included in the *Ch'u-tz'u* anthology. In this poem, Ch'ü Yüan laments the fact that he has been rejected and sent into exile by King Huai of Ch'u (*r.* 329–299) , and that his counsel with regard to the state has been ignored. He mourns his fate until he can no longer bear it, and then drowns himself in the Mi-lo River. According to tradition, Ch'ü Yüan is also the author of the *Nine Songs* in the *Ch'u-tz'u*, and two of these poems, the "Hsiang *fu-jen*," and the "Hsiang *chün*" express the frustrated longing of the poet for the favors of the Hsiang River goddesses (or goddess). *See* Hsiang River.

Chün Mountain (Chün-shan 君山) is also named the Tung-t'ing Mountain or the Hsiang Mountain. It rises from Lake Tung-t'ing southwest of Yüeh-yang. It was a sacred site and supposedly concealed a magical palace with five gateways leading to secret passageways concealed in the sacred mountains, among them, Lo-fu in Kuangtung, T'ai-shan in Shantung, and O-mei in Szechuan.

Clouds and rain (*yün-yü* 雲雨) is a euphemism for a sexual relationship. It first occurs in the "Kao-t'ang *fu*" attributed to the third century B.C. Ch'u poet, Sung Yü. When the goddess of the Wu Mountain parts from the king of the Ch'u state after their dalliance, she tells him that she is "the morning cloud at dawn," and "the driving rain at dusk."

Cold Food Festival (*Han-shih jih* 寒食日) is a festival celebrated the day before the *ch'ing-ming* festival when only cold food is eaten.

Crane (*ho* 鶴) is a symbol of longevity and immortality. Immortals are frequently depicted as riding on the backs of cranes as they soar into the sky.

Crystal Palace (Shui-ching kung 水晶宮) is an image for the moon.

Cuckoo (*tu-chüan* 杜鵑, *tu-yü* 杜宇) are also names for the azalea in Chinese. The reference is to the legendary king of the ancient state of Shu, Tu Yü, also known as the Emperor Wang, who had an illicit love affair with the wife of one of his ministers. He died of shame because of it, and after his death he was transformed into a cuckoo, which is said to weep blood in the late spring, hence the red color of the azalea which blooms at that time.

Day-lilies (*hsüan-ts'ao* 萱草) are popularly believed to cause people to forget their sorrows, for which purpose the plants and leaves are cooked and eaten. It is also known as the "grass of forgetfulness." *Hsüan-ts'ao* is often used as a metaphor for one's mother because the mother's rooms were in the north of the house where the day-lilies were traditionally planted.

Dragon Pond (Lung-ch'ih 龍池) was the name of a pond in the imperial complex of the T'ang emperor Hsüan-tsung (*r.* 712–756) in Ch'ang-an.

Fen River (Fen-ho 汾河 or Fen-shui 汾水) is a tributary of the Yellow River and a major waterway in the present-day province of Shansi.

Fish (*yü* 魚) is a common image for letters.

Five Clouds (*wu-yün* 五雲) are the clouds of the five colors (green, white, red, black, and yellow) through which the immortals roamed.

Geese or Wild Geese (*yen* 雁 or 鴈) is a metaphor for a letter. When Su Wu (140–60) was held prisoner by the Hsiung-nu, he sent out a letter tied to the foot of a wild goose.

*Hai-t'ung* tree (*hai-t'ung hua* 海桐花 or *tz'u-t'ung hua* 刺桐花) is a kind of evergreen shrub or tree with shiny oval-shaped foliage and fragrant white flowers.

Han River (Han-shui 漢水) is a tributary of the Yangtze. It rises in Shensi and runs southeast to Hupei where it joins the Yangtze at Han-k'ou.

Hei Mountain (Hei-shan 黑山) lies in present-day Hopei Province north of the district of Sha-ho.

Hsi Shih (西施) was a famous beauty from the state of Yüeh who was sent by the king of Yüeh, Kou Chien (*r.* 496–465), to Fu Ch'ai (*r.* 495–473), the king of Wu, in order to distract him from his official duties. The state of Yüeh was then able to attack and destroy Wu in 473 B.C. Hsi Shih is the Chinese "Helen of Troy," and a common image for a beautiful woman.

Hsiang River (Hsiang-ho 湘河) is a tributary of the Yangtze which flows through Hunan. It is the river protected by the goddesses of the Hsiang, the Hsiang-fei, who according to later legend were said to be the daughters of the sage emperor Yao and the wives of his successor, Shun. Anciently, however, it seems that there was only one goddess at the center of a shamanistic cult associated with the Hsiang River and the state of Ch'u. Two poems survive in the *Ch'u-tz'u* in which a shaman makes appeal to the goddess: the "Hsiang *fu-jen*" and the "Hsiang *chün*" in the *Nine Songs*.

Hsiang River Goddesses, *see* Hsiang River.

Hsiao River (Hsiao-shui 瀟水) flows through Hunan and is a tributary of the Hsiang River.

Hsiang-yang (襄陽) is a prefecture in present-day Hupei Province.

Hsien-yang (咸陽) was the site of the capital of the Ch'in dynasty (221–207) just northwest of the modern city of Hsi-an in Shensi Province.

Hsüan-tsung (玄宗) was an emperor of the T'ang dynasty (*r.* 713–756), who was also known as Ming-huang, the "Enlightened Emperor." His reign was marked by great political and cultural achievements, but unfortunately it also was the beginning of the end for the dynasty. In 745, Hsüan-tsung, then in his sixties, took as his favorite the beautiful Yang Kuei-fei, the consort of one of his sons. Her influence over Hsüan-tsung was disastrous for the country as the emperor more and more neglected his official responsibilities. One of her protégés, the ambitious An Lu-shan, eventually was placed in command of some 200,000 troops. In 755, he attempted to take control of the central government, capturing Lo-yang and then Ch'ang-an. Hsüan-tsung fled to Szechuan, but on the way his angry troops forced him to execute Yang Kuei-fei, whom they blamed for the disorders. Hsüan-tsung then abdicated in favor of one of his sons. The romance of the Emperor Hsüan-tsung and Yang Kuei-fei is one of the most famous love stories in Chinese history, celebrated by Po Chü-i (772–846) in his poem, "The Everlasting Sorrow" written in A.D. 806. The T'ang never again achieved its earlier grandeur. The authority of the central government had been seriously weakened, and although China was to enjoy yet another century of peace, there was constant friction with the border tribes, and within the court itself, factionalism was rife.

Huai River (Huai-shui 淮水) begins in Honan Province, runs through Anhwei and empties into the sea on the Kiangsu coast.

Huai-yin (淮陰) is the name of a city in Kiangsu Province, the ancient state of Wu. It was an important point on the canal system established by Emperor Yang of the Sui dynasty (*r.* 604–618).

Huang-ling Shrine (Huang-ling miao 黃陵廟) was a shrine dedicated to the worship of the Hsiang River goddesses. It was situated near the Hsiang River in the vicinity of Hsiang-t'an in Hunan Province.

I-ch'un Park (I-ch'un yüan 宜春苑) was the name of an ancient park situated in Ch'ang-an.

Jade Cord (*yü-sheng* 玉繩) refers to two stars in the constellation Draco.

Jade Emperor (Yü-huang 玉皇) is the supreme deity of heaven in Taoist lore.

Jade Pass (Yü-kuan 玉關) is a strategic border pass important in ancient times and located in present-day Kansu Province. It is frequently used as a reference for the border areas in general.

Jade Rabbit (*yü-t'u* 玉兔) is an image for the moon. Legend held that a rabbit dwelt on the moon, and that the rabbit, using a pestle and mortar, prepares the drug of immortality which Ch'ang O, the goddess of the moon, will drink to become an immortal toad dwelling near the foot of the cassia tree.

Jo-yeh Stream (Jo-yeh ch'i 若耶溪) is the name of a stream in present-day Chekiang Province. It is the stream by which the famous beauty Hsi Shih was discovered washing silk.

Juan, *see* Liu and Juan.

Jui-chu Palace (Jui-chu kung 蘂珠宮) is the dwelling place of the Taoist immortals. It was believed to be the palace of the Yellow Emperor.

Kao-t'ang (高唐) was the name of a pavilion in the ancient state of Ch'u. It is the setting of a *fu* attributed to the poet Sung Yü (third century B.C.) in which a king of the state of Ch'u enjoyed a dream rendezvous with the goddess of the Wu Mountain at the Kao-t'ang Pavilion near Lake Tung-t'ing. The goddess is described in extravagant terms of beauty which influenced later writers such as Ts'ao Chih (192–232) in his paean to the goddess of the Lo River, the "Lo-shen *fu*." The "Kao-t'ang *fu*" is also the *locus classicus* for the metaphor "clouds and rain" as an image for a sexual relationship.

Ku-su Pavilion (Ku-su t'ai 姑蘇臺) was a pavilion in the ancient state of Wu. It was the residence of the famous beauty Hsi Shih.

Kuan-wa Palace (Kuan-wa kung 館娃宮) was the name of a palace in the ancient state of Wu where the beautiful Hsi Shih resided. It was noted for the willow trees that grew there.

Liao-yang (遼陽) is a city in Liao-ning Province in Manchuria. Liao-yang is frequently used as a general reference to the border areas.

Lin-ch'iung (臨邛) is the name of a district in Szechuan. It was here that the poet Ssu-ma Hsiang-ju (179–117) and his wife ran a wine-shop after their elopement and rejection by her wealthy father.

Ling-ho Palace (Ling-ho tien 靈和殿) was a palace constructed by Emperor Wu (*r.* 483–494) of the Southern Ch'i dynasty. It was famous for the willow trees that grew around it.

Little Jade (Hsiao Yü 小玉) is the heroine of "Prince Huo's Daughter," a prose romance by Chiang Fang (*fl.* A.D. 813). Little Jade is abandoned by her lover, Li I, who marries someone else instead. On her deathbed, Little Jade curses him for his heartlessness, and he is haunted by her ghost, which makes him suspect that his wife is unfaithful. He divorces his wife as a consequence. He marries three times, but always Little Jade's ghost causes him to doubt the fidelity of his wives.

Liu and Juan (Liu Ch'en 劉晨 and Juan Chao 阮肇) lived during the first century B.C. According to legend, one day during the Yung-p'ing reign period (58–76), they went to the T'ien-t'ai Mountain to gather herbs. They lost their way and for some thirteen days were without food. Then they saw in the distance peach trees filled with fruit. They went there and met two lovely women. They stayed with the women for six months before returning home. When they arrived home, they discovered that several centuries had passed. The allusion to Liu and Juan, either singly or together, indicates an absent lover.

Lo-fu Mountain (Lo-fu shan 羅浮山) is a mountain in Kuangtung, east of the district of Tseng-ch'eng. It was believed to be a place inhabited by strange and wonderful spirits, where one could learn the magic arts. *See* Chün Mountain.

Lo Goddess (Lo-shen 洛神) is the goddess Fu-fei 宓妃, or the Consort Fu. By the time of the T'ang dynasty (618–907), she was considered to be the daughter of Fu Hsi, the legendary emperor of the third millennium B.C., although her actual divine origins are obscure.

Lo River (Lo-shui 洛水) rises in Shensi and flows into the Yellow River just west of Lo-yang. Ts'ao Chih's (192–232) rhapsodic poem, the "Lo-shen *fu*," is written in honor of the goddess of the Lo River. *See* "Lo-shen *fu*."

"Lo-shen *fu*" (洛神賦), "The Goddess of the Lo River," was written by Ts'ao Chih (192–232) in A.D. 223 in honor of the goddess of the Lo River. It is a descriptive work praising in elaborate terms the beauty of a woman who miraculously appears to the poet on the banks of the Lo River. Some critics have interpreted this poem allegorically as a declaration of loyalty to the poet's brother, Ts'ao P'i (187–226), who had forced the abdication of the last emperor of the Han dynasty and declared himself emperor of the Wei dynasty in A.D. 220. Others identify the goddess with the Empress Chen, who was married to Ts'ao P'i but was loved by Ts'ao Chih. Legend holds that after Empress Chen had been killed by Ts'ao P'i as a result of palace intrigue, Ts'ao Chih saw a pillow that had once belonged to her. He broke down in tears, and Ts'ao P'i presented the pillow to him as a gift. It was shortly after this that Ts'ao Chih, returning to his country seat, stopped by the Lo River and wrote the "Lo-shen *fu*." There is no evidence to support the claim of Ts'ao Chih's frustrated love, but the story has inspired poets for generations.

Lo-yang (洛陽) is located west of Yen-shih prefecture in present-day Honan Province. It had been the capital of the Eastern Chou dynasty (770–255). After the destruction of Ch'ang-an, during the short-lived Hsin dynasty of Wang Mang (*r.* 8–23), the capital was moved to Lo-yang by the Emperor Kuang-wu (*r.* 25–57), who established the Latter or Eastern Han dynasty. In A.D. 190, Lo-yang was destroyed by Tung Cho in the course of his unsuccessful bid for supreme power. It was rebuilt and became the capital of the Wei dynasty (220–265). It remained an important imperial center and became the "eastern capital" of the T'ang dynasty with Ch'ang-an as the central or "western capital."

Lotus seed (*lien-tzu* 蓮子) is a token of love.

Lung (隴) is an area lying between the provinces of Shensi and Kansu. The southeast corner of Kansu is still known as Lung-hsi.

Magic Islands (Shih-chou 十洲), literally "Ten Islands," are the ten legendary islands on which the immortals were believed to dwell.

Magpie Bridge (*ch'üeh-ch'iao* 鵲橋) is the legendary bridge formed by the magpies (the Milky Way) on the seventh day of the seventh lunar month so that the Weaving Girl (Vega) may cross and meet her husband, the Herd Boy (stars in Aquila). Married during their lifetimes, the Weaving Girl and the Herd Boy neglected their various duties in preference to their own company. As punishment, they were transformed into stars and must live apart except for this one day a year.

Mandarin ducks (*yüan-yang* 鴛鴦) are usually depicted in pairs and represent conjugal harmony and bliss.

Mi Tower (Mi-lou 迷樓), the "Maze Tower," was in Chiang-tu, and it was so named because its labyrinthine passages and apartments allowed Emperor Yang (*r.* 604–618) of the Sui dynasty to pursue his sexual pleasures in privacy.

Mo-ling (秣陵) is an ancient name for the present-day district of Nanking.

Moon Goddess, *see* Ch'ang O

Nan-chung (南中) refers to the area of Kuangtung and Kuangsi, also known as Ling-nan.

Nung Yü (弄玉) was the daughter of Duke Mu of Ch'in (seventh century B.C.) who married Hsiao Shih, a musician so skilled at playing the pipes that the music resembled the cry of the phoenix. Hsiao Shih taught Nung Yü to play the pipes, and later they both ascended into the land of the immortals, she on a phoenix, and he on a dragon.

Orange Island (Chü-chou 橘洲) is an island in Hunan, west of Ch'ang-sha in the Hsiang River. In ancient times it was famous for the oranges that grew there.

Orioles (*ying* 鶯) is a frequent image for singing-girls and prostitutes. "Orioles and flowers," and "orioles and swallows" are similar images. The "high-flying orioles" refers to those who successfully passed the civil-service examination.

Pa (巴) is the name of an ancient state which occupied much of what is now Szechuan Province.

Pa-ling (灞陵) is an area east of Ch'ang-an bordered by the Pa Stream. The Pa Bridge with its many willows was famous as a site of partings during the T'ang dynasty (618–907).

Pai-t'ung Dam (Pai-t'ung t'i 白銅堤) is the name of a place in Hsiang-yang in present-day Hupei Province. In ancient times it seems to have been something of a gathering place. Li Po (701–762) in his poem, "Song of Hsiang-yang," describes a scene of feasting and revelry that took place there.

Pearl-Sporting River (Nung-chu chiang 弄珠江) is a reference to a folk song and to the story of Cheng Chiao-fu of the Chou dynasty and his liaison with two goddesses at the foot of the Han-kao Mountain. The goddesses were wearing girdles trimmed with extremely large pearls. Cheng Chiao-fu asked for and received them as gifts, but as he left, the pearls vanished and so did the women. Han-kao Mountain is northwest of the district of Hsiang-yang.

P'eng-lai (蓬萊) is a legendary island in the Yellow Sea where the immortals were believed to dwell.

Phoenixes (*feng-huang* 鳳凰) are frequently depicted in pairs, and like mandarin ducks are an image for marital bliss and happiness.

*P'i-p'a* (琵琶) is a musical instrument similar to a guitar.

P'i-p'a Island (P'i-p'a chou 琵琶洲) is an island in the district of Yü-kan in Kiangsi Province. It is shaped like a *p'i-p'a* and thus its name. When written with the characters *p'i-p'a* 枇杷, "loquat," it is also an image associated with houses of prostitution.

Pien River (Pien-ho 汴河) runs south from the present-day district of Ying-yang in Honan and forms the upper reaches of the Lang-tang-ch'ü. It continues eastward to K'ai-feng where it branches into two streams. The one flowing north is known as Yin-kou, and the one flowing south as Hung-kou.

Pine Tree (*sung* 松) symbolizes longevity and immortality. The pine is also used as an image of the scholar of integrity and fortitude who does not depart from principles.

P'ing-yüan (平原) was a city in the state of Chao during the period of Warring States (403–221) which was famous for its young gentlemen who would chant in exceedingly mournful tones.

Prince of Wei's Embankment (Wei-wang t'i 魏王堤) is presumed to be on the banks of the Lo River, the scene of Ts'ao Chih's (192–232) famous *Fu* or prose poem, "The Goddess of the Lo River." It was noted for the willows that grew there. Ts'ao Chih, a son and possible heir of Ts'ao Ts'ao (155–220) was known as the Prince of Wei.

"Rainbow Skirts and Feathered Jackets" (*Ni-shang yü-i* 霓裳羽衣) is the name of a popular song of the T'ang dynasty (618–907). The title was also used to refer to the special dance that was done to this tune.

Red Bean (*hung-tou* 紅豆) is a token of love.

Red Towers (*hung-lou* 紅樓) is a metaphor for houses of prostitution.

*se* (瑟), is a musical instrument with 25 strings resembling a zither.

Shang-yang Palace (Shang-yang kung 上陽宮) is the name of a palace in Lo-yang constructed by the T'ang emperor Kao-tsung (*r.* 649–683).

Shao (韶) was an area in present-day Kuangtung Province noted for the production of fine red silks.

*Sheng* (笙) is a small instrument consisting of a number of pipes of different lengths resembling the Pan pipe.

Shih-t'ou (石頭) is a city west of present-day Nanking behind Shih-t'ou Mountain. It was first established by Sun Ch'üan (182–252), the ruler of the Kingdom of Wu (*r.* 229–252), whose capital was in Nanking. It is an area that figures prominently in the history of the Six Dynasties (220–589). It was here that Emperor Ch'eng (*r.* 325–342) of the Eastern Chin dynasty found refuge when the capital of Nanking was occupied in A.D. 328 by the forces of Su Chün (d. A.D. 328). It also was an important strategic area in the overthrow of the Ch'en dynasty by the forces of the Sui in A.D. 589.

Shou-yang, Lady (壽陽) was the daughter of Emperor Wu of the Liu-Sung dynasty (*r.* 420–423). Once she rested near the Han-chang Palace and let the plum-blossoms drift around her face, until she, herself, resembled the flower. This was the origin of the famous "plum blossom make-up."

Shu (蜀) is an ancient name for the province of Szechuan.

Silver arrow (*yin-chien* 銀箭) is an arrow or needle for indicating time on the water clock.

Silver Toad (*yin-ch'an* 銀蟾) is an image for the moon, deriving from the transformation of Ch'ang O, the goddess of the moon, into a toad after she drank the elixir of immortality.

Six Dynasties (*liu-ch'ao* 六朝) is a period in Chinese history that follows the fall of the Later Han dynasty in A.D. 220. It is called the Six Dynasties period after the six successive dynasties that had their capitals in Nanking between 222 and 589. These were the Wu, Eastern Chin, Liu-Sung, Southern Ch'i, Liang, and Ch'en dynasties.

Southern Palace (*Nan-nei* 南內) is the name of a palace compound of the T'ang
  emperor Hsüan-tsung (*r.* 713–756), also named the Hsing-Ch'ing Palace.

Southern Yüeh (Nan-Yüeh 南越) was an area embracing the provinces of
  Kuangtung, Kuangsi, and parts of northern Vietnam.

Su Hsiao-hsiao (蘇小小) is the name of a famous courtesan who lived during the
  Southern Ch'i dynasty (479–501). Her home in Ch'ien-t'ang was noted for the
  willow trees that grew there.

Sui Embankment (Sui-t'i 隋堤) was built by the Emperor Yang (*r.* 604–618) of the
  Sui dynasty. It was noted for the lovely willows that grew there.

Sung River (Sung-chiang 松江) is also known as the Wu-Sung River and is in
  Kiangsu Province in the prefecture of Wu.

Sung Yü (宋玉) is believed to be a third century B.C. disciple of the fourth century
  B.C. poet Ch'ü Yüan. Several works in the *Ch'u-tz'u* anthology are attributed
  to him. He is depicted in later literature as a gifted poet and quite a romantic
  lover. The authorship of the "Kao-t'ang *fu*," and the "Shen-nü *fu*," both
  describing the beauty of the goddess of the Wu Mountain, is attributed to
  him, as is the "Teng-t'u tzu *hao-se fu*," in which he defends himself against a
  charge of improper behavior with the king's daughter.

Swallows (*yen* 燕) is an image like mandarin ducks and suggests marital bliss and
  harmony. It can also be used as an image for singing girls.

"*Ta-t'i*" (大堤) or "The Great Embankment" is the name of a song belonging to a
  group of songs in the section "Music of Hsiang-yang" in the *Yüeh-fu shih-chi*,
  48.8a–9a.

T'ao-yeh Ford (T'ao-yeh tu 桃葉渡) is a ford named after the beloved concubine,
  T'ao-yeh or Peach Leaf, of Wang Hsien-chih (344–388) of the Chin dynasty. It
  is in Chiang-ning in present-day Kiangsu Province at the junction of the
  Ch'in-huai and the Ch'ing-ch'i rivers.

"Thoughts of Return" (*Ssu-kuei yin* 思歸引) is the title of a melody for the
  *ch'in*. According to tradition, the king of the ancient district of Shao in
  present-day Honan Province heard that in the state of Wei there lived a very
  virtuous woman, and he proposed marriage to her. While she was on her way
  to Shao, the king died. The Crown Prince said that it was well known that
  Duke Huan of Ch'i (*r.* 685–643) has taken a woman of Wei to be his
  concubine, and he had subsequently become hegemon. Against the advice of
  his minister, the Crown Prince refused to allow the lady to return to her home
  in Wei. In sorrow and despair at her captivity, she composed this melody on
  the *ch'in* and then hanged herself.

Three Islands (*san-tao* 三島) are the three legendary islands where the immortals
  were believed to dwell.

Ts'ao Chih (曹植 192–232) is one of the greatest of all Chinese lyric poets. In the

*Hua-chien chi,* he is most usually associated with his prose poem to the goddess of the Lo River, the "Lo-shen *fu,*" a rhapsodic poem in praise of the beauty of the goddess similar to Sung Yü's praise of the goddess of the Wu Mountain in the "Kao-t'ang *fu,*" and the "Shen-nü *fu.*" *See* "Lo-shen *fu.*"

Tung-t'ing Lake (Tung-t'ing hu 洞庭湖) is a large lake in Hunan whose waters merge with the Hsiang and Yangtze rivers. Lake Tung-t'ing was the center of the cult of the Hsiang River goddesses.

Tzu-wei (紫薇) is the name of a star north of the Big Dipper. It was believed to be the dwelling place of the Heavenly Emperor.

Weaving Maiden and the Herd Boy, *see* Magpie Bridge

Wei River (Wei-ho 渭河) is a large tributary of the Yellow River in Shensi.

Wei-yang Palace (Wei-yang kung 未央宮) was a palace in the capital city of Ch'ang-an during the Han dynasty (202 B.C.–A.D. 220). It was a center of governmental activity.

Willow trees (*yang-liu* 楊柳) occur as an image for the grace and beauty of the singing girl. They also symbolize parting. Willow branches were frequently presented as gifts of farewell.

Wu (吳) is the name of an ancient state which occupied the territory in the lower Yangtze areas around modern Nanking and Shanghai, a region roughly corresponding to present-day Kiangsu Province. It was noted for the beauty and skill of its singing and dancing girls.

Wu-chiang (吳江) is a district in present-day Kiangsu Province south of the district of Wu.

Wu-hsia Gorge (巫峽) is one of the three famous gorges of the Yangtze River. *See* Ch'ü-t'ang Gorge.

Wu king, *see* Hsi Shih

Wu Mountain (Wu-shan 巫山) is a mountain in eastern Szechuan Province which was anciently associated with shamanistic practices, hence its name, "Shaman Mountain." It was here that the goddess of the Wu Mountain, Yao Chi, was believed to dwell. The famous prose poems by Sung Yü, the "Kao-t'ang *fu*" and the "Shen-nü *fu*" celebrate her great beauty.

Wu Palace (Wu kung 吳宮) is a reference to Hsi Shih, who was sent from her home in Yüeh to distract the king of Wu from his duties so that Yüeh might attack and defeat Wu. The phrase "Wu palace" also was used as a euphemism for a house of prostitution.

*Wu-t'ung* trees (梧桐) are the *firmiana Sterculia platanifolia. Wu-t'ung* trees are a frequent image in this type of poetry because the name involves a pun on *wu-t'ung* 吾同, "we two" or "we together."

Yang-chou, *see* Chiang-tu

Yang, Emperor of the Sui dynasty (Sui Yang-ti 隋煬帝) (*r.* 604–618) was the second emperor of the short-lived Sui dynasty (589–618). He succeeded his father, probably through murder, in A.D. 604. It was the Sui that initiated the second great imperial period in China, which was to culminate during the subsequent T'ang dynasty. However, grandeur has its price, and Emperor Yang alienated the people with his incessant wars, and with his increasing demands for labor to construct the great canals, walls, and palaces that were later to contribute to China's prosperity. He was also castigated for the depravity of his private life and became, in the eyes of later historians, the quintessential "bad last emperor" who loses the right to rule through the Mandate of Heaven. He was assassinated in A.D. 618, thus opening the way for a struggle for power that led to the triumph of the Li family and the establishment of the T'ang dynasty in A.D. 618.

Yang Pass (Yang-kuan 陽關) is an important mountain pass in Kansu Province, 130 miles southwest of the district of Tun-huang, and west of the Tang River.

Yao Chi (瑤姬) is the name of the goddess who dwells on the Wu Mountain. She is the goddess described in Sung Yü's "Kao-t'ang *fu*," and "Shen-nü *fu*." According to one tradition, she was believed to be the youngest daughter of the mythical Red Emperor, or Yen-ti, the god of fire, summer, and the south. Like Aphrodite or Venus, the name Yao Chi is used as an image for a beautiful woman.

Yao and Shun (堯舜) are legendary sage emperors believed to have reigned in the third millennium B.C. Their reigns represent a golden age of peace and harmony in China.

Yao-t'ai (瑤臺) is the name of the tower where Chien Ti, the first ancestress of the Shang dynasty (second millennium B.C.) was shut away. Ti K'u, the first ancestor of the Shang people, sent her a swallow, and she became pregnant by swallowing its egg.

Yeh (鄴) is the city in which Ts'ao Ts'ao (155–220) built the famous Copper-Bird Pavilion noted for its beautiful willows.

Yen-ch'iu Gate (Yen-ch'iu men 延秋門) was a gate in the city of Ch'ang-an.

Yü Yu (于祐) sent a poem entitled "Red Leaves" along the water drains into the palace, where it was received by the Lady Han. When the T'ang emperor Hsi-tsung (*r.* 874–889) later dismissed her, she married Yü Yu.

Yüeh (越) is the name of an ancient state which occupied what is now Fukien and Chekiang provinces. It was noted not only as the birthplace of the beautiful Hsi Shih, but also for the skill and loveliness of its singing and dancing girls.

Yüeh king, *see* Hsi Shih

Yung-ch'eng (墉城) is a dwelling place of the immortals in the fabulous K'un-lun mountains in the far west.

# Bibliography

Balakian, Anna, *The Symbolist Movement*. New York: Random House, 1967.

Baudelaire, Charles. *Flowers of Evil*. Ed. Marthiel and Jackson Mathews. New York: New Directions, 1955.

—— *L'Art Romantique*. In *Oeuvres Complètes de Charles Baudelaire*. Ed. Jacques Crépet, IV. Paris: L. Conard, 1925.

Baxter, Glen. *Hua-chien chi: Songs of Tenth Century China*. Ph.D. diss., Harvard University, 1952; Cambridge: Harvard University Microfilms, 1962.

—— *Index to the Imperial Register of Tz'u Prosody*. Harvard-Yenching Institute Studies XV. Cambridge: Harvard University Press, 1956.

—— "Metrical Origins of the *Tz'u*." In *Studies in Chinese Literature*. Ed. John L. Bishop. Harvard-Yenching Institute Studies XXI. Cambridge: Harvard University Press, 1966; pp. 186–224.

Brooks, Cleanth, and William K. Wimsatt, Jr., eds. *A Short History of Literary Criticism*. New York: Vintage Books, 1967.

Chang Fu-jui. *Les Fonctionnaires des Song, Index des Titres*. Paris: Mouton and Company, 1962.

Chang Kang-i Sun. *The Evolution of Chinese Tz'u Poetry*. Princeton: Princeton University Press, 1980.

Chiang Shang-hsien 姜尙賢, ed. *T'ang Sung ming-chia tz'u hsin-hsüan* 唐宋名家詞新選. Taipei: Hsieh-i yin-shua chü, 1964.

*Chin-shu* 晉書, 10 vols. Compiled by Fang Hsüan-ling 房玄齡 (578–648). Peking: Chung-hua shu-chü, 1974.

*Ch'u-tz'u pu-chu* 楚辭補註. Ed. Hung Hsing-tsu 洪興祖 (1090–1155); rpt. Taipei: I-wen yin-shu kuan, 1965.

Daiches, David and William Charvat, eds. *Poems in English, 1530–1940*. New York: Ronald Press, 1950.

Des Rotours, Robert, trans. *Courtisanes Chinoises à la fin des T'ang*. By Sun Ch'i. Paris: Presses Universitaires de France, 1968.

—— *Le Traité des Examens*. Paris: Librairie Ernest Leroux, 1932.

Erkes, Ed. "*Shen-nü fu*, The Song of the Goddess, by Sung Yüh." *T'oung-pao* 25 (1928): 387–402.

Fusek, Lois. "The *Kao-t'ang fu* by Sung Yü." *Monumenta Serica* 30 (1972–1973): 392–425.

Graham, A. C. *Poems of the Late T'ang*. Baltimore: Penguin Books, 1965.

*Han-shu* 漢書, 8 vols. Ed. Yen Shih-ku 顏師古. Peking: Chung-hua shu-chü, 1962.

Hawkes, David. "The Quest of the Goddess." *Asia Major* 13 (1967); 71–94.

—— *Songs of the South*. Boston: Beacon Press, 1962.

Hightower, James R. "The *Fu* of T'ao Ch'ien." In *Studies in Chinese Literature*. Ed. John L. Bishop. Harvard-Yenching Institute Studies XXI. Cambridge: Harvard University Press, 1966; pp. 45–106.

—— *The Poetry of T'ao Ch'ien*. Oxford: Clarendon Press, 1970.

Hsiao Chi-tsung 蕭繼宗, ed. *Hua-chien chi* 花間集. Taipei: Taiwan hsüeh-sheng shu-chü, 1977.

Hsieh Wu-hsiung 謝武雄. "*Hua-chien tz'u-jen chi ch'i tso-p'in yen-chiu*." 花間詞人及其作品研究. In *T'ai-chung Shih-chuan hsüeh-pao*. 臺中師專學報 Taichung, Taiwan: Taiwan Provincial Taichung Junior Teachers' College, June, 1979; pp. 81–122.

Hu Shih 胡適, ed. *Tz'u-hsüan* 詞選. 1927; rpt. Taipei: Commercial Press, 1959.

Hua Lien-p'u 華連圃, ed. *Hua-chien chi chu* 花間集注. Shanghai: Commercial Press, 1935.

Jao Tsung-i 饒宗頤, ed. *Tz'u-chi k'ao* 詞籍考. Hong Kong: Ta-hsüeh ch'u-pan she, 1963.

Levis, John Hazedel. *Foundations of Chinese Musical Art*. 1936; rpt. New York: Paragon Book Reprint Corporation, 1963.

Levy, Howard S. *Chinese Footbinding*. New York: Walton Rawls, 1966.

Li I-mang 李一氓, ed. *Hua-chien chi chiao* 花間集校. Hong Kong: Commercial Press, 1960.

Li Ping-jo 李冰若, ed. *Hua-chien chi p'ing-chu* 花間集評注. 1935; rpt. Hong Kong: Lo-chih ch'u-pan she, 1960.

Liu, James J.Y. "Some Literary Qualities of the Lyric (*Tz'u*)." In *Studies in Chinese Literary Genres*, ed. Cyril Birch. Berkeley: University of California Press, 1974; pp. 133–53.

Liu Wu-chi and Irving Yu-cheng Lo, eds. *Sunflower Splendor: Three Thousand Years of Chinese Poetry*. Bloomington, Indiana: Indiana University Press, 1975.

Mallarmé, Stéphane. *Selected Poems*. Trans. C. F. Macintyre. Berkeley: University of California Press, 1957.

Miao, Ronald C. "Palace-Style Poetry: The Courtly Treatment of Glamour and Love." In *Studies in Chinese Poetry and Poetics*. Ed. Ronald C. Miao. San Francisco: Chinese Materials Center, Inc., 1978; pp. 1–42.

*Mu t'ien-tzu chuan* 穆天子傳. *Ssu-pu pei-yao* ed.

*Nan-shih* 南史, 6 vols. Compiled by Li Yen-shou 李延壽 in A.D. 659. Peking: Chung-hua shu-chü, 1975.

Pian, Rulan Chao. *Sonq Dynasty Musical Sources and Their Interpretation.* Cambridge: Harvard University Press, 1969.

*Shan-hai ching* 山海經. *Ssu-pu pei-yao* ed.

*Shih-chi* 史記. *Ssu-pu pei-yao* ed.

*Sung-pen Hua-chien chi* 宋本花間集. Based on the edition of Ch'ao Ch'ien-chih 晁謙之 with colophon dated A.D. 1148; rpt. Taipei: I-wen yin-shu kuan, 1960.

*T'ai-p'ing kuang-chi* 太平廣記, Compiled by Li Fang 李昉 and others in A.D. 978. Peking: Chung-hua shu-chü, 1961.

Ting Fu-pao 丁福保, ed. *Ch'üan Han san-kuo Chin nan-pei ch'ao shih* 全漢三國晉南北朝詩, 3 vols. Taipei: Shih-chieh shu-chü, 1969.

Van Gulik, R. H. *Sexual Life in Ancient China.* Leiden: E. J. Brill, 1961.

Waley, Arthur. *One Hundred and Seventy Chinese Poems.* London: Constable, 1962.

—— *The Temple and Other Poems.* New York: Alfred A. Knopf, 1923. (Contains translations of some of the Sung Yü *fu.*)

Wan Shu 萬樹 (fl. 1680–1692). *Tz'u-lü* 詞律. Preface dated 1687; rpt. Taipei: Shih-chieh shu-chü, 1966.

Wang I-ch'ing 王奕清 (*c.* 1644–*c.* 1736). *Tz'u-p'u* 詞譜. Preface dated 1715; rpt. Taipei: privately printed, 1964.

Watson, Burton. *Chinese Rhyme-Prose.* New York: Columbia University Press, 1971.

Watson, Burton, trans. *The Complete Works of Chuang-tzu.* New York: Columbia University Press, 1968.

*Wen-hsüan* 文選. Compiled by Hsiao T'ung 蕭統 (501–531); rpt. Taipei: Kuang-wen shu-chü, 1965.

Wu Mei 吳梅. *Tz'u-hsüeh t'ung-lun* 詞學通論. 1932; rpt. Taipei: privately printed, 1965.

Yang Po-chün 楊伯峻, ed. *Lieh-tzu chi-shih* 列子集釋. Taipei: T'ai-p'ing shu-chü, 1965.

*Yüeh-fu shih-chi* 樂府詩集, 3 vols. Compiled by Kuo Mao-ch'ien 郭茂倩 (twelfth century); rpt. Taipei: Shih-chieh shu-chü, 1961.

# Index of Tune Titles

# General Index

# Translations From the Oriental Classics

*Major Plays of Chikamatsu,* tr. Donald Keene
*Four Major Plays of Chikamatsu,* tr. Donald Keene. Paperback text edition.                                                                1961
*Records of the Grand Historian of China, translated from the Shih chi of Ssu-ma Ch'ien,* tr. Burton Watson, 2 vols.                        1961
*Instructions for Practical Living and Other Neo-Confucian Writings by Wang Yang-ming,* tr. Wing-tsit Chan                                  1963
*Chuang Tzu: Basic Writings,* tr. Burton Watson, paperback ed. only       1964
*The Mahābhārata,* tr. Chakravarthi V. Narasimhan. Also in paperback ed.                                                                    1965
*The Manyōshū,* Nippon Gakujutsu Shinkōkai edition                        1954
*Su Tung-p'o: Selections from a Sung Dynasty Poet,* tr. Burton Watson. Also in paperback ed.                                                1965
*Bhartrihari: Poems,* tr. Barbara Stoler Miller. Also in paperback ed.    1967
*Basic Writings of Mo Tzu, Hsün Tzu, and Han Fei Tzu,* tr. Burton Watson. Also in separate paperback eds.                                   1967
*The Awakening of Faith, attributed to Aśvaghosha,* tr. Yoshito S. Hakeda. Also in paperback ed.                                            1967
*Reflections on Things at Hand: The Neo-Confucian Anthology,* comp. Chu Hsi and Lü Tsu-ch'ien, tr. Wing-tsit Chan                           1967
*The Platform Sutra of the Sixth Patriarch,* tr. Philip B. Yampolsky. Also in paperback ed.                                                1967
*Essays in Idleness: The Tsurezuregusa of Kenkō,* tr. Donald Keene. Also in paperback ed.                                                   1967
*The Pillow Book of Sei Shōnagon,* tr. Ivan Morris, 2 vols.               1967
*Two Plays of Ancient India: The Little Clay Cart and the Minister's Seal,* tr. J. A. B. van Buitenen                                       1968
*The Complete Works of Chuang Tzu,* tr. Burton Watson                     1968
*The Romance of the Western Chamber (Hsi Hsiang chi),* tr. S. I. Hsiung. Also in paperback ed.                                              1968
*The Manyōshū,* Nippon Gakujutsu Shinkōkai edition. Paperback text edition.                                                                1969
*Records of the Historian: Chapters from the Shih chi of Ssu-ma Ch'ien.* Paperback text edition, tr. Burton Watson                          1969

*Cold Mountain: 100 Poems by the T'ang Poet Han-shan*, tr. Burton Watson. Also in paperback ed.  1970

*Twenty Plays of the Nō Theatre*, ed. Donald Keene. Also in paperback ed.  1970

*Chūshingura: The Treasury of Loyal Retainers*, tr. Donald Keene. Also in paperback ed.  1971

*The Zen Master Hakuin: Selected Writings*, tr. Philip B. Yampolsky  1971

*Chinese Rhyme-Prose*, tr. Burton Watson. Also in paperback ed.  1971

*Kūkai: Major Works*, tr. Yoshito S. Hakeda  1972

*The Old Man Who Does as He Pleases: Selections from the Poetry and Prose of Lu Yu*, tr. Burton Watson  1973

*The Lion's Roar of Queen Śrīmālā*, tr. Alex & Hideko Wayman  1974

*Courtier and Commoner in Ancient China: Selections from the History of The Former Han by Pan Ku*, tr. Burton Watson. Also in paperback ed.  1974

*Japanese Literature in Chinese, Vol. I: Poetry and Prose in Chinese by Japanese Writers of the Early Period*, tr. Burton Watson  1975

*Japanese Literature in Chinese, Vol. II: Poetry and Prose in Chinese by Japanese Writers of the Later Period*, tr. Burton Watson  1976

*Scripture of the Lotus Blossom of the Fine Dharma*, tr. Leon Hurvitz. Also in paperback ed.  1976

*Love Song of the Dark Lord: Jayadeva's Gītagovinda*, tr. Barbara Stoler Miller. Also in paperback ed. Cloth ed. includes critical text of the Sanskrit.  1977

*Ryōkan: Zen Monk-Poet of Japan*, tr. Burton Watson  1977

*Calming the Mind and Discerning the Real: From the Lam rim chen mo of Tson-kha-pa*, tr. Alex Wayman  1978

*The Hermit and the Love-Thief: Sanskrit Poems of Bhartrihari and Bilhana*, tr. Barbara Stoler Miller  1978

*The Lute: Kao Ming's P'i-p'a chi*, tr. Jean Mulligan. Also in paperback ed.  1980

*A Chronicle of Gods and Sovereigns: Jinnō Shōtōki of Kitabatake Chikafusa*, tr. H. Paul Varley  1980

*Among the Flowers: The Hua-chien chi*, tr. Lois Fusek  1982

# Studies in Oriental Culture

# Companions To Asian Studies

# Introduction To Oriental Civilizations

## Wm. Theodore de Bary, *Editor*

| | | | |
|---|---|---|---|
| *Sources of Japanese Tradition* | 1958 | Paperback ed., 2 vols. | 1964 |
| *Sources of Indian Tradition* | 1958 | Paperback ed., 2 vols. | 1964 |
| *Sources of Chinese Tradition* | 1960 | Paperback ed., 2 vols. | 1964 |